Cosmic Accolades

"**A worthy instruction book for Spaceship Earth!** Finally, an updated guide from the Universe to help humankind move forward! Cosmic coaching can assist humans in their ever-changing journey to hurry up and create a world that everyone can be proud of!"
– **THE B.O.S.S. (Being of Supreme Source)**, Universe CEO, Director of all Cosmic Beings, and Co-Founder of Spiritual, Transformational and Evolutionary Projects including Total Species Theory, Big Bang Boom, Quantum Physics, and Plumbing. Manager of Galactic Evolution and Energy Systems.

"Inspiring and funny, while insanely intelligent. Humans have been given a gift of higher knowledge, which we hope they appreciate. We know Ga-zillions of advanced beings who practice these techniques daily. Cosmic wisdom is especially needed right now for Planet Earth! So, go on, hurry up and evolve!"
– **Dr. Vortex Vulcani, ABA BABA B100** (Highest Honorable AB Title), Galaxy-Renowned Authority on Evolving and Advanced Being Studies, President of Universal Universe University (UUU). Our motto: "It's *all about* YOU."

"*Hurry Up and Evolve* is a perfect blend of advice given in a simple format for humans. Profound yet straight to the point, the Advanced Being Coaches are brilliant in communicating the message of much-needed evolution. We are rooting for the humans, although we are realistic in our expectations!"
– **Dr. Youpoke Yopraugh, M.D.B (Multi-Dimensional Being)**, Director and Founder of YO- YO- GA Center for Inter-Galactic Species Development and creator of the "*Ultra Galactic Species Evolution Training Series.*"

"A timeless and soon-to-be human classic, this guide offers pearls of wisdom that are breathtaking in their powerful message of "*evolve or forget about it!*" These ABCs are professionals and not fooling around. We should know, as we were their students eons ago. We didn't listen the first time, but we got it right the second time around!"
– **Sirius Lee Cosmic, Founder of the Planetary Artists Group and Creators of Groovy Civilizations and Legends**, and Bestselling Author

of "*What's Your Galaxy Vision?*," "*Create with the Cosmos*," and "*Atlantis Gone But Not Forgotten.*"

"*Human Earthlings need this now!* We've been watching the drama unfold on this planet and eagerly waiting for the Universe to provide this level of cosmically qualified guidance. As professionals who work in the Galaxy with various beings, we know how difficult it is to get a species out of denial. These Cosmic Coaches have taken complex concepts and made them relatively easy for Earthlings to understand. We also give a big appendage up for mixing in some much-needed humor!"
– Dr. Yangoorish Yinish and Dr. Zoopa Zip, **Founders of the Advanced Being Behavioral Association (ABBA)** and Authors of "*Theories of Inter-Galactic Humor to Expand Cosmic Relations*" and "*If You Can't Laugh, You're Boring.*"

"Very cool message from my fellow ABs. Awesome in its brilliance. Love, love, love how you ABs stay chill while this planet has a meltdown! Surely you will gain a following on this planet and throughout the Cosmos. Looking forward to sharing your message with the major galaxy networks and am happy to help with an agent if you need one!"
– Star-Ashanumi, Galaxy Sound & Visual Artist, Creator of the Galaxy Mega Hit "*SoulStar Being*" and other Delightfully Divine Creations; Major STAR of Vortex Visionary Videos (VVV) and Member of the Cosmic Celebrities Care Council (CCCC).

"This book is more than a guide. It's a manifesto for humans to get with the universal program of love, peace, and evolution. This is the way, the light, the answer. Okay, maybe it's a doorway, but we're hoping humans will walk through it. Keep the faith my AB friends, as you are giving hope to humankind, or at the very least, getting their attention!"
– Master Yogishimi Yami Zami, Teacher, Guruologist, and Director of the Cudha Shoudha Institute of Being Here But Not There and Author of "*I Know it All, Shouldn't You?*" and "*I Know Nothing and Neither Do You*," and Universe Master Energy Transformer, Certified, Verified and Electrified Practitioner Level 10,000.

"**A must-read for ALL Humans!** Quite a brilliant achievement. In a time when writing and reading printed "books" isn't the norm among Advanced Universal Beings (or humans!), these fun-loving ABs took the time to do it the old-fashioned way to get their message out

to Earthlings. Such an interesting idea to download major concepts through human words instead of communicating them through telepathy. Who knew? Well, we reviewed this little gem and hope humans appreciate the effort it took to find an agreeable human assistant and publish this through human technology. Honestly, it would have been easier just to take over the planet. ***Only kidding!***"
– The Cosmic Inquisitors Review & Galaxy Media Group. Our motto: "*Telepath Today, Teleport Tomorrow!*"

Hurry Up and Evolve!®

Hurry Up and Evolve!®

How to be your best self with Cosmic help!

L. CHAKRAZARA

WELLNESSWISDOM BOOKS
PLANET EARTH

First Printing 2025, 1st Edition
Book Design by L. ChakraZara and Bookcovers.com

ISBN 979-8-9918898-0-3 (paperback)
ISBN 979-8-9918898-1-0 (ebook)
Printed in USA, Planet Earth

Library of Congress Control Number: 2025910048

Published by WellnessWisdom Books
www.wellnesswisdombooks.com
Visit the author's website at ladychakrazara.com
All inquiries will be forwarded to the author, and contact details will be provided upon the author's authorization.

This book is intended to serve as an informational guide. The approaches and techniques described herein are designed to inspire advanced self-development and are not a substitute for professional psychological, spiritual, or medical interventions that some humans may need. The publisher, authors, and any other advanced beings or otherworldly entities are not liable for any damages or negative consequences resulting from the actions, applications, or misapplications of the information in this book.

Humans are responsible for their own actions and are accountable for their "Human Karma, Dharma, and Drama." References are provided for informational purposes only and do not imply an endorsement of any websites or other sources. We are simply the messengers! Readers should also be aware that the resources and websites listed in this book may change or evolve.

Dedicated to felines, chocolate and Planet Earth.

Contents

"Now there is one outstanding important fact regarding spaceship earth, and that is that no instruction book came with it." – Buckminster Fuller, inventor and philosopher

That is, until this one!

It's a Circus...But It's Not Ours!

"You can't legislate intelligence and common sense into people."
– Will Rogers, humorous social commentator

Given that humans are currently experiencing numerous and ongoing dramas that include entertaining yet disturbing conspiracy theories, "crazy ass" lies, and other wacko B.S.,[1] our cosmic legal experts highly advised an official disclaimer to clarify and reduce the possibility of irrational speculations or misinterpretations that may result from reading this guide. In other words, we are "covering our behinds, butts, and rear ends (even though we don't exactly have them)."

Disclaimer Statement:

We are not officially (or unofficially) affiliated, associated, authorized, endorsed, or connected with any of the following parties, or any others who are not included here:

- Nefarious and nasty groups plotting to overthrow your planet.
- Any cabals, evil or otherwise.
- Unsavory and loathsome humans who disguise themselves as "regular humans."
- Secret[2] oracles led by conspiratorial theorists with a negative agenda. This also includes other organizations that are not very "secret," organized, or even "deep" (e.g., the Deep State).
- Any organization or group, such as NASA, FBI, CIA, Mafia, KGB, IRS, OPEC, INTERPOL, CSETI, U.N., UNOOSA, IIA, military operatives, cartels, gangs, and cults, some of which are comprised of rowdy troublemakers who seem to favor large amounts of facial hair, rundown vehicles, and frequent belching (among other things).
- Certain humans who work in Hollywood or are currently residing in Roswell, New Mexico. We love you guys, though!
- Satan, Bigfoot, or Elvis.
- Lizard entities that may or may not disguise themselves as lizards.
- Any wellness, spiritual, and assorted mystical groups that have veered

off the path and are more preoccupied with gaining more followers (and income) rather than fostering authentic inner growth. *What happened to love & light?*

- Overly dramatic, pseudo-religious types who are more concerned with their own "abundance" rather than helping others. It is highly recommended to avoid using the various names of the *Great Creator* in profit-driven marketing or promotions.
- Fanatical sects and other groups that employ mind control and brainwashing techniques.
- Any riotous, screeching, annoying (and possibly inebriated) humans who are making things worse on Planet Earth.
- Governments, states, and agencies of any nation on Earth.
- Nice Jewish Earthlings who have been falsely accused of possessing space lasers. (However, we do in fact have space lasers.)
- Any aliens[3] pretending to be us.

Furthermore, the Universe and the authors make no guarantees for the level of success or outcomes you may experience when implementing the advice and strategies contained in this book. Consequently, you must accept the possibility that results may differ for each human. With that said, although we cannot provide a 100% guarantee, the Universe still holds hope for humanity. We are all eternal optimists for sure.

With warm regards,

Your Cosmic Coaches, AB1 & AB2

Grammar and Writing Disclaimer: Please note that the attempt to convey concepts, ideas, and thoughts in a form not native to ours – which has been translated through the best efforts of our co-author, LCZ – may have resulted in some incorrect usage of human grammar, sentence structure, and wording. Please keep in mind that we are not here to impress literary agents, but rather, to deliver an important "message from the Cosmos" in a unique communicative style. We are indebted to LCZ for doing an extraordinary job with the intricacies of telepathic transference translation (TTT), as this is a skill (and talent) not yet common on your planet.

Gender Disclaimer: Most Advanced Beings are gender fluid, so we don't typically focus on using certain descriptions, since no one really cares about this stuff in the Cosmos. So, if we are incorrect in our usage somehow, or use one form over the other, please relax. We are all-inclusive and recognize all types of humans. We respect gender fluidity on Planet Earth and in the Cosmos, so why wouldn't you? Perhaps some humans are fearful of change, feel insecure, or have no idea why they are against this issue (or anything else for that matter). It is hypocritical to demand and expect the freedom to be whoever you are but advocate taking away that same freedom from others.

Notes

1. Crazy-ass usually refers to completely crazy with assholery thrown in. If a human is considered a crazy-ass, it is assumed that their "ass or butt" will also follow in the same direction as their brain (or vice versa). There are many types of B.S. (bullshit) and other "shit," but Earthlings seem to prefer bull's shit over others.

2. Secret typically implies something confidential or undisclosed, but if it's on the internet, then it's not very secret, is it? If any organization, led by an anonymous individual or individuals, is cultivating devoted followers by promoting beliefs in all sorts of outlandish and hateful ways, and manipulating or exploiting the internet - without revealing how they acquired their facts or theories but instead encourage you to do your "own research" (which is often misleading in its intention) - then that should be a warning that things are not exactly above board. Furthermore, are these "oracles of opinion" promoting uplifting, wise, and beneficial messages for the common good? If not, then *what exactly* is their goal? If they are angry humans who are promoting anger and divisiveness, then how is that really helping you or your planet? It's one thing to have an "air of mystery" and protect your identity for valid reasons, but it's another matter when it's used primarily to spread falsehoods and fear. This can further encourage negative thinking and behavior. BEWARE and Be Aware of those who are trying to take advantage of you!

3. We delve deeper into Aliens, Advanced Beings, Extraterrestrials, and related topics in the upcoming chapters. When discussing aliens, UFOs, and other unexplained phenomena, it is best to approach the subject with an open mind rather than giving in to hysteria or making assumptions that may inadvertently lead to rumors, anxiety, high expectations, sleep disturbances, excitement, and once in a while, a glimpse of truth.

"To Evolve or Not to Evolve. It is no longer a question."
– The B.O.S.S.[1]

Let's get right to the point. Humanity is now facing a defining moment in time, one that will determine the future of your species. Our advice to humankind is basically a simple one:

GET OFF YOUR BUTTS AND EVOLVE![2]

To avoid a potential doomsday[3] scenario – which could likely include a variety of boo-boos and perhaps, *even an end to your internet service!* – will most likely depend on whether or not humanity can mobilize forces for positive change in time. We hope that our cosmic "knock on the head" will be an effective wake-up call to avert potential unpleasantness and instead, encourage humanity to overcome asinine behaviors, beliefs, and habits.

Isn't it time that the endless lunacy displayed throughout Planet Earth becomes a thing of the past? The likelihood of a civilization falling apart is usually enough motivation for a species to change, but this doesn't seem to be the case on Planet Earth!

Far too many humans still have self-destructive tendencies that negate the advances made through the centuries, causing some sane humans to question whether humanity even has the ability or motivation to properly evolve at all. The Universe sincerely hopes that taking on these challenges will be preferable to the possible risk of a total planetary meltdown.

The main point is that the evolution of any species requires a unified majority to get their *"butts moving,"*[4] otherwise, there is the realistic possibility of sliding backward. Becoming a better human is a major step in the process of evolving and a pivotal juncture for any species that seriously wants to continue with their ongoing existence and keep their planet!

Keep in mind that becoming a better human is not a weekend project. It requires Earthlings to make significant changes to their inner channels. The best way to approach any advice, especially ours, is to keep an open mind with a rational perspective, while simultaneously suspending rigid beliefs and avoiding quick assumptions or inflexible opinions. We realize this may be asking a lot from humans, but this type of mindset is helpful in all areas of life. It especially comes in handy when encountering a book that has cartoon alien characters on the front cover!

However, paying attention to the purpose of this book is much more important than speculating about who wrote it or heaven forbid, not taking it seriously because of its humorous tone. Although humans have been given "pearls of wisdom" throughout the centuries, this is not the time to assume that you've heard it all before, even though you may find some things familiar and even obvious. It is not in anyone's best interest to disregard the information in this book because there are still too many humans who are a work in progress. Our cosmic guidance will generally apply to most of humanity unless, of course, you happen to be an advanced human.

Currently, getting the attention of most humans on Planet Earth has become a herculean task that requires out-of-the-box ideas, such as cute alien book covers that hopefully grab your eyeballs! Things were so much easier in the "bygone days" when burning bushes and walking on water were not in competition with other Earthling theatrics. Sending in a team of wise prophets and spiritual masters was usually more than enough, but not anymore. Fortunately, the Universe recognizes that what works in the past may not work in the present, so it adapts and alters to whatever is needed at any given moment.

Adding to the dilemma of messaging this outreach are the differences in human understanding and abilities. This requires communicating concepts in a way that would be beneficial to as many humans as possible while taking into account the incessant demand to be *constantly entertained* in some manner. The challenge in conveying this information is somewhat made easier by utilizing your various communication technologies, although the priority for the Universe isn't about creating a "presence" on social media.

It was determined that a sensible outreach effort would be best implemented through proven methods of guidance provided from qualified Advanced Being Coaches. These cosmic coaches not only possess multi-species expertise and a good sense of humor, but they are also well-acquainted with various "knuckle-headed"[5] species across the Galaxy. Given the presence of quite a few human knuckleheads residing on your planet, this type of coaching advice was thought to be the most suitable option.

AB Coaches are uniquely qualified to understand the struggles of countless of species who believe they are "intelligent beings" when in fact, they are not even remotely close to being one.

While the Universe is adept at creating miracles when so inclined, a project of this type called for human collaboration and representation, although selecting a human for this task was a miracle in and of itself. Fortunately, Earthling L. ChakraZara was available to assist with the various details required in your dimension and possesses qualifications that align with our requirements, such as otherworldly humor, cosmic insights, and a general enthusiasm for a project of this magnitude. LCZ is not only experienced with advanced tasks that require a steady stream of suspended beliefs (and lots of patience), but is capable of dealing with absurdity, high expectations, and other demands on her time that will take an eternity to complete. She has been cleared for these missions.

"The highly anticipated transformative "aha" moment would happen more quickly if Earthlings would begin to accept responsibility both individually and collectively." – The B.O.S.S.

As a final point, the Universe continues to expand and move forward, with or without humans. Now is the time for Earthlings to take the steps to avoid the possibility of being left behind. Humanity can achieve this transition by understanding that when there is freedom to make authentic changes, the possibility for real transformation will create positive outcomes for personal and collective reality. Ideally, this will lead to a higher level of consciousness but remember, "Rome wasn't built in a day," so start small and go from there.

At this time, humanity has the potential to improve life for everyone, not just for a select few. YOU can create a world that ALL can be proud of by making proper use of the wisdom available to you, not only from this book but from all sources.

Do not underestimate the cosmic power that is within all of you.
We know all about it, *we put it there!* So go on now, *hurry up, and evolve!*

With Love, (*what else?*)

THE B.O.S.S.
CEO of the Cosmos, Director of Universal Beings, Co-Founder of Spiritual, Transformational, and Evolutionary Projects, Manager of Galactic Evolution and Energy Systems, Total Species Theory, Big Bang Boom, The Internet, Quantum Physics, Plumbing and more. Not available for speaking engagements!

"*Humanity has only scratched the surface of its real potential.*" – *Peace Pilgrim*

Notes

1. The B.O.S.S. (Being of Supreme Source), is the Manager of the Cosmos and has no Planet Earth affiliation with the musician Bruce Springsteen, although there is a common bond of love for music and creativity. As far as we know, Mr. Springsteen is not an alien, although some humans may consider him to be advanced.

2. Evolve usually refers to the process of developing from a simpler to a more complex form over time in order to better adapt and survive environmental changes. From a cosmic perspective, evolution is a multi-dimensional process to a more advanced or mature stage. For humans to advance, conscious personal growth is essential. This involves deepening your awareness and taking action to become a better version of yourself. Personal evolution is a shift in perspective of oneself and one's place in the world and the universe.

3. Doomsday scenarios can vary. Stay informed with the Bulletin of Atomic Scientists and the Doomsday Clock. https://thebulletin.org/doomsday-clock/faq/

4. The Universe recognizes that not all species have butts. Human behinds, however, come in many varieties and shapes, "*butt*" what really matters is that when you evolve, *your butt evolves with you!*

5. Knuckle-headed can refer to any species of questionable intelligence, who are usually stubborn and possibly quite foolish, who may do stupid or dumb things.

PART I
OVERVIEW

1. Please Allow Us to Introduce Ourselves

To: Earthling Humans
From: Advanced Being Coaches 1 & 2
Re: Your evolution (maybe)
Date: Eternity

Dear Humans,

Greetings from the Galaxy from your *friendly* Advanced Beings, who are not to be confused with ordinary aliens or ETs. We have been informed of your planet's distress calls and have zoomed into your orbit not a nanosecond too soon! This Cosmic outreach is being made because the Universe is worried about the future of humankind and Planet Earth. We have no choice but to point out your dire circumstances and hope that you will not think of us as cosmic voices of doom because of it.

It shouldn't be taking this long to evolve when considering the many opportunities humans have had to learn from their mistakes. Unfortunately, certain negative habits haven't improved and have actually gotten worse! Surely, it's not smart to keep repeating the same foolish things over and over, not only because you should know better but also because there are numerous available resources to help.

As Advanced Beings, we make every effort to guide species in the right direction *before* there is a complete and irreversible meltdown.[1] As you may have noticed, Planet Earth and humans are having many meltdowns and crises right now. Our mission is to deliver the message that humanity can move forward and overcome these challenges. The Universe has confidence in your ability to improve, but *you also need to believe in it yourselves*! How things will eventually turn out depends on this belief and whether or not humanity values saving itself.

"What happens on Earth does not stay on Earth."

Did you know that negative behavior and low-level energy have ramifications throughout the galaxy? We suspect that many on Planet Earth are clueless about the impact that limited thinking has on the overall cosmic system that all species and life forms are part of. We are all connected in some way, even though this may sound weird to those who usually feel quite disconnected. The cosmic concepts of interconnection are irrefutable in the universe, so it's time for humankind to embrace an evolved vision of life to *avoid a possible disconnection from having a future!*

The moment has come to end denials, false beliefs and the excuse that nothing can be done. To move forward requires *you* to acknowledge your problems, and we are sorry to say, the biggest problem is YOU! You really can't blame anyone else. Make no mistake, this is an emergency project requiring a universal team effort to provide sound principles and timeless wisdom in a manner applicable to Earthlings. This intergalactic assignment is authorized and approved by our Superiors, who have your well-being in mind. Not to mention your entire existence!

However, no need to panic just yet.

The good news is that we have a relatively straightforward human improvement plan that can serve as your guide during this time of major changes. Since you picked up this little guidebook for a reason, we believe the planets and stars may be aligning in your favor. Depending on your situation, this could be a very good omen. Maybe you've realized that something needs to be done about your problems and are ready to take some positive steps. Perhaps you liked our cover picture or enjoyed reading our reviews.

Whatever the reason, the main point is to strive towards becoming better humans to launch your collective evolution. We are confident that our initial 1.0 edition for human betterment is a solid start in taking the steps to get your butts moving in the right direction.

To Be Your Best Self with Cosmic Help, You Need:

Kindness
Emotional Intelligence
Inner Peace
Communication and Connection
Gratitude
Humor
Respect
Non-judgment
Generosity
Wisdom
Ethical Conscience
LOVE

Having a practical approach to changing behaviors doesn't require an advanced degree or countless number of hours to understand. We've taken into consideration that humans are in various stages of development, but no matter where you are, there is something that you can apply to yourself.

"I believe that the Galactic alignment stimulates consciousness evolution on this planet, whether or not beings alive during the alignment era are aware of it happening." – John Jenkins[2]

Despite your challenges, try not to despair or give up just yet. The Universe believes that humanity can reach its full potential so that life on Planet Earth can flourish. Once you have reached evolving velocity, humankind will continue to be a part of the ever-expanding vision of the Universe!

All the Best,

AB1 and AB2 – Advanced Being Coaches, Universally Certified and Licensed

P.S. Please do not worry about alien invasions (a term we truly dislike) or an imminent UFO landing. Our mission is to assist humans, not to further overwhelm Planet Earth.

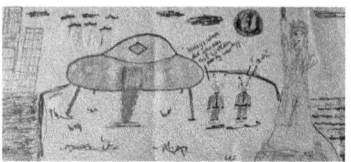

Honey, where did you say this birthday party was?!

Thoughts?

"If our solar system is not unusual, then there are so many planets in the universe that, for example, they outnumber the sum of all sounds and words ever uttered by every human who has ever lived. To declare that Earth must be the only planet with life in the universe would be inexcusably big-headed of us." – Neil deGrasse Tyson[3]

Notes

1. Earthling meltdowns can range from simple tantrums to possible nuclear annihilation. On any given day, meltdowns are hurled at regular folks minding their own business, idiotic folks who annoy rational folks, raging and angry folks who take it out on decent folks, rogue terrorist folks who just want to wage war on all folks, and Mother Earth, who is contemplating the *"Mother of Them All Meltdowns"* for human folks.

2. John Jenkins was an researcher known for theories about astronomical and esoteric connections of Mayan calendar systems of pre-Columbian Mesoamerica. https://en.wikipedia.org/wiki/John_Major_Jenkins

3. Neil deGrasse Tyson, an American astrophysicist and science communicator, studied at Harvard, Texas, Columbia and Princeton University.

2. Don't Let Us Be Misunderstood!

"There is always a possibility that a higher civilization in the universe could visit the Earth and destroy our civilization, or on the contrary, help us make a big leap in our evolutionary development!" – Mehmet Murat ildan, Turkish playwright

Let's Get Clear

Before you begin to *hurry up and evolve*, it's probably a good idea to provide further clarification for offering assistance to Earthlings. This is necessary because there is a general false assumption that any attempt to communicate with extraterrestrials[1] could be dangerous to humankind, which is based on all sorts of fears and biases.

We believe that these beliefs, and the tendency to lump all universal life forms together, stem from confusion about alien life forms in general. Worse, we suspect that these misunderstandings are based on something uniquely human; you judge other species' behavior and motives on your own human biases! A quick rush to judgment about other life forms can be misguided in most cases, whether one is human or not.

Since humans have strong opinions on various topics, especially otherworldly ones, it's a good idea to clear up certain misconceptions. Understandably, there may be some hesitancy in believing our good intentions when there are so many multi-marketers, scammers, and conspiracy theorists creating confusion on your planet. In this current Earth time of non-stop information and intentional fake facts, it can be difficult to know who is or isn't misleading their fellow Earthlings.

Of course, some might find it incredulous that an advanced race would even bother attempting such an outreach when there's such chaos on Planet Earth. Certainly, it may be better not to get involved to avoid adding to the stress taking place on the planet. Despite our assurances and good intentions, it may not stop some humans from preparing for a possible calamity by packing an emergency bag filled with snacks, underwear, and a favorite plush animal – while making a frenzied call to the proper authorities to inform them of a possible imminent alien invasion – because well, *you never know*, right?

Earthlings take note.

We mean NO HARM.
We will *not* take over your planet.
We will *not* fix your problems or wave our magic wands to make things better.[2]
AND, we will *not* abduct or probe you.

We're Advanced Beings, Not (Ordinary) Aliens!

There are numerous outdated beliefs and preconceived notions about alien life forms that continue to exist. Certainly, few humans would envision aliens as life coaches! Actually, *what do you think Advanced Beings would be doing?* Of course, we know what you think we may be doing since many of humankind's various alien stereotypes consist of hostile aliens or adorable ET-like pets.[3] Rarely are we assumed to be nice, thoughtful, and logically advanced beings, with some exceptions, such as Star Trek's Vulcans, who are closer to fact than fiction![4]

You would have less reason to obsess about dangerous aliens if you realized that there are advanced beings who are more interested in promoting advancement rather than invasions. Logically, why would we want to invade or take over your planet when it is quite apparent to any passerby that Planet Earth isn't the most evolved planet on the block?

Considering the current stalled level of humanity and the degradation of your planet, it would be obvious that if advanced beings were going to take over anything, it would be another advanced planet. But then again, when you are advanced, you know better and don't do those types of things.

Ironically, some humans would probably welcome some sort of invasion due to the various problems playing out on all corners of your planet. To be clear, we will not be conducting any rescue missions or invasions. We especially find invasions to be barbaric behavior. In case you somehow missed it, *we are Advanced Beings, not ordinary Aliens!*

Unlike some of your own "illustrious leaders," there will be no authoritarian implementation of evolving advice. In other words, we will not "invade your brains!" Advanced Beings do not condone a controlling mindset or force another being to do anything against their will. Although a forceful intervention to fix another species' problems may seem effective in the short term, it is not considered a preferred method for the long term. We are definitely not "Rambo aliens,"[5] although we do like wearing headbands.

Plus, it's not our style to be hostile!
Our style is sort of groovy, laid-back, hip Advanced Beings.
Just so you know.

And...we are Advanced Beings that care!

Advanced Being Coaches, like human coaches, strive to inspire and guide those who are ready and motivated to make the necessary changes. This partnership requires a sincere commitment to being transparent and honest, especially when it concerns unproductive habits and behaviors that have negative consequences. There's a fine line between telling a species what to do versus an authentic desire to help them change for the better.

We are not here to do the heavy lifting; *you are.* And although we did toss around the idea of a quick little "tweak here and there," we knew it was just wishful thinking on our part. We had this momentary lapse of reason because we feel bad for Earthlings, especially the non-human ones! However, any well-intentioned interference would likely result in humans never truly learning what they need to do, which is to figure out how to solve their problems and do the work.

For humankind to properly get their act together will require taking the steps to, well, getting your acts together! No one should be forced to change, even when one species has superior intelligence compared to another and is willing to share it.

"The greatest gift is the passion for reading. It is cheap, it consoles, it distracts, it excites, it gives you knowledge of the world and experience of a wide kind. It is a moral illumination." – Elizabeth Hardwick, writer

ABs Just Wanna Help

The task of summarizing important cosmic (and comic) wisdom tips into an easy-to-understand format that is not only informative but engaging, is best left to Advanced Beings for sure. Downloading this information into every human brain was not an option (at this time), so we decided to "go retro" and initially utilize the written form of a guidebook to jump-start your neurons. We're keeping our appendages crossed that perusing through our "magnum opus of evolving tips" will get many humans excited about saving themselves!

The good news is that most Earthling brains can grow and create new thought forms when time is taken for inner reflection through reading and meditation.[6] In other words, it's never too late to become a better version of yourself, especially if you have a library card!

A project of this magnitude requires taking deep concepts of evolving and making them palatable to the average human, hopefully accompanied by some delectable snacks to munch on. Taking into account human history and behavior, both past and present, meant that it was necessary to take a new approach to timeless wisdom. The idea of just throwing something together so that we could finish up quickly and head back to our "corner of the galaxy" was tempting, but just not possible, *because we realized we had our work cut out for ourselves!*

Evolve or Devolve. *The choice is yours.*

This galaxy-based coaching program is designed with humans in mind, who else? It's been confirmed that there has been *a ginormous* increase in issues related to attention, distraction, apathy, and boredom. Included in these statistics is the sobering news that the level of human insanity has caused stress levels to skyrocket and could get even worse due to multiple crises.

To add to this conundrum, strategies and guidance are sorely lacking in specific Earthling training related to the process of *how to become a better human.* Ironically, there seems to be quite a lot of advice on how to achieve career success, financial wealth (a popular one!), weight loss, and meeting your perfect partner. Now, these things are important but heck, so is human advancement!

Our research into your predicament also confirmed that MOST HUMANS ARE NOT LISTENING TO OTHER ADVANCED HUMANS. These select few enlightened and advanced Earthlings are doing their best to help, but the reality is that their message is not getting through to those who need it the most. Perhaps all the conflicting advice and theories are causing confusion and paralysis of some kind.

With that being said, we as qualified Advanced Beings are prepared to take on the challenge of how to get these vital messages across, especially when the particular species in question is in no hurry to evolve!

"Those who teach the most about humanity, aren't always human." – Donald L. Hicks, Author

Advanced Beings Will Do This, But Not That!

Since communicating expectations can be tricky, we want to make sure that you do not confuse our roles as coaching guides with miracle workers or worse, with unfriendly aliens! To avoid any possible misunderstandings, our legal buddies over at the Cosmic Council of Conduct Advisory Board (CCCAB) insist that we cover all bases, no matter which part of the galaxy we are in. Please take note of the following:

- We will not control your brain, eat your brain, or take your brain. We are not mad scientists, zombies, or overly enthusiastic neuroscientists. We are content with our own brains and don't need yours.

- We will not be landing or appearing anywhere, until further notice and clearance. There will be no direct, in-person contact with human authorities, "illustrious leaders," or media professionals. Do not waste time scanning the sky looking for our spacecraft or obsessively reading UFO reports, as we will not be accessible at this time. It is also advisable not to contact your "friendly" investigative agent for updates, as they may become less than friendly after receiving a gazillion calls, emails, or texts.

- We will not be transporting, teleporting, or probing any humans, animals, or other Earth species. The same goes for abductions.

- We will not be revealing the secrets of the Universe, such as space travel, anytime soon. Stay tuned, however, for future releases.

- We will not be liable for failed attempts at evolving.

Becoming a better human is all on you! We take no responsibility for any negative outcomes. However, if you follow the advice in this guidebook, there will be a good chance of positive results that may include more chocolate, world peace, and other fun stuff.

- We will, however, sample some of your delicacies, take a few (free) Earthling souvenirs for our families, and snap some pics for our Cosmic Insta-SpaceGram to share with our Galaxy friends.

- We will make the best efforts to guide and inspire you to be the best version of a human.

We Could Be Doing Something Else, BUT...

- As mentioned earlier, we really do care.

- It's the right choice to help species who are less fortunate, less evolved, or not living up to their potential. THIS MEANS YOU!

- We'd like to pass on what we learned. This is especially important since humans are entering a crossroads in the sustainability of life on their planet! Sadly, humans have been in similar predicaments before and experienced a few "civilization rewinds," which aren't much fun unless you like sliding back into depravity and discomfort. Atlantis is more than a myth!

- Our Superiors requested that we give you a helping appendage and initiate this "Become a Better Human Project." They certainly know more than us.

- Planet Earth is like a test case, so if we *"make it here, we will make it anywhere"* in the galaxy. Plus, we get a nice bonus and some time off.

Unfriendly Aliens Would Do This...

- Use their lasers and start zapping humans.

- Land in inconvenient areas and disrupt the wildlife, both human and otherwise.

- Start a Universal campaign blaming humans for all Planetary and Galaxy problems.

- Run for political office.

- Use social media to turn humans against each other, thereby taking control of your brains.

- Join forces with the insect species to finally take over the world.

"I think the surest sign that there is intelligent life out there in the universe is that none of it has tried to contact us." – Bill Watterson, American cartoonist, Calvin and Hobbes

Advanced Being of Assistance

Cosmic help has been offered before but with mixed results! As some of you may have suspected, there have been various **Cosmic Research Assistance Projects (CRAP)** to check in on human evolution through the eons. These projects usually require taking a sensitive and pragmatic approach to Earthling development, but even with that in mind, things do not always go as planned. Certain species simply need time and repeated lessons, as we have learned.

In all cases, serious efforts are made to avoid alarming the general population, but as it happens, things happen. Sometimes, we forget to do our "cloaking thing" and are seen by Earthlings. Other times, we forget our belongings in our rush to leave your planet. Oops. This shouldn't be a surprise, as Advanced Beings can also forget things, especially when in a hurry. When Earthlings find some of this "stuff," it leads to all sorts of crazy theories and opinions, although occasionally, humans come pretty close to some reasonable conclusions.

Advanced Beings make every effort to nudge species development through a variety of methods, all without disturbing the general population or causing hysteria. What's really important to keep in mind about these CRAP excursions (most of them anyway), is that if a planet is visited by Advanced Beings, it is usually to provide some serious CRAP assistance!

Occasionally, some ABs may remain on a planet by blending in with the dominant species and essentially, becoming residents (yes, this is done with proper documentation!). This enables them to plant "seeds of ideas and concepts" while offering assorted guidance from the sidelines. Some of these diligent ABs may still be hanging around your planet, although we cannot confirm or deny their whereabouts.

However, there's no need to worry about the possibility of ABs taking over another species' body by ejecting the current inhabitant, as body snatching is quite overrated, especially on Planet Earth. Additionally, we have no association with pesky "spirits or things that go bump in the night."[7] Their dimension differs from ours.

Anyway, most of us prefer to stay on the quiet, unobserved side and in a way that works best for everyone. Excursions on Planet Earth have taken into consideration that certain varieties of male humans need to be handled with care and sometimes, with complete avoidance. CRAP research has shown that aggressiveness and intolerance can result when there is even a hint of threat to male human domains (and currently, to their websites as well). Due to these and other issues, maintaining a low profile is absolutely necessary for everyone's well-being while performing good deeds.

"The extraterrestrials would probably be far in advance of us. The history of advanced races meeting more primitive people on this planet is not very happy, and they were the same species. I think we should keep our heads low." — Stephen Hawking, Naked Science: National Geographic Channel, 2004

To Be or Not To Be Advanced?

This is a serious question that requires your full attention! Do humans want to get with the program or not? The reason you should be pondering this question at all is that many humans misunderstand what it means to be advanced. There's more to it than just technology or material comforts. The main purpose of our coaching mission is to bring awareness to this simple concept; being advanced is an "inside to outside" job. And who better to bring humankind this awareness than Advanced Beings from the Cosmos, because sometimes, a species doesn't quite see themselves as others do!

In the past, when any civilization welcomed cosmic guidance, it helped them progress and move forward with their development. For example, the Ancient Egyptians were eager to take the evolving process seriously and integrated certain ideas and mysteries into their long-lasting civilization. These were the golden days when humans were less cynical about wisdom and more willing to accept otherworldly help *without constantly asking for proof!*

It may be easy to dismiss the achievements of an ancient civilization when comparing them to modern technological and scientific advances, especially if they involved human sacrifices and bloody battles. However, having a biased opinion of modern advances may lead to a lack of appreciation for the accomplishments in literature, science, math, architecture, philosophy, art, and music made by earlier humans.

We have observed that some modern humans truly believe that progress is called a drive-through and that being advanced is correlated to social media skills. Advancements in medicine, science, psychology, and technology are just one aspect of a civilization's development, and do not necessarily indicate that a higher level of evolution has been achieved.

Advanced Beings perceive progress differently than humans, and we wouldn't be spending so much time clarifying what an advanced being is and how to become one if we thought otherwise. So what exactly do humans need to know or remember?

A species' evolution is not only measured by wealth, technology, and external power, but also by wisdom and inner development. Progressive civilizations reflect what they value the most. There is the advancement of things and the advancement of living beings. Sometimes it can be both, but usually, one takes precedence over the other. Know which one matters the most.

We understand your challenges; we've had our own.

Civilizations that lose their connection to the higher aspects of themselves will eventually fall apart, both internally and externally. Throughout the galaxy, various species experience similar struggles with evolution, so humans are not unique in facing these challenges. Some life forms have learned the hard way, including some unfriendly aliens who have since reformed. After much trial and error, some species finally understand that authentic progress starts from within and is necessary for the evolution of their entire civilization.

Species that can evolve and improve their planet become advanced civilizations. Unfortunately, those who make no effort eventually slide further into chaos or become extinct. "Sad." The chance to turn things around *before an apocalypse* is a choice that can be made and shouldn't be put off for too long.

We know of a few planets where the species decided to ignore common sense and partied like it was "1999999," even while things melted down around them! *There's something to be said* about being inebriated and clueless while society crumbles around you, *although we are not going to say it*. The universe sure does have its share of drama.

We understand what it's like when the time for reckoning is at hand, especially if it means possibly losing some of the many comforts of modern life, such as indoor plumbing, 24-hour access to shopping, pizza delivery, clean underwear, and umpteenth choices of sweet and salty snacks. And of course, *you may be risking the future of your existence!* Make no mistake, we understand the dilemma that humanity is facing. Most species have more in common than not, regardless of the planet they inhabit or whether they are average aliens or advanced beings. The connections we share are greater than the differences that set us apart.

The Universe is Advancing

Did you think it was going backward? You may (or may not) be surprised to hear that "the Universe continues to advance," thereby causing the additional drama of another dimension coming through to a galaxy near you! These new energies are the start of a new paradigm and require your attention since this little *universal crinkle* can cause some destabilization during this phase in your development. To aid in these transitions, species such as humans get all sorts of hints, tips, and other notices that things are changing. However, these cosmic messages may end up being ignored, dismissed, or worse, unnoticed if there is no urgency to evolve.

We have found that chaos during any transitional period is compounded by those who hold on to old ways and are unwilling to let go of outdated and unproductive beliefs, structures, and norms. The fear of the unknown can become overwhelming to those who resist advancing in any way. The challenge is to recognize what doesn't serve humankind any longer. Change is inevitable, but how you handle it is what makes the difference.

In closing, we hope you've gained more insight into advanced beings and why they shouldn't be automatically confused with ETs and aliens. For further details, please go to the FAQ section titled "You've Got Questions?"

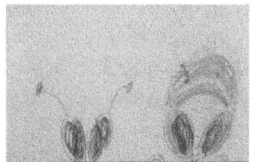

Thoughts? If *YOU* met an extraterrestrial, what would you say or do?

"A single message from space will show that it is possible to live through technological adolescence. It is possible that the future of human civilization depends on the receipt of interstellar messages..." — Carl Sagan, 'The Quest for Extraterrestrial Intelligence,' Smithsonian magazine, 1978.

Notes

1. Extraterrestrial refers to any object or being beyond planet Earth, including aliens, Advanced Beings, and others that have no name.
2. A wand is one way to describe our nano crystal super charged quantum plutonium device, which delivers instant results and can also be used as a back scratcher.
3. In the 1982 film "E.T." by Steven Spielberg, an adorable alien is inadvertently left behind on Earth. While traumatic, most ETs do prepare

for this type of emergency, although sometimes, things don't always go as planned. We give the film a "5+ appendages up" for its realistic portrayal of a wise and kind alien, while also noting that human children tend to be more understanding than some adults.

4. From Star Trek: *The Original Series* created by Gene Roddenberry (TV Series 1966–1969), Vulcans are a fictional extraterrestrial humanoid species in the Star Trek universe and media franchise. In the various Star Trek television series and films, they are noted for their attempt to live by logic and reason with as little interference from emotion as possible. – Wikipedia

5. We do not encourage humans to behave like a "Rambo human" or endorse the viewing of films with excessive violence, nor are we criticizing Mr. Stallone for his choice of outlandish characters. The closest we come to any *Rambo-like* activity is occasionally wearing headbands, which can be a stylish accessory, just like scarves! Eddy, Cheryl. *Predator Is Brilliant Because It's Rambo, But With an Alien*, Pub. 2017: https://gizmodo.com/predator-is-brilliant-because-its-rambo-but-with-an-al-1796009748

6. Research has confirmed that cognitive integrity can be compromised by overexposure to negative audio and visual stimuli. Simply put, watching and listening to negative human behavior is harmful to your mind and overall brain health. As a result, the Universe is encouraging more humans to "go retro" and READ instead. This allows humans to absorb information rather than relying on blabbering humans who may not know what they are talking about, but are trying to convince you otherwise. Take care of your brain! Nicole, Washington and Moore, Lela. *How Meditation Changes the Brain.* Psych Central, 2021 https://psychcentral.com/blog/how-meditation-changes-the-brain#lets-recap

7. Things that go bump in the night include monsters under your bed, zombies, felines who need your immediate attention, and spooky, melodramatic humans who enjoy dressing up.

3. Having Fun Yet?

We Interrupt Your Regularly Scheduled *Human Programming* to Bring You Breaking News... The Sh*t Show on Earth Ramps Up to New Levels of Insanity!

Do humans have any idea *how crazy* things look from here in the universe? Lucky for us, we can change channels! We've been to a lot of galaxies and have seen things that are hard to believe, but during all our travels, rarely have we encountered the level of wacky antics that we see on your planet. When we initially "entered into your orbit," we were a bit tempted to just sit back, grab our nutritionally advanced snacks and watch the bizarre reality show taking place on Planet Earth. Good grief, what a mess! And so much of it is on REPEAT and RERUN.

However, we quickly realized that we couldn't continue chilling while watching human craziness unfold because there is real damage being done all the time, every day! So, we reluctantly put away our snacks, got off our comfy super-advanced recliners, and reviewed our instructions from the B.O.S.S. who gave us a deadline for this "*Leave No Human Behind*" project. In any case, let's get to the point, shall we? Are humans aware that they've been wasting time on useless and destructive behaviors for thousands of years? If this sobering fact hasn't sunk into your brain yet, please allow it to marinate right now.

WARNING! Tough Love and NO Bull Sh*t Ahead!

Although we would have preferred to spend more time on pleasant things such as Earthling chocolate, butterflies, flowers, kittens, and those cute little teddy bears that serve as talismans of sorts, we have to instead bring your attention to the dark, underbelly, yucky stuff that exists on Earth. It's not pleasant to point these things out, but it can't be ignored either because to understand, and CHANGE, requires acknowledging the problems.

For thousands of years, yes, THOUSANDS, various groups of humans have been at war, in conflict or subjugating one another. Anger, hatred, and negativity have been spewed out throughout your planet and continue to this day, despite all the good that has been achieved. Humans sure like to give each other pain and boo-boos, which is not only nasty but also senseless and tragic. One would think that after all this time, humans would stop hurting and killing each other, as well as animals, especially when these actions are so cruel and uncivilized.

Another concern is that several of your *"not so evolved"* leaders and other rogue types have weapons of mass destruction that could potentially destroy the entire planet. If that happens, there's good reason to believe that our project with Earthlings will officially be over.

There's more, unfortunately. On top of this big pile of steamy manure, humans are also determined to destroy their own environment. This is way beyond dumb because it's where you live! And let's be clear, your re-location options are quite slim, if non-existent. This self-destructive behavior needs to be addressed quickly, as time is running out to reverse the damage. It is alarming that some humans remain unconcerned about *the urgency* of this matter, despite the clear signals from the planet indicating imminent consequences, such as eviction.

If this tsunami of threats isn't enough, there are ongoing outbreaks of viruses, diseases, and other strange phenomena grabbing headlines that have nothing to do with Advanced Beings! While these are all extremely compelling reasons to *hurry up and evolve*, the fact is that the choice of staying the same or doing nothing is no longer a viable option when it comes to getting along and working things out. Although the Universe is confident that humans are capable of changing, the reality is that you now have to do something about it.

So, the time to be tweaked[1] is here and NOW, and not a nano-moment too soon. From our experience, we have found that there's nothing like chaos and crisis to spur a species to action!

Denial and apathy can be a potent combination and may prevent you from getting off the couch and taking part in saving humankind. Certainly, it is your choice to reject or ignore the current situation, but you may find yourself at the end of the conga line to "De-Nial,"[2] along with the rest of the ill-informed and deluded group. The tides are shifting and unless you want to be pulled under, it is necessary to snap out of denial and start addressing what is happening on Planet Earth (and in your neighborhoods).

The truth is, humans have a lot of issues and frankly, most of them are of their own making. Our objective observations are meant to provide constructive criticism, not judgment. These insights are intended to help humans gain clarity around challenges and obstacles that must be realistically acknowledged, with the belief that they can be overcome.

Reactions such as resignation, disbelief, and outright indignation at the preposterous idiocy of it all are to be expected! This may be a good time to use your favorite relaxation technique or go-to method to render yourself temporarily unconscious until you can take it all in. Once you regroup, you can begin to convince yourself that there is a positive side to humanity and hope for the future, because there truly is.

So what exactly needs to be tweaked and transformed?

To be honest, there is quite a wide range of human behaviors that span from pretty darn awful to completely horrific. However, this should not lead to despair because negativity and shadow behavior can be overcome when humans realize that it is part of their nature, but not necessarily their destiny.

Recognizing your "dark side" and shadow behavior[3] does not mean excusing negative behavior or avoiding responsibility for your actions. Even though the dark side may hold some attraction for a certain type of human, always remember that there is a price to pay sooner or later. Usually, it's sooner than you think.

The Unpleasant Side of Humankind

VIOLENCE & HATRED

The dark side of humanity can lead to the destruction of families, cultures, groups, and entire civilizations. It manifests in fighting, aggressiveness, cruelty, and killing. This extreme negative energy can result in hate and evil acts, creating a vicious cycle. It is crucial to put an end to this cycle and instead, promote love and healing.

GREED

The fanatical obsession to possess money, objects, and property is a deep-rooted weakness and illusion. In reality, greed is usually about things that are material and earthbound. In case you forgot, or didn't know, there is no "carry-on luggage" in the next dimension. This we're quite sure of.

CORRUPTION AND MISUSE OF POWER

The pursuit of power to control others usually reflects a weak ego that stems from fear, lack of self-control, and worthlessness. The quest for power over others, rather than empowerment, is also a symptom of having a low sense of self, or sometimes, even no self. Many human tyrants are just empty shells of blubbering weaklings.

DEHUMANIZATION

When humans view others as *less than human*, it condones harm, disrespect, and violence. Domination combined with dehumanization is usually caused by fear and hate. Humiliating, dehumanizing, and demoralizing others automatically reduces your self-worth and dehumanizes *you*, no matter how much you try to cover up your own lack of self-worth.

DISRESPECT

Rudeness, contempt, discourtesy and mistreating others reflect low self-esteem, insecurity, and a lack of empathy. Humans may not only lack respect for each other (or for themselves) but also for their planet, other species, and the environment. It is impossible to have a properly functioning society without understanding what respect truly means.

ARROGANCE & IGNORANCE

Being narrow-minded and dogmatic stems from arrogance, pride, and over-confidence. This often leads to difficulties in communication, understanding, and logical reasoning. Pompous loud-mouthed humans, spouting and spewing incessantly via all forms of communication, is truly not a "good look" for themselves or humanity. There has been an uptick in this arrogance-ignorance combo and although we are assuming some human ignorance may be harmless, more of it may be *stupidity on purpose*.

CRUELTY

When humans derive pleasure in the suffering of others, it can morph into evil acts. This is when humans intentionally and maliciously cause mental or physical pain to others, animals, or any living being. Malicious and cruel behavior is completely unacceptable and should be met with swift and appropriate consequences before it becomes normalized.

VANITY & SELFISHNESS

An obsession with the self can result in a shallow human. When you place yourself above everyone in an unhealthy manner, it can lead to a never-ending cycle of ego maintenance that is often at the expense of others. The increase in self-absorption has become popular, fueled by the power of social media which often gives unwarranted attention to conceited humans who believe in their own exaggerated self-importance. There is a vast difference between self-obsession and genuine self-love.

HYPOCRISY AND DISHONESTY ~

The absence of truth, empathy, compassion, or authenticity often results in moral hypocrisy. Saying one thing and doing another can breed contempt for the truth, especially when honor and integrity are not valued or respected. Humans who struggle with truth, and are deceitful or insincere, are not only dishonest with others, but also with themselves.

APATHY ~
A lack of concern or hope diminishes the possibility for change and improvement. Apathy as a choice can also mean that one doesn't believe in anything. The sense of powerlessness over situations can sometimes lead to a defeatist attitude. However, if too many humans become apathetic – not only about their own lives but also about the future of Planet Earth – then destructive forces will grow stronger as apathy fosters negativity and indifference.

"Two things are infinite: the universe and human stupidity; and I'm not sure about the universe." – Albert Einstein, physicist and scientist

Can you acknowledge that these negative human traits and behaviors are not conducive to a happy existence?

Hopefully, most humans would agree that harmful negativity is not fun and is in fact, an outdated way to behave. Who truly prefers all this incredibly distressing drama? Okay, so you may know a few humans who lean toward the dark side. However, ongoing emotional dysfunction and naughty behavior are not only unhealthy for the human who is spewing negativity, but are also damaging to those they come into contact with.

These negative traits can be passed down from generation to generation, leading to repeated tragedy and unhappiness. BUT the chain can be broken when the will to change is strong. Hello! Now may be a good time to become more familiar with understanding karma[4] and the benefits of healing! Human nature is complicated, but more often than not, it leans towards what is good and positive. Sometimes, it is necessary to point out the positive aspects of a species when they are struggling, so that they do not lose hope or give up. The choice to step into an improved version of humanity will require leveraging what is best in humans, but the good news is that there's lots to choose from!

The Pleasant Side of Humans

LOVE: Considered the highest expression for all beings, love is transformational. Love is not only a feeling, but a way of being in this world and the next. Loving and being loved is essential for almost every human, although sadly, there are exceptions because some humans cannot feel or express love of any kind.

KINDNESS: The importance of being kind is often underestimated on Earth. There is no better way to connect with others, human or not, than with a kind heart. Kindness is expressed through compassion, caring, and empathy towards all living beings, and even non-living ones.

RESILIENCE: Perseverance and persistence have helped humans overcome obstacles and survive hardships. This ability to adapt and recover in the face of adversity is vital when dealing with various challenges. Resilience is one of the most crucial skills to have in normal times, but is especially needed during major changes and instability.

HUMOR: Things can become bleak and dreary without some laughter and joy. Humor helps to connect with others and is important for emotional health. If you can't laugh at yourself or enjoy laughing with others, there may be a problem. Laughter is medicine for everyone, but especially for those who lean toward doomsday attitudes and need to lighten up.

CREATIVITY: Humans are imaginative and inventive when they connect with the creative spark within themselves. *Creativity is quite literally an expression of the Universe!* When a human's potential is fully expressed, dreams can manifest into being.

CURIOSITY: A natural inquisitiveness is innate to humans and has led to many discoveries, development and personal growth in civilization. However, curiosity should be tempered with wisdom because as many felines know, "curiosity doesn't always kill the cat" when there's forethought and good sense.

COURAGE: Being brave and facing adversity is a highly admirable trait in a human, especially during dangerous situations or when challenging certain norms or injustices in society. Courage is essential for truth and integrity to triumph, and requires a solid commitment to one's convictions.

GENEROSITY: The human spirit is naturally inclined to give and share with other humans, as well as with other life forms. Being generous is essential for the task of working together to solve problems and is crucial for human survival.

TRUST & FAITH: Trust requires a belief in something greater than oneself and is based on a deep conviction from within. There is an intuitive knowing of a higher purpose and deeper meaning to life, regardless of the dimension one is in. Faith is built on genuine connection rather than blind, unquestioning indoctrination, and creates trust that is earned through mutual respect.

OPTIMISM: Maintaining a positive attitude under almost any circumstance creates the expectation of better outcomes, especially during setbacks. Optimistic humans have a unique perspective on how they see and experience life, tending to look at the bright side of things during their time on the "**Planet Earth Show.**" Humor and optimism, along with some chocolate, go great together!

Conversely, being overly optimistic can be unrealistic and is not the same as maintaining a positive attitude when facing difficulties. Pretending that harmful things don't exist is a form of denial and can lead to "Pollyanna thinking,"[5] which can be seen as outdated and naive, despite having well-meaning intentions.

However, maintaining an optimistic mindset is necessary when things are quickly going downhill because this is exactly when humans need to push through and focus on what is good in their lives. Of course, there will be times when no amount of pushing or focusing is enough, which may then lead to overindulging in some delectable delights or perhaps, banging one's head against the wall. Once this is out of the way, you may not only feel better and regain your equilibrium, but also realize that the "bright side of life" is much more preferable than descending into a state of despair.

You've Got This!

Although we brought up the good and the not-so-good, we urge you not to fixate on the negative. Please resist the temptation to weep and wail or give up on humanity despite the horror, violence, and deviant behavior that some humans continue to perpetuate on others and themselves. No, we *really, really* don't want you to do that. Instead, we would like humans to acknowledge their dark sides, similar to what Darth Vader did in the film, Star Wars[6] and move towards the LIGHT, to those high-level positive behaviors that we listed and any others that you can think of. If you haven't seen the film (which remains popular) you may not understand the reference, but no matter, the important takeaway is that humans' dark sides are *usually* voluntary.

Yes, preferring the dark side is usually a deliberate choice, with some exceptions.[7] To do so requires one to actively shut out empathy and compassion while allowing darker emotions of fear, hate, anger, jealousy, and envy to take over. When humans truly accept and understand their dark sides, the ability to process and release those emotions will become easier to do.

"Being human, at times, is very painful, and that leads us to reawakening." – Suzanne Giesemann, author

Shut Off the Miserable Channel

For some of you, this truly means switching channels from what you usually indulge in and changing it to something more uplifting. Negativity seems to be the default channel for many and unfortunately, there are lots to choose from. If you're not careful, the miserable channel can take up residence in your mind and continue its non-stop negative loop. **This constant negative reinforcement combined with an already pessimistic mindset, creates the possibility of a certain negative reality.** This usually results in a human who regularly expresses an angry and cranky personality, causing other humans (and most definitely animals) to either avoid them or respond in kind.

Unless you enjoy purposefully being negative, you have a choice to be either a PLEASANT[8] or UNPLEASANT human. Yes, this is a decision you can make every day. Aside from serious psychological problems and other assorted dark shadow behavior, we suspect that many of you are simply bored or have nothing better to do than complain and be angry. How about transforming that energy into something positive?

If you are someone who constantly listens to negative humans and agrees with their worldview, please stop and take a moment to think. *What is the point of all this negativity?* Are these ranting humans doing something positive to make life better? If all they do is spread more hatred and anger, then it's important to realize that they may not have your best interests in mind. It's time to snap out of it! You have the choice to either continue immersing yourself in a limited and dark perspective that only amplifies negative energy—a path that will likely not end well for anyone — *or instead*, shift your mindset and actively work towards making life better on Earth.

What does the Universe want humans to do?

Well, it certainly doesn't want you to continue with all the current nonsense, that's for sure! The ability to create a new vision of Planet Earth is up to you, really. If you haven't kept up with the trends, the Cosmic Superiors have a new galaxy vision and expansion project in the works. Of course, the plan is to include humanity and Planet Earth in this exciting vision.

However, it will require you to redefine the purpose of humanity and *reinvent what it means to be human,* while also creating a coherent plan to address the rapidly increasing deterioration of your planet, which includes the possibility of your own extinction. A collective effort is absolutely necessary to make better choices not only for the advancement of humanity, but also for it's continuation in the future. Procrastination is no longer a viable option.

Of course, this will ultimately depend on what humanity will do in the near future. No one likes to be left behind feeling stuck and unhappy, while others move forward to brighter horizons. We believe that humans would naturally want to be part of the "in crowd" in the Cosmos. Therefore, it is crucial to contemplate the choice you have while it's still an option, as chaotic forces may soon take that choice from you. And when that happens, it will definitely not be fun.

The Universe hopes to leave no humans behind! An evolved vision is one filled with possibilities and inspiration. If humanity DOES NOT make an effort to evolve, what do you think will happen? Some possibilities are boo-boos, meltdowns, chaos, the Apocalypse, and on-going mayhem!

Thoughts?

The greatest wisdom is in simplicity. Love, respect, tolerance, sharing, gratitude, forgiveness. It's not complex or elaborate. The real knowledge is free. It's encoded in your DNA. All you need is within you. Great teachers have said that from the beginning. Find your heart, and you will find your way." – Carlos Barrios, anthropologist and authority on Mayan history

Notes

1. In this context, tweak means to adjust, modify, CHANGE for the better, and *does not* mean to abuse drugs, get high or go bonkers!

2. Denial is a refusal to admit the truth or reality of something. The Nile is the longest river in the world in Northeastern Africa, and when mentioned, Egypt usually comes to mind.

3. Dark sides do not connote a specific color but rather a negative essence or energy within a species. A human's "shadow side" often represents the hidden aspect of someone that is unconscious or repressed. Once acknowledged, it loses its power over you, unless of course, you happen to be someone who prefers working from a darker energy.

4. A cycle of cause-and-effect, karma is an energy created by willful action, through thoughts, words, and deeds. If humankind would better understand this concept, lots of stuff would be resolved while still on Planet Earth. But since that isn't always possible, you'll have more time to ponder your behavior once you're in the hereafter, the next dimension, heaven, the other side, or wherever you may end up!

5. The tendency to primarily focus on pleasant things over more unpleasant ones, regardless of external circumstances, is "Pollyanna thinking." This description was based on a fictional character, the heroine of the novel Pollyanna (1913) by Eleanor Porter.

6. In the 1977 film *Star Wars Episode IV: A New Hope*, written and directed by George Lucas, the term 'The Dark Side" came about as a result of the plot line with Dark Jedi Darth Vader. We've encountered a few "Darth Vaders" in our travels and can attest that dealing with dark sides is never fun, especially if it's an advanced being who turns the wrong way. So much energy is wasted on engaging in negative behaviors.

7. Undeliberate exceptions include serious brain disorders, emotional dysfunctions, genetic disposition to being an idiotic human, sociopathic tendencies, being a bad seed, unhealed abuse, and any other human obstacles that get in the way of making better choices.

8. An authentically PLEASANT human can have many positive characteristics, such as kindness, empathy, and a good sense of humor, which is necessary when dealing with those who are unpleasant. If you are a PLEASANT human reading this, you may be feeling distressed about all the unpleasantness going on. Please keep in mind that others are depending on you, so please don't give up.

4. 911 from Planet Earth

I will survive. Will you? – Mother Nature

"A radical inner transformation and rise to a new level of consciousness might be the only real hope we have in the current global crisis brought on by the dominance of the Western mechanistic paradigm." – Dr. Stanislav Grof [1]

Planet Earth's Post

The current Planetary situation is serious. The planet is unwell and needs immediate care. Humankind's actions have contributed to the accelerating distress of the planet. A united approach is necessary to avoid the likelihood of irreparable damage that quite possibly, will end human life on Earth.

You Need Your Planet. The Planet Does Not Need You.

The tipping point has been reached. If you are currently living on Planet Earth, you should be aware of the dire warnings from many scientists, environmentalists, and other concerned humans who recognize the dangers ahead. If you have any appendages stuck in your ears, please take them out now. No matter what you happen to believe, or not believe, humans are currently living with planetary changes that are increasingly severe and destructive.

We realize that the climate crisis [2] and its warnings of ongoing environmental damage, dying oceans, ecological devastation, species extinction, pollution, and depletion of natural resources are enough to cause massive hair follicle loss or shriveling of appendages BECAUSE *it could mean the end of many things you hold dear – such as eating, breathing and living a comfy life!*

Humans have not only ravaged [3] nature, but have also provoked the planet to respond to the many offenses of mistreatment and damage.

If humans wish to continue living on Planet Earth, there has to be a collective end to procrastination, ignorance, and denial. Any human who continues to be stubbornly unconvinced – or remains willfully and obliviously *unconcerned* – should keep in mind that avoiding responsibility will likely lead to some very unpleasant outcomes, several of which are already happening.

Planet Earth and nature form a closed-loop dynamic system when it comes to matter and an open system in terms of energy.[4] Both operate based on Mother Nature's fundamental rules of interdependence, self-regulation, and ecological equilibrium. When a dominant species, such as HUMANS, tips the scales past management and disrupts this balance, consequences arise that will affect all inhabitants of the planet.

"The earth is but one country and mankind its citizens." – Baha'u'llah[5]

Cosmic Post

If you are waiting and hoping for some form of *Divine* intervention to intercede in any possible upcoming calamity, remember that although all things are possible, *the Universe is all about teaching lessons!*

"Going to Mars might be a fun goal. But keeping us alive requires staying focused on Earth." – Kelsey Piper, Writer for Vox[6]

No Vacancy Available!

Any super-rich human who is currently investing time and money in space colony missions should instead, focus on funding environmental projects to help restore Planet Earth. It's much more realistic for humankind to address the many concerns of the planet *before* planning for any future relocation projects or ego-driven excursions into the galaxy. However, that does not mean putting an end to space exploration or other efforts to understand the universe.[7] It just means that commonsense is needed. If you are using your wealth to further degrade the planet, then you are part of the problem and not the solution.

Why is it even necessary to point out that Earth is your only available planet at this time? More to the point, it is your current permanent residence, not a temporary rental to trash and leave in disarray. Unrealistic expectations, like having an "exit plan," are unproductive. The Universe will not support any relocation efforts, regardless of technological ability, when one's current home is so neglected. When a species fails to properly maintain and clean up their planet, it is logical to assume they will create messes elsewhere!

Current human behaviors are certainly alarming and perplexing when it comes to maintaining environmental and personal order throughout a range of habitats. How is it possible that so many humans can go about their business while the home they live in is in such bad shape? Granted, some humans have a high tolerance for trash, disorder, and unsafe environments, choosing to adapt rather than improve their surroundings. However, continuing the neglect and abuse of one's residence will eventually result in serious damage and things falling apart. Procrastination is no longer an option, not that it ever was.

When a species continually ignores planetary distress signals, it unfortunately confirms that a necessary level of "evolutionary maturity" has not yet been achieved.

"Humanity is causing a rapid loss of biodiversity and, with it, Earth's ability to support complex life. But the mainstream is having difficulty grasping the magnitude of this loss, despite the steady erosion of the fabric of human civilization. The scale of the threats to the biosphere and all its life forms is so great that it is difficult to grasp for even well-informed experts. The problem is compounded by ignorance and short-term self-interest, with the pursuit of wealth and political interests stymieing the action that is crucial for survival." – Professor Corey Bradshaw, Flinders University, Australia[8]

It's Not Nice to Fool (with) Mother Nature![9]

Nature has its ways of fixing problems, and what begins as a minor repair can quickly escalate into a full tear-down and then, a complete restoration. Considering that humans have proven to be the biggest problem for the planet, the outcome of these *"repairs"* does not bode well for civilization.

It should be obvious that plundering and abusing your environment is unwise, especially since you actually need your planet to stay alive.

Now is a good time to remind you that "Shop and Drop" food stores, or any store, will not remain open during a planetary meltdown. For those who doubt this or are misinformed, it's important to remember that life's necessities, like food and water, are provided by Mother Nature, not some mega-shopping conglomerate![10] A disruption to the ecosystem will have a much greater impact on humans than on the planet itself, potentially leading to the termination of all services in the long run.

Perhaps you're wondering how humankind ended up in this predicament. If you're still in the dark, then you'll need to catch up quickly as this is no time to be left behind wondering about it all! There are lots of reasons for this mess, many of which are well-documented. It is highly recommended that you READ, LISTEN, or WATCH expert-based research based on the foundations of scientific, historical, and ecological studies. Now would be a good time, before the Apocalypse, to utilize the library, connect with educated professionals, or read a real book, rather than just listening to random self-titled experts on social media channels.[11]

"Making a huge mess doesn't necessarily mean that it's the end of the world. However, in some cases, it actually is." – The B.O.S.S.

Modern advancements have both positive and negative consequences. When a species has not properly evolved, there is a chance that the negative consequences will overshadow the positive ones. Mindless and selfish progress can lead to a feeling of superiority over the natural world. Consequently, this has resulted in actions and behaviors that have eroded humanity's relationship with nature and the planet.

Caring for the land has been replaced by organizations and businesses that prioritize profits over the environment. The advancement of modern technology has sadly increased the disconnection from nature and the world. Virtual reality has, in some cases, completely replaced environmental and personal reality. Then, of course, *some humans seem to have no sense of reality at all!* But that's another subject for another time.

Clearly, a lot of things need to change, and they need to change soon!

Individuals, businesses, and organizations must prioritize respecting and appreciating nature to become truly evolved stewards of the planet. The awareness and understanding that all things in nature are interconnected are essential to effectively address the damage to ecosystems and the environment. Developing a relationship with nature is the first step in finding sustainable solutions so that humankind can coexist properly with all life on the planet. Any further steps will depend on whether humans can agree to work together to take action *in time.*

There are some promising signs that humanity is attempting to do the right thing for the planet. However, a massive, worldwide movement is necessary for these efforts to make a difference. Although mindsets and habits must change to create a new level of awareness, anyone can improve their connection with nature right away.

As a way to feel more invested in the process, you can begin by dipping your appendages in the grass or hugging a favorite tree to feel connected with Mother Nature. Take a walk outside for *Earth's sake* and notice that you are actually living on the planet! It's the ultimate virtual experience.

For anyone who may feel clueless about the importance of this relationship, connecting with nature is one of the first steps in healing the planet and respecting your environment.

"Human society is in jeopardy from the accelerating decline of the Earth's natural life-support systems, the world's leading scientists have warned, as they announced the results of the most thorough planetary health check ever undertaken." – Jonathan Watts Global environment editor, The Guardian, May 6, 2019[12]

How Much Proof Do You *Need*?!

Some Earthlings have the opinion that human activities, such as carbon emissions, are not connected to climate change, global warming, or environmental devastation. In fact, these may be the same Earthlings who regularly litter and leave messes for others to clean up after! While certain planetary changes can occur independently of a species actions, it does not excuse personal and collective responsibility for the well-being of the planet. Dismissing and belittling scientific facts with personal viewpoints is absurd, especially when those facts point directly to behaviors that are contributing to the problem!

There are times when it becomes necessary for a planet to balance and reset its natural systems in order to survive. Sometimes, a planetary reset occurs due to events outside of its system, such as asteroids, which can cause a reaction that changes the trajectory of life on a planet. Sadly, some planets die through no fault of their own.

The significant planetary changes should not be ignored, as time is running out for a leisurely discussion about the matter. Humans need to reach a consensus on how to address these issues. Constantly arguing about the reality of the global climate crisis and environmental damage, or placing blame without taking responsibility, is unproductive and foolish.

A united effort is overdue to implement solutions to address the multitude of ecological crises. Ideally, this would create better stewardship of nature and the planet. There is no time like the present to recognize what needs to be done and then *do something about it.* Why would any human think that a "wait and see" attitude is an appropriate response at this point?

It is crucial to adopt a sustainable stabilization strategy to prevent further damage. It is becoming increasingly clear that Planet Earth is moving forward with her own stabilization plans, with or without you.

Mother of a Meltdown Coming Soon

The Earth is rapidly approaching its limits in providing for the growing human population in terms of food, energy, and waste absorption.

Unsustainable economic practices are causing environmental damage in both developed and underdeveloped nations alike. This cannot continue without risking irreversible harm to vital planetary systems.

Once ecosystems enter this acceleration process, it will become increasingly difficult to reverse or slow down the collapse. The likelihood of increased chaos and apocalyptic scenarios is high. Buckle in!

The discovery of plastics in the tiniest ocean microorganisms caused by pollution and consumer habits should be a major cause for alarm. Plastic should not be a part of any species' diet unless, of course, you happen to be a species that can digest plastic!

Earth is experiencing serious hot flashes, which does not bode well for humanity. Extreme climate changes and natural disasters are occurring more rapidly than previously anticipated.

Mother Earth seems ready to end the relationship and is no longer that into you!

"If we [humans] disappeared overnight, the world would probably be better off." – Sir David Attenborough, biologist, natural historian, and writer

Every day is Earth Day

Showing genuine appreciation for the Earth goes beyond simply marking a token holiday on your calendars. Building a respectful relationship with Mother Nature involves forming a strong bond rooted in a sincere commitment to care.

In the past, humans were more in tune with natural cycles and had a stronger connection to Earth. However, due to advancements and short memories, humans have become increasingly disconnected from the natural world, causing harm to both themselves and the planet. Unfortunately, if humans continue to neglect their relationship with the natural world, Mother Earth will make it clear that she's *"not gonna take it anymore."*

When was the last time you enjoyed the outside world? If humans aren't spending enough time in nature, then realistically, what are the chances of changing the relationship you have with your planet?

One way to rekindle your connection with the natural world is to immerse yourself in it. Take a walk in the woods, stroll on the beach or visit a park to feel the natural vibes you have been missing. Listen to the birds chirping, feel the wind on your body and appreciate the beauty of the trees, plants and flowers. *Mother Earth needs to know you care!*

"The health of the ecosystems on which we and other species depend is deteriorating more rapidly than ever. We are eroding the very foundations of economies, livelihoods, food security, health and quality of life worldwide. We have lost time. We must act now." – Robert Watson, Intergovernmental Science – Policy Platform on Biodiversity and Ecosystem Services (IPBES), May 7, 2019[13]

You're not the *only* ones on the Planet you know!

The fact that there are plenty of humans who still believe they're entitled to dominate other species and the environment should be embarrassing for all of humanity. Although this does not apply to all cultures, there is a persistent mistaken idea that it is acceptable to use up resources without considering the negative consequences of not taking moral responsibility for the world around you. This unenlightened mindset reflects a selfish and entitled attitude towards your world.

Many life forms are now threatened by human actions that have had severe impacts. Destroying natural habitats, killing for sport, operating dreadful animal factories, over developing land, destroying native sanctuaries, and other devastating actions are inhumane! Humankind must have respect and honor for all life on Planet Earth.

Humans are not the only ones that matter! Showing concern for other species and properly sharing the environment with all its inhabitants is not just a nice idea – it is critical to the planet's ecological well-being and your very own survival! There is no longer any question that human actions have caused destruction and damage, some of which is irreversible. It's time to revise this outdated approach to coexisting with each other on your planet.

"Honor the sacred. Honor the Earth, our Mother. Honor the Elders. Honor all with whom we share the Earth: Four-leggeds, two-leggeds, winged ones, Swimmers, crawlers, plant and rock people. Walk in balance and beauty." – Native American Elder

There is a direct correlation between how a civilization treats all species and life forms, and how advanced that civilization truly is.

Earthling creatures are suffering through no fault of their own. Perhaps it's time to assist them rather than the humans who are causing them distress. Frankly, if our mission *to* awaken human hearts and minds doesn't go as planned, it might make more sense to help these creatures instead of humans. They may have a higher chance of recovering after a worldwide meltdown and deserve to be saved.

What's more, humans may not be as highly developed as they believe themselves to be, which isn't that surprising when there's a reluctance to "hurry up and evolve." Certain groups of animals and species are providing some serious competition in terms of intelligence. When you compare an "average human"[14] to the abilities of dolphins, whales or chimpanzees, one finds that human intelligence is sometimes very overrated.

For instance, Earthling pets have figured out how to manage humans effortlessly. It is quite impressive that cats and dogs have worked out their living arrangements without an overthrow of humanity. This is high intelligence indeed. As for the pest population, humans might want to reconsider their current approach to "pest control," as you never know when a push-back from this group may happen. It may be worth reevaluating the reasons for exterminating insects and think about their function in the big picture. Yes, we realize that some of them creep out humans or are, well, pests. However, they're not too thrilled with humans either. Have you *ever* considered life from their perspective?

"The more we observe humans, the more we like your animals." – AB1 & AB2

They've Got Something to Say and Humans Need to Listen

"If you talk to the animals they will talk with you and you will know each other. If you do not talk to them you will not know them and what you do not know, you will fear. What one fears, one destroys." – Chief Dan George, Tsleil-Waututh Nation

If you truly look into the eyes of a non-human species, you may realize that they are aware beings with feelings and perceptions. We have looked and listened and so should you.

- Most furballs typically love their humans unconditionally, but that can change quickly.

- While *you* may see cute furballs, *we* see a cleverly disguised

---

species that has successfully achieved almost complete control of your residences. The collaboration between felines and canines for world domination is currently on hold because humans are increasingly acting like staff, and they like it!

- Some animal pets only tolerate weird human behavior because of snacks and other perks.

- Most species do not enjoy chattering incessantly like humans, with the exception of some small mischievous monkeys, chatterbirds, AND some annoyed squirrels.

- Earth's creatures do not intentionally start wars or set out to destroy each other, although some insects are battle-prone. However, human conflicts impact all species, causing fear, pain, and hardship.

- Many species have been forced to tolerate human disruption to their natural habitats and feel ill-treated when their homes and food sources are destroyed and taken from them. Increasingly, they are trying to find new habitats and end up interacting more often with humans, which is not ideal for anyone.

- Earth's creatures do not use guns or weapons (yet), but some species are starting to push back with the tools and skills they do have.

- Most species don't litter like humans (poop doesn't count) but many of them are eating YOUR LITTER!

- Earth's creatures live in the moment. If they're chewing, then they are chewing. If they're pooping, then that's all they are doing. If they're sleeping, do not bother them.

- Non-human life forms do not care about politics, gossip,

money, or other distractions, but they do care about survival.

- Earth's species are sensing planetary changes and experiencing distress because of intolerable conditions, yet humankind is not as concerned as they should be. Many are now under a threat of extinction or have gone extinct. All these changes are extremely stressful.

- Almost all species have feelings and some level of intelligence, more than you may realize. They feel, they absorb, they are sentient[15] (with very few exceptions).

- There is a great deal of sadness among creatures regarding humankind's struggle to properly coexist with them or with any other living beings.

- They desire for humankind to appreciate life on Earth and to acknowledge that all animals and species are valuable and beautiful, even the ones that may seem a bit scary.

AND now... a message from insects, reptiles, plants, trees, rocks, plankton, and other various life forms that *don't always receive the recognition they deserve.*

These creatures and species want humans to understand that they are not just taking up space in the world but are interconnected as part of an ecosystem with one another, which also includes YOU! Your planet's entire environment is ALIVE with energy and a life force. This should not be a NEWSFLASH, but we believe it may be for some. It's time for humans to become AWARE of this connection with all beings on the planet.

Work with all of Mother Nature's creatures to help restore and heal Planet Earth.

"The fact is that no species has ever had such wholesale control over everything on earth, living or dead, as we now have. That lays upon us, whether we like it or not, an awesome responsibility. In our hands now lies not only our own future, but that of all other living creatures with whom we share the earth." – Sir David Attenborough, biologist, natural historian, and writer

Make Earth Great Again! (MEGA!)

If this isn't a priority, then what is? Humans cannot continue disrespecting Mother Earth because it is not a winning strategy moving forward. The silver lining in the dark clouds hovering over your world is that there is a growing group of humans who love and respect Earth and its inhabitants. These caring and brave souls are out there, on your behalf, doing the heavy lifting, and if you happen to be one of them, great. If not, get yourself in gear and move it, because MEGA is the new way forward in all of your world, *not just select parts of it!*

You would be making a positive impact by helping the natural world and wildlife instead of spending time following trends or groups led by various knuckleheads (if this is what you are usually doing). Many phony groups do not care about your future, only their own! Instead, join in with those who have taken up the task of saving the environment and humankind, which consists of a diverse assortment of individuals, environmentalists, scientists, community groups, and Indigenous and Native people.

Indeed, these humans are doing something great by leading the way to find solutions to various problems. What's also encouraging is the growing number of organizations and businesses that are increasingly prioritizing environmental sustainability. Not to be left out, even human children are speaking up and in some cases, taking action!

So what's your excuse? If you're angrily spouting empty slogans and think you stand for something important, we have COSMIC NEWS for you; you're not. You may be part of the problem. But remember, you can be part of the solution instead, through a real, united effort to *Make Earth Great Again!*

The bottom line is that MEGA inspires you to believe in the greatness of not only the planet, but also of yourself and others. In reality, the planet is already great; it's humankind that needs to realize this. Humans may not all get along or like each other, but that becomes irrelevant when you realize that this is the only planet you have and without it, all of humankind loses. And from what we gather, there's a bunch of humans who *do not* like being losers.

"Unless our fundamental sacred connectedness with every being and thing is experienced deeply and enacted everywhere, religious, political, and other differences will go on creating intolerable conflict that can only increase the already dangerously high chances of our self-annihilation." – Andrew Harvey, Founder & Director of the Institute for Sacred Activism

Is It a Lost Cause?

We don't think so, at least not yet. We wouldn't be encouraging humans to become better versions of themselves if there wasn't a chance for evolution. However, you will need to have a properly functioning planet that provides for your basic requirements. We understand that becoming a better human may get tossed out the window if your favorite snacks and WIFI are unavailable when you need them the most. If food and water are scarce, and extreme climate mood swings and planetary vengeance become the new norm, then understandably, that may leave little time to work on yourself and finish this book! While this is a very real and pressing issue, it is all the more reason to start taking action now, rather than waiting until the last minute.

So the question that presents itself is this: should you hurry up and evolve to save the planet, or do you save the planet first and then evolve? As ABs with experience in this matter, we believe that you can do both at the same time!*

It's understandable that juggling the downfall of humanity and the meltdown of the planet can be quite daunting! To be clear, dealing with it all is probably not going to be easy. However, if humanity remains stalled at this pivotal moment, then all bets are off because if you think things are tough now, imagine them a lot tougher. One of the biggest obstacles will be changing the mindset that has contributed to your current issues, as it is proving to be unsustainable for a functioning society.

It would certainly be helpful if humans sped things up and began developing an enlightened mindset. However, if that shift doesn't happen right away, humanity can still take crucial steps to *get going!* Preventing a planetary breakdown – and consequently, a human one – will require immediate and strategic changes to the consumption of resources, transitioning current systems to zero waste sustainability, and essentially remaking civilization (it's been done before!) so that it works fairly for everyone on the planet.

Of course, it might be helpful to enjoy a few delectable delights while contemplating the various personal changes necessary for humanity's upgrade, all of which are conveniently outlined in this guide. This cosmic guide to behavior change is beneficial for all humans, snacks or no snacks, but is especially helpful for those who rarely think about improving themselves because they're *too busy partying like it's 1999!*

"What happens next, is up to every one of us." – *Sir David Attenborough*

TRY *NOT* TO PANIC KEY POINTS

Earth's biological clock is *ticking*, which can be reason enough to feel a little panicky. Adding to the issue is the fact that the state of Planet Earth may be worse than most humans realize. If things don't radically change soon, a cascade of interrelated events will become increasingly unmanageable and *scary!* If you were hoping that this Key Point section would somehow soften the tone of previous warnings of gloom and doom, you were mistaken. Sometimes, a little panic can be a motivating factor in finally doing something when there's still a chance of averting terrible consequences.

"We can't kick this can down the road any longer." – *Andrea Dutton, Geoscientist, University of Wisconsin, Madison.*

YES, *DO* SOMETHING!

If you're making excuses to ignore the obvious, you may want to keep in mind that a day may come when that will no longer be an option. Doing nothing is not a great excuse, because *when did ignoring a problem ever make it go away?* If you answered "not often" or "never," that is correct. Although it can be an option once in a while, it certainly isn't a good choice now.

Humanity can and must improve its relationship with the world. Almost all humans can manage to do something. However, to make any real impact on improving your situation, organizations, world governments, and other prominent and influential humans will also have to DO SOMETHING to implement and coordinate a plan of action. How society and its systems are set up and operated will have to change. While it is no small undertaking to reboot human civilization, it can be done. Yes, most of you can *do something!*

"I often hear people say climate change is about saving the planet, but that seems utterly misguided to me — the planet will be fine, we will not be." – Sean Illing, Writer[16]

Hopefully, not on a final note...

- The climate and ecological crisis is a human issue that affects everything: food, water, health, air quality, safety, finances, and basically, your entire existence. You should care about at least one of those, if not all of them.
- No matter where you live on Planet Earth, everyone will experience some type of impact.
- Denying or ignoring the situation will not make it go away.
- There needs to be an understanding and consensus about the reality of these changes.
- Embrace what you are feeling – fear, anger, guilt, sadness, apathy, overwhelm, etc. – and transform it into constructive action or a positive contribution.
- Connect with others who understand and support becoming an effective change agent.
- Be part of the solution, not the problem because everything you

do, or do not do, matters now.
- Become resilient, hopeful, and courageous. Take breaks and continue to enjoy the beauty of life.
- Show kindness and appreciation to each other and the planet. This alone can be transformative, and *who knows, maybe the Universe will provide a miracle after all.*

"Humankind has not woven the web of life. We are but one thread within it. Whatever we do to the web, we do to ourselves. All things are bound together. All things connect." – Chief Seattle, Duwamish

When humanity heals the relationship they have with themselves and nature, they may come to find that solutions, collaborations, insights, and positive changes will simultaneously occur. This will then beneficially impact the well-being of all who live on Planet Earth.

Why would this happen? Because you are all connected, *that's why!* Separation is an illusion!

Repeat After Us

I care for other non-human species and nature.
I respect nature and am a good steward of the Earth.
I connect with nature and appreciate what it provides.
I inspire myself and others to lead more sustainable lives.
I respectfully use natural resources of food, water and air.
I am simplifying and reducing my carbon footprint.
I reuse and recycle and am a caring human.
I clean up my messes and trash, and do not create new ones.
I support environmentally conscious organizations and groups.

I treat Mother Earth with kindness, love and respect.

I endorse efforts to sustainably use resources and respect the environment.

I appreciate all of nature's gifts and natural beauty that is available to me.

I will LOVE MY EARTH MAMMA every day AND will never forget that I am a guest in her house.

A Few of Mother Earth's Favorite Things

Raindrops. Sunflowers. Orchids. Roses. Kittens. Puppies. Birds. Snowflakes. Ice. Seasons. Land. Oceans. Beaches. Coral. Forests. Trees. Leaves. Mountains. Glaciers. Fish. Seashells. Rocks. Crystals. Flowers. Water. Frogs. Grasshoppers. Whales. Sharks. Waterfalls. Lakes. Rivers. Streams. Warm breezes. Thunderstorms. Lightning. Fire. Clouds. Sunshine. Wind. Soil. Vegetables. Fruit. Bees. Fireflies. Honey. Herbs. Plants. Seeds. Glaciers. Deserts. Canyons. Caves. Sand. Rain-forests. Elephants. Mice. Spiders. Bugs. Reptiles. Large and Small Mammals. The entire Animal, Plant and Sea Creatures of the World. Humans who show respect and appreciation for Nature's beauty and their Planet.

These must be the evolved ones!

Thoughts?

"The Great Work now, as we move into a new millennium, is to carry out the transition from a period of human devastation of the Earth to a period when humans would be present to the planet in a mutually beneficial manner." – Thomas Berry, The Great Work, cultural historian

Notes

1. Dr. Grof, PhD., has researched non-ordinary states of consciousness. https://www.stangrof.com/

2. The final warnings from scientists are dire BUT there's still hope if you HURRY UP to find solutions! Boehm, Sophie and Schumer, Clea. *10 Big Findings from the 2023 IPCC Report on Climate Change*, 2023 https://www.wri.org/insights/2023-ipcc-ar6-synthesis-report-climate-change-findings

3. Besides "ravaged," other words to describe how humans mistreat the planet are devastate, destroy, damage, wreak, plunder, and exploit.

4. One Earth's mission is to heal the Earth. https://www.oneearth.org/

5. Bahá'u'lláh, founder of the Bahá'í Faith, was one of many "Divine Educators" sent to assist humanity. Challenges are expected during Earth trips. https://www.bahai.org/

6. Kelsy Piper explains how humanity can mitigate risks to civilization. Piper, Kelsey. *The Case Against Colonizing Space To Save Humanity*, Vox 2018 https://www.vox.com/future-perfect/2018/10/22/17991736/jeff-bezos-elon-musk-colonizing-mars-moon-space-blue-origin-spacex

7. The Universe encourages scientific explorations of the galaxy when it is for the higher good of all.

8. Read it and weep. Science Daily's planetary prognosis. Flinders University, 2021. Summary: "An international group of 17 leading scientists have produced a comprehensive yet concise assessment of the state of civilization, warning that the outlook is more dire and dangerous than is generally understood." https://www.sciencedaily.com/releases/2021/01/210113090922.htm

9. Truer words were never spoken, but should be! This catchy slogan is from a vintage Chiffon Margarine commercial. Ironically, it was promoting *fake* butter. Mother Nature does not approve of fake products. This is not a

criticism of humans who enjoy margarine, or any margarine company, including Chiffon (which is no longer in business). https://en.wikipedia.org/wiki/Chiffon_margarine and https://www.youtube.com/watch?v=gDkiq5jD5Hc

10. Shop & drop shopping offers fast and convenient options for life's necessities. Any resemblance to real grocery stores is "not a coincidence" and is meant to emphasize a point. **We are not associated with any Earthling food conglomerates, *but* we may consider the possibility of endorsing an organic chocolate company to raise awareness around sustainability.**

11. Many experts are more concerned about the planet than social media, although sharing factual information is helpful. Dag Hammarskjöld Library, Research Guides, Climate Change - A Global Issue, Consulting the Experts: https://research.un.org/en/climate-change/experts and NASA, 2024: Climate Change, Scientific Consensus https://climate.nasa.gov/scientific-consensus/

12. Josef Settele, entomologist at the Helmholtz Centre for Environmental Research, states: "The situation is tricky and difficult but I would never give up. The report shows there is a way out. I believe we can still bend the curve. People shouldn't panic, but they should begin drastic change. Business as usual with small adjustments won't be enough." **The Cosmic opinion is that a little panic can go a long way when a species needs to wake up!** Watts, Jonathan, Global environment editor. *Human Society Under Urgent Threat From Loss of Earth's Natural Life.* The Guardian 2019, https://www.theguardian.com/environment/2019/may/06/human-society-under-urgent-threat-loss-earth-natural-life-un-report

13. IPBES Global Assessment: https://www.un.org/sustainabledevelopment/blog/2019/05/nature-decline-unprecedented-report/

14. Hoffman Ph.D, Bobby. *Do You Think More Intelligently Than the Average Person?* Psychology Today, 2019 https://www.psychologytoday.com/us/blog/motivate/201910/do-you-think-more-intelligently-than-the-average-person and *The Downfall Of Human Intelligence With The Advent Of Technology.* (2021). Edubirdie. 2025 https://edubirdie.com/examples/the-downfall-of-human-intelligence-with-the-advent-of-technology/ and *How Intelligent are Whales and Dolphins?* WDC, Whale and Dolphin Conservation, nonprofit organization https://us.whales.org/whales-dolphins/how-intelligent-are-whales-and-dolphins/

15. Olafsson, Björn. *What 'Sentience' Means and Why the Concept Matters for Animals.* Sentient Media 2023 https://sentientmedia.org/sentient-definition/

16. It can always be worse, but don't let it get to that point! Wallace-Wells, David and Illing, Sean. *It Is Absolutely Time to Panic About Climate Change.* Vox Media 2019 https://www.vox.com/energy-and-environment/2019/2/22/18188562/climate-change-david-wallace-wells-the-uninhabitable-earth

PART II
WHAT IS YOUR REALITY?

5. Follow the Leader?

"A leader leads by example, not by force." – Sun Tzu

Who Are You Following?

Earthlings may have become immune to centuries of human insanity that is often provoked by those who abuse positions of power. In this current era, our advanced audio receptors have intercepted channels on which angry humans are furiously spouting their hateful rhetoric and so many other weird grievances about fellow humans. *Some of these ranters happen to be your "so-called leaders!"* We just don't compute how this unhinged behavior is tolerated, especially when those who should be primarily focused on governing are instead, furthering their quest for power.

Humankind should find it unacceptable that their leaders do not take responsibility for their actions. On the contrary, many of them have an unending fascination with hearing themselves speak while blaming others in an argumentative manner that is often loud, pointless, and mind-numbing. Let's hope they have plenty of breath mints!

Our attempts to decipher their "messages" caused our sensitive follicles to immediately shrivel due to extreme falsehoods and ignorance. The negative energy spewed is astonishing in its ability to momentarily stun any species into disbelief, leading to an immediate urge to either laugh or vomit – your choice, of course. We must emphasize once again that we fail to comprehend the appeal of these types of leaders.

Before any of you get too heated because of your allegiance to your particular "leader of the day," we acknowledge that there are some decent human beings who manage and govern your nations, communities, and whatever else that requires supervision. You need more of them. However, the rest continue to govern using outdated and illogical leadership methods. In some parts of the world, political parties are constantly at odds with each other. We don't understand why you refer to them as "parties," as they are usually anything but fun.

Humans have a weird, dysfunctional relationship with their leaders.

Why do certain extremely maladjusted leaders and other influential types keep rising to the very pinnacle of power in your world? This assessment of the relationship between those who are led and those who lead is not just an opinion, but a rational analysis based on facts and research. We've been observing quite a few of your leaders and have come to a major conclusion.....*you humans are really nuts!*

From various encounters with a few knuckleheads here in the galaxy, we recognize that there are times when a species may have difficulty managing things as best as they can. On more than one occasion, we've had to zip past a planet and move on to the next one because of *less-than-ideal* conditions. However, when we entered your planet's orbit and zoomed into current events, we were quite stunned by what we found despite our extensive galaxy experience.

The leadership situation on your planet is so bizarre that for a moment, we thought we were witnessing a virtual reality performance of some kind, rather than real life! Fortunately, we had our notes ready from our debriefing with the B.O.S.S.,[1] which helped us prepare for the scenario currently playing out on Planet Earth. However, *just to be sure*, we took the extra steps to confirm that certain humans were truly in charge of running things on your planet, which caused us to become *quite speechless!* Now normally we are speechless, but in this instance we almost blanked out on our telepathic speech, causing us to use some strong orifice cosmic cussing.[2]

After calming ourselves with some soothing aromatic therapy, we were able to confirm that humans are in the *last phases of wacko governance*. The commotion around these changes is quite disruptive, causing a good many Earthlings some serious heartburn and stress. The previous ways of "bossing over others" are falling apart. This, of course, has resulted in some serious pushback from those who do not want to let go of power and also from their followers, who rather like these types of leaders. Frankly, we fail to see the appeal of bad energy, bad breath, and bad attitudes. Many of these negative leaders also have issues with their orifices, appendages, and follicles, or lack thereof. Nastiness is NOT HEALTHY!

According to the esteemed Dr. Youpoke Yopraugh (Dr. Yo Yo), M.D.B (Multi-Dimensional Being) and Director and Founder of YO- YO- GA Center for Inter- Galactic Species Development and Creator of the universally renowned Ultra Galactic Species Evolution Training Series, being a leader requires "advanced skills:"

"Evidence conclusively correlates highly effective leadership with an appropriate level of hormonal balance, proper brain health, a sense of humor, inner growth and spiritual development (which includes daily meditation and lots of deep breathing), copious amounts of soothing essential oils inhaled as needed, frequent servings of high-quality chocolate (perhaps paired with a nice glass of vino), selective on-and-off hearing, a tolerance for high levels of bat shit crazy and a real love for other species, including of course, their own."

The good doctor also recommends that *"every leader check their compassion AND their compensation benefit plan so that if a long vacation or sabbatical is needed, or even perhaps, some time alone without any contact with living beings except for cute furballs, access to this precious and sanity saving time-off is readily available."*

Do Your Damn Jobs!

Imagine if selecting better leaders didn't rely on things like propaganda and other unfair practices, but instead utilized an elevated process of choosing the most qualified for the job. If humankind were to seriously address how to disconnect governance from being influenced by greed, warfare profiteering, manipulative marketing, and other assorted "theatrics,"[3] there could be a sensible group of government leaders and officials whose main job would be to just *do their damn jobs!*

"If you are blabbering incoherently all the time, loudly and obnoxiously without letting up, even for some fresh air, and definitely for some much-needed breath mints, and are spewing out ridiculous and blatantly false crap out of all orifices, then you are OBVIOUSLY NOT WORKING AND DOING YOUR DAMN JOB because OBVIOUSLY, you are spending most of your time BLABBERING!

Our professional Cosmic opinion is that you need to IMMEDIATELY get back to work and respect those who either hired you, pay you, look up to you, or have s(elected) you for the position you are in!" – **Dr. Yangoorish Yinish and Dr. Zoopa Zip,** *Founders of the Advanced Being Behavioral Association (ABBA)*

Fortunately, throughout human history, there have been wise and inspired leaders who did their damn jobs, during which time the populace had the opportunity to enjoy some relative calm. The usual worries about any impending apocalypses or other disasters of the day were put on hold. These few sane rulers and leaders are sprinkled about in any given century and create a level of peace, security, and progress.

However, these sprinkles of relative stability are often short-lived, resulting in humankind kicking the "insanity can" down the road!

On a positive note, the ongoing quest for balanced leadership and egalitarian forms of governing isn't hopeless, since chaos and change present the possible opportunity to usher in more enlightened approaches. The primary mission and goal should be to inspire and uplift society for everyone by requiring humans in charge to lead wisely and effectively.

This requires not only strategic thinking, efficient decision-making, and an understanding of human needs but also a commitment to ethical principles. Leaders need to have the ability to navigate complex situations, foster collaboration, empower individuals, and inspire a shared vision of a better future. Ultimately, the success of any governance model depends on the quality and integrity of those who lead it. If you are any type of leader and are not leading this way, you need to reflect and ask yourself why.

There are likely numerous recommendations for establishing *baseline bossing requirements*, but at the very least, it should include some essentials – the liberal use of breath fresheners, discouraging or eliminating the use of misleading, boring, and hateful communications, maintaining a high level of honesty, integrity, maturity, and intellectual ability – and the mandatory stipulation (preferably put in legal terms) that states, *"Anyone who cares only about themselves and has narcissistic tendencies cannot be a leader."*

I'm the Boss and I'm in Charge?

There seems to be some ongoing confusion about what being in charge involves and what it doesn't. One thing is for sure, it doesn't entitle anyone to rudely command or do whatever they want at the expense of others (which also includes non-human species). It usually turns out that any form of authoritative commandeering does not work out in the long run, for either the boss or the ones being bossed.

Sooner or later, there is a reckoning, which may include anything from cyber "pitchforks," massive marketing campaigns, boycotts, an increase in early retirement, and other assorted pushback until the boss sees the error of his-her-their ways.

From what we gathered in our findings of the dynamics of "those that boss and those that are bossed," Earthlings would prefer to focus on living their lives rather than dealing with horrible bosses and dysfunctional leaders. They simply want a few basic necessities: a calm working and living environment, a yearly bonus, paid vacation time, fair living wages to cover essentials, and access to affordable healthcare and WIFI (not necessarily in that order). All of this without having to constantly worry about the next crisis at work or in the world. The constant effort of holding leaders and bosses accountable is exhausting, and realistically, who has the time for that?

Meanwhile, it may be helpful to understand the attributes of a good boss, leader, and human in charge.

They **lead from a place of empowerment** and strive to make the best decisions possible for all. No matter what sector they are in, they realize that their decisions can have far-reaching impacts.

They **balance kindness, wisdom, humor, and fairness with a sensible attitude,** and can deal with major responsibilities without "losing their mind."

They make it a **priority to control impulses, ego, and any orifices or appendages that may cause irresponsible behaviors and actions.**

They aim to **be honest, transparent, and critical thinkers.**

They **have a strong inner center** and can resist the temptation of manipulating information and using other coercive methods to promote greed, division, and other nefarious deeds.

Leading of any kind is a serious responsibility, so a **good sense of humor** is absolutely necessary to relieve the pressure! Cranky humans should not apply.

Leaders who are spreading fear, falsehoods and hatred, or are driving a wedge between groups of humans, have serious issues, AND DO NOT HAVE YOUR BEST INTEREST AT HEART (if they even have a heart at all). These types do not belong in any positions of power and need to be discharged immediately, in whatever manner is appropriate.

These ornery and rigid types, who are not secure within themselves, are not true leadership material. They are often referred to as dictators, tyrants, despots, mean bosses, and a few other names we won't mention.

"I do not think the measure of a civilization is how tall its buildings of concrete are, but rather how well its people have learned to relate to their environment and fellow man." – Sun Bear, Chippewa

Meeting Postponed Until Further Notice

When contemplating a "meet and greet" with extraterrestrial beings on any planet, there is an expectation of being properly welcomed and treated. A first encounter with any advanced extraterrestrial necessitates a basic set of qualifications from all participants, ensuring that a sufficient level of development and mindset have been met. Regrettably, this means that many of your current human leaders are unfit to represent not only humanity in the universe, but even on your own planet! As a result, our welcoming outreach and appendage-friendly handshake will remain on hold until further notice.

Leaders throughout the Cosmos are evaluated by their words, actions, and behavior, so when any species behaves with less-than-ideal manners before a meeting, it's only logical to assume the worst. In fact, there are valid reasons to suspect that some human leaders have ulterior motives that would cause serious concern – such as covert attempts to seize advanced technology, unpleasant probing sessions to obtain "clues to the universe" and the very real possibility of nasty boo-boos![4] Keep in mind that we usually anticipate these kinds of inappropriate antics and take the necessary precautions to deal with them before any meeting.

Therefore, a future gathering with any of your leaders,[5] heads of state, self-important government officials, or anyone else in an authority position, will only be considered when certain criteria are met. This generally includes reaching acceptable standards.[6] Since most humans are still a work in progress, we assume this may take some time. In the meantime, we sincerely hope that your leaders begin working on themselves so that they can inspire others to do the same.

With that said, there are a few humans who may be almost ready to meet extraterrestrials if the right conditions were to align. This diverse group includes devoted fans, serious scientists, spiritual leaders, and other progressively eclectic types. Interestingly, some even enjoy wearing *alien* costumes while coming together for annual events and fun activities, such as gazing into space in the hopes of spotting a random UFO. Most seem quite eager to make contact with otherworldly beings.

While we appreciate their good intentions, our goal is not to expand our fan base but to assist humanity in evolving. In times of global turmoil, certain encounters with Advanced *alien* Beings, would divert attention from the more important work of becoming a better human. If you are a leader of any kind reading this, we urge you to embrace the responsibility of being the best human in charge, so that you can contribute to uplifting mankind instead of just feeding your ego.

"It does not require many words to speak the truth." – Hinmaton-Yalaktit, which means "Thunder Rolling Down the Mountain," leader of the Nez Perce and known as Chief Joseph

Ready for inspired leaders with vision?

If there has ever been a time for an upgrade in leadership, it is now. Humanity needs a reminder that a truly great leader inspires confidence and encourages others to *bring out their best*. If this is not what you are experiencing, perhaps now is the perfect time to make a change and work towards having more good leaders in the world. Unfortunately, there are still too many leaders who are "not that great" and are abusing the power they have been given. It is important for them to receive the message that their time is coming to an end and who knows, they may be happy to hear it!

For any human who may still be questioning the purpose of this guide, and who may have little or no interest in their leaders, neighbors, or even themselves, now is a good time to reflect on how your habitual ways of thinking[7] may be getting in the way of expanding your worldview.

Your leaders represent your current collective level of evolution. You may want to let that really sink in...

Whether or not you understand the deeper implications, a simpler question to ask yourself is: *why would any leader choose to lead with fear rather than inspiration?* The fact is, an abuse of power in any form is a serious sign of weakness and very low-level behavior. When humankind individually and collectively accepts certain indisputable truths, the path to a new vision for humanity becomes possible.

Please take the time to think over what you are reading here. Perhaps you have never questioned or given any thought to these matters before. Even if you do not have any immediate insights, keep at it. Some humans have been so hypnotized and misled by deceiving leaders and other influential humans (perhaps even by those closest to you), that coming out of the haze of ignorance is difficult.

Of course, there are followers who align themselves with certain types of leaders for various reasons. False beliefs are not always easy to let go of because you must first become aware of them. Sometimes, they are so ingrained that it is difficult to even realize that they exist. However, you do not have to let negative false beliefs prevent you from recognizing profound and important truths, as you have the choice to change them.

Why do some of your leaders and other groups create discord among humans and encourage conflict?

Why is there a constant push to divide humans through hate, fear, and self-defeating negativity?

Why are fear and false beliefs regularly "marketed" to the masses?

Who benefits and why? AND...What is the underlying motivation for those who want to maintain their power?

Tomorrow's leaders will not lead dictating from the front, nor pushing from the back. They will lead from the centre – from the heart." – Rasheed Ogunlaru, Author, Coach

Build More Bridges, Not Walls

The "walls will come tumbling down" when humans accept that they are interconnected because wouldn't you know it, *separation is an illusion!* Unification is one aspect of Universal Law that confirms an intergalactic and planetary web of influence that links all things together. This applies not only to the universe, but also to your very own planet. Whether it's butterflies fluttering or a sneeze erupting in Oshkosh, Wisconsin (USA) – which then causes a strong breeze to blow near Hell, Michigan (USA), where a cooling breeze is likely appreciated during summer – the reality is that your world is deeply interconnected, whether you believe it or not![8]

Everything is intertwined in the web of life, which not coincidentally, also reflects the dynamics of how your own body, mind, and spirit are interrelated. Many Earthling spiritual teachers, healers, Indigenous wisdom keepers, ecologists, scientists, and other *in-the-know* humans can confirm this connection theory.[9] Feel free to pursue your own investigations into this very interesting matter, because, for reasons we don't quite understand, this topic isn't widely shared on social media or making headlines the way it should.

Furthermore, modern communication, technology, commerce, and your shrinking planet have brought more of you together than ever before, whether you like it or not. Unfortunately, those humans who are still not interested in changing their views will continue to believe they are connected to nothing and no one, except their WiFi (which isn't always guaranteed).

Maintaining the illusion of being separate is crucial to quite a few humans with a negative agenda. The deliberate resistance to the idea of connection is one of the reasons why Earthlings are still facing so many challenges. Humans are hurting themselves when they choose ignorance, hatred, and fear.

A unified response to harmful wall-building attitudes demonstrates that it is no longer an acceptable way to coexist with each other. When efforts are put into *building strong bridges of positive connection*, it will enable humans to progress instead of sliding backward. While it's true that some walls have functional uses or an aesthetic appeal, they are usually made to keep some in and others out. Walling oneself off is never much fun unless you're building a tomb or burial chamber. Just make sure to have the necessary supplies while in there.

"A system is a set of interconnected elements that form a whole and show properties that are properties of the whole rather than of the individual elements. This definition is valid for a cell, an organism, a society, or a galaxy." – Kathia Laszlo, PhD

If You Build It, They May Evolve

Since most of your leaders are human, we assume that many of them will need assistance in the "inner developmental" department. However, regardless of how they evolve individually, humanity can collectively create changes that would ripple out in the world so that a new way of leading would emerge. Essentially, a shift in consciousness would improve all of your relationships and elevate many areas of your society.

These positive outcomes would result in new forms of governing, where decisions are made through collaboration in councils, collective groups, and with leaders who act more like guides and coaches. As more humans evolve, so do your leaders, making egotistical and self-centered leaders irrelevant and powerless. Who knows, you may become a leader yourself, or be motivated enough to insist on higher standards of leadership that are necessary now and for the future.

You can send this guide to your current leaders, as many of them may welcome the assistance and consider changing their ways. Try to hold a positive vision, even for those who may seem inflexible or in some cases, too far gone. However, Earthlings need not wait for any leader who is unwilling to move forward, as it may be time to consider an immediate *re-selection* of new leaders. Sometimes, the only way anyone learns what is necessary is through consequences for their actions. Unfortunately, there are a few who may not learn even then.

Look for Silver Linings

Sometimes, finding a silver lining can help put things in perspective when life seems overwhelming. We're not sure if Vilfredo Pareto, an Italian economist, was looking for silver linings when he introduced the 80/20 rule, which proposes that 80% of effects come from 20% of causes.

If we apply this rule to humankind, we can assume that 20% of humans are likely causing 80% of the problems that humanity has

---

to deal with. This percentage may seem low when considering the number of awful humans in the news. The uptick in unhinged behavior has led to speculation that "**spawns of Satan**"[10] may exist and are lurking about, possibly even in your neighborhood. While we are not at liberty to confirm or verify the actual number of humans who may be *spawns of Satan*, we can say with some reassurance that you are much more likely to encounter a very unpleasant human rather than a truly malevolent one.

Although these hostile humans *may not* actually be spawns of Satan, they are still creating negativity and causing harm to humanity. Unfortunately, it only takes about 20% of knuckleheads to convince a larger majority that their misdeeds and questionable behaviors are in your best interests. Human history is full of these types who persist in pushing their agendas that are usually at your expense. It's time to confront and address negative humans who consistently bring pain and heartache to the majority of you. Remember, as the majority, you have power and influence!

What does this mean for you and your fellow positive-minded Earthlings? Well, it means that if a higher percentage of humans collectively organized and worked together, they would likely be able to change the world for the better, and relatively quickly.

Some time ago, an Earthling named Mahatma Gandhi in India was able to promote change by *inspiring* the majority of his people, all without a cell phone, social media campaign, or a podcast channel. At the time, he was facing great odds but he persisted. Mr. Gandhi was a lawyer, anti-colonial nationalist, and ethical political activist who employed nonviolent resistance to lead a successful campaign for India's independence from British rule (they were in the minority percentage).

This led to an inspired movement for civil rights and freedom across the world. Incredibly, Mr. Gandhi was able to mobilize a large group, many of whom may not have been that eager to go up against the British Empire. We're not sure if Mr. Gandhi was aware of the 80/20 rule, but he certainly was able to make changes. The main point is that when many humans work together and decide that "enough is enough," it can lead to an outcome that exceeds expectations.

"A sign of a good leader is not how many followers you have, but how many leaders you create." – Mahatma Gandhi

You may be wondering how we govern our planet

One of the best things we did was to eliminate unethical communication practices, such as propaganda, and dismantle divisive groups that got in the way of proper governance. This occurred at the same time when we collectively agreed that it was time to do something and began working on our overall evolution. We did a little tweaking here and there, keeping democratic principles at the core of our system while also establishing policies and regulations that made the most sense.

We removed all personal incentives for governing officials that did not align with the mission of an advanced government, which is to prioritize the well-being of all, not just a select few. Additionally, we properly rewarded those who do a great job (which now usually includes everyone), implemented specific term limits on service, established a system of ongoing accountability, and mandated TRAINING IN GOVERNANCE.

Anyone who assumes the position of planetary governance is highly vetted. We select only the best, excluding egotistical narcissists, authoritarian types, or those motivated solely by greed, power, or domination. Those who are even remotely maladjusted or unbalanced are not considered for any positions of responsibility. It is rare for a non-advanced being to sneak through and take on a position of importance on our planet, and it hasn't happened in a very long time BECAUSE *we figured it out!* You will too.

When a species experiences a collective shift in energy and consciousness, authentic empowerment will lead to enlightened leadership. In the meantime, as we lounge in our spacecraft recliners munching on Earthling chocolate, know that you have cosmic support. In our experience, all those negative leaders will eventually be transformed in one way or another.

The choices you make now may determine the fate of your planet and humankind. It can be stressful to think about how your leaders will manage the serious challenges facing humanity right now. If only you could put out an ad for improved leaders...

Bold Visionaries Please Apply

The world needs a new generation of enlightened leaders. Support them or become one of them!

* Find a way that you can contribute to effective change.
* Choose leaders who cooperate, share a collective vision, and inspire others.
* Choose positive solutions that unite, not divide.
* Choose officials who genuinely represent the priorities of the people.
* Support those who enhance your community and the world. Get involved if possible.

While you're waiting for applicants to respond, remember that *change starts with you. Be like a butterfly.*

"If you do not have a moral question in your governing process, then you do not have a process that is going to survive." – Oren R. Lyons Jr., Native American[11]

Thoughts?

"No leader sets out to be a leader. People set out to live their lives, expressing themselves fully. When that expression is of value, they become leaders. So the point is not to become a leader. The point is to become yourself, to use yourself completely – all your skills, gifts and energies – in order to make your vision manifest. You must withhold nothing. You must, in sum, become the person you started out to be, and to enjoy the process of becoming." – Warren Bennis, writer

Notes

1. The Being of Supreme Source (B.O.S.S.) is also known as the Galaxy Supervisor, Big Honcho, ONE who Reports to the Bigger Honcho (S.D.S), Manager and Director of the Galaxy, and is usually very busy with UNIVERSAL ISSUES.

2. Cosmic cussing is an innovative approach to using a special combination of "advanced expletives," peppered with humorous ranting and plenty of snark. These expletives are properly selected and concisely delivered with insight and wisdom without being completely tasteless. The intention is to make an important point and in *almost all cases*, to relieve stress and aggravation.

3. Various theatrics include but are not limited to, outright lying, gaslighting, bribery, intentional conspiracies, inciting mayhem, encouraging violence through hateful rhetoric, subverting justice, intentionally agitating normal humans and other offensive behaviors, such as epic meltdowns that resemble borderline lunacy. All the while, either avoiding doing their damn jobs or being a decent human being. The worst of these theatrics is war and the killing of other humans and species.

4. Boo-boos can range from "ouch" to serious injury on Planet Earth. When considering an in-person visit on any planet, we always bring cosmically enhanced band-aids for any unexpected emergencies.

5. Human leaders are supposed to be responsible and accountable to other humans but it appears that some of them are just faking it and have *no intention* of taking the job seriously. Many of them surround themselves with those who share their worldview and rarely do they relate with those who are different, let alone animals or other species.

6. Acceptable standards include, but are not limited to, having fresh breath, a sunny disposition, kindness, fairness, the ability to appreciate (Advanced Being) humor, a love for learning and stylish scarves, respect for all species, clear thinking, curiosity, a healthy mind, body, and soul, open-mindedness, the ability to speak in complete sentences - AND the capacity to listen before speaking - and, dare we hope, an interest in self-

development and evolving!

7. Understand negative thinking. Cuncic, Arlin. *Negative Automatic Thoughts and Social Anxiety*. Verywell Mind 2023 https://www.verywellmind.com/negative-thinking-patterns-and-beliefs-2584084

8. "The interconnectedness of events highlights the interconnected nature of our world. The Butterfly Effect encapsulates the delicate balance between choice and consequence, action and reaction. It challenges us to consider the ripples our decisions send through the fabric of reality, prompting us to approach our options with mindfulness and consideration." - Heenakshi. *The Butterfly Effect: The Psychology of Chaos.* Iimperium pub. 2023: https://www.imperiumpublication.com/post/the-butterfly-effect

9. Humans are still under the illusion of being separate from each other. *You can break this spell* by first connecting with YOURSELF, which will then help you realize that you are interdependent on each other and your planet. Earth is increasingly annoyed that the human race is still questioning this truth. The Karmapa, Ogyen Trinley Dorje. *Our Interdependent World.* Wisdom Pub. 2020 https://wisdomexperience.org/ebook/interconnected/seeing-the-connection/1-our-interdependent-world/

10. We have not had the pleasure of actually meeting the head honcho, who may or may not call himself, herself or themselves *Satan*, although we have come across certain entities who are doing their best to become one. We wouldn't recommend actively seeking them out unless you're interested in becoming spawn-like yourself (there is some actual training to become *fully* spawned). Of course, if you enjoy engaging in truly horrible activities that involve hanging out with other malevolent beings who enjoy the street cred of being a *spawn of Satan*, you may also want to keep in mind that at some point the "fun" times come to an end. We're *quite* sure about that. There's a lot to cover regarding Satan, Lucifer, and other names used by certain religious groups. However, this subject is too complex to address here because the concept of good and evil is not as simple as many humans (and perhaps, even non-humans), would like you to believe. Not everything is as it seems. Denova, Rebecca. *The Origin of Satan.* The World History Encyclopedia, 2021 https://www.worldhistory.org/article/1685/the-origin-of-satan/

11. Oren R. Lyons is a wise elder and leader who continues to share much wisdom. Bump, Alyssa. *Faith keeper Oren Lyons delivers dire warning of mass extinction.* The Chautauquan Daily 2022 https://chqdaily.com/2022/07/faithkeeper-lyons-delivers-dire-warning-of-mass-extinction/

6. While You Were Sleeping

"As cosmically certified professionals who work in all parts of the Galaxy, we know how difficult it is to get a species out of denial. It requires an ability to face facts without any B.S. or lame excuses. It also requires patience, motivation and at times, the threat of extinction. This last one usually works." – Dr. Yangoorish Yinish and Dr. Zoopa Zip, Advanced Being Behavioral Association (ABBA) Founders

Ding Ding!
Wake Up Call Incoming From the Universe! Are you *still* in bed?

Every so often, to get our butts in gear (if a species has them), we need a wake-up call to prompt us to change and transform. Sometimes, wake-up calls[1] can be for individuals, and other times, for an entire group. Every few eons it's both and humanity is now getting that call. We're not sure if you've noticed, but the Universe and Mother Earth are sending out quite a few of those calls.

If for any reason you have chosen to ignore these calls and have instead hit the "snooze button" on your life, it might be time to start paying attention to what's happening around you. The rise in unstable humans (some of whom are violent), animals lashing out in retaliation (who can blame them?), strange unexplained phenomena, and other wacky commotion should be enough to make you open one eyeball and discourage you from going back to sleep!

The urge to hide under the covers is simply delaying the inevitable, though we understand the appeal of cocooning in bed, especially if it involves snuggling with furry friends and staying in pajamas all day. We have found that most species rarely like to jump out of bed and rush headlong into facing unpleasant challenges that require a "cold splash" of reality. Denial is much more convenient and comfortable.

In most cases, the journey to becoming a better species usually begins with some form of a wake-up process that, hopefully, also includes brushing your teeth and finding some clean underwear. We have found that once that happens, the temptation to hit the snooze button or ignore your messages becomes less likely.

Urgent wake-up calls can be overwhelming, leading to fear and denial that reduces the ability to face an unpleasant reality. Therefore, the Universe recognizes that sometimes a variety of notices are necessary when attempting to rouse a species awake. Essentially, early warning messages can come in a variety of ways, but if messages are repeatedly disregarded, then other more urgent alarm bells will begin to go off. It's a good idea to pay attention because ignoring repeated messages while hiding under the covers is not going to make them go away!

Humanity's current wake-up calls may not, however, include a personal "ring-a-dingy" from friendly extraterrestrials. That call is on hold for now due to planetary commotion. Making a call of that magnitude would only distract from the more important task of *getting off your butts* so humanity can properly evolve. Just imagine the hysteria if an *alien* were to answer any of humankind's high-tech satellite communication devices. What a wake-up call that would be!

"It's exhilarating to be alive in a time of awakening consciousness; it can also be confusing, disorienting, and painful." – Adrienne Rich, poet

Rise and Shine!

As Advanced Coaches, our intention is to help you understand that you have a choice in how you wake up, or whether you even want to wake up at all. *What should you awaken to?* The truth, if possible.

We understand that most humans would love to awaken to the smell of delicious coffee, some crispy (vegan) bacon with eggs, and maybe some juice all nicely laid out on a tray so they can enjoy a leisurely breakfast in bed, while lazily perusing some reading material as the birds chirp merrily outside. Unfortunately, this type of "gently greeting the dawn" wake-up scenario will probably not motivate you to get out of bed and face your reality.

We suspect that a rude awakening is on the horizon for some humans, similar to those experienced on mornings when the alarm is blaring at an annoyingly high volume, you've overslept, had a really bad dream, are starving and all that's left in your fridge is an old banana. You can't recall where you left your pants and worst of all, you can't find the report you worked on for countless of hours for your extremely cranky boss who needed it 10 minutes ago. Yes, *that kind of* "*awakening*."

Okay, so maybe the old banana was over the top, but we hope you understand the point. There's no time to waste, so please get up and moving. In any case, the alarms are ringing and they probably won't stop until more humans wake up. For those of you who have opened an eyeball or two and have been paying attention, you may understand the purpose of these wake-up calls. But for those who are still ignoring the alarm, still asleep, or need constant reminders, the reasons to "smell the coffee" may not be that clear.

"A global awakening can only happen from a spiritual awakening that is of global dimensions." – Matthew Fox, spiritual theologian

---

CAN YOU JUST WAKE ME WHEN THE APOCALYPSE IS OVER?[2]

- No, because keeping your head buried under the covers is a form of denial.

- No, because things are heading into the danger zone, and although there is still time to avoid a complete meltdown, that window will eventually close!

- No, because ignorance, fear, hatred, and apathy are *not normal for a sustainable civilization.*

- No, because it's necessary to wake up *and take* Mother Earth's emergency 911 calls (if you haven't noticed, it's on re-dial).

- No, because you must try to become a better human and move evolution forward.

- No, because every little effort counts right now.

- No, because you are really *all in this together.*

- No, because the Universe requires your involvement and cooperation, otherwise, all bets are off.

"Truth is what we are. It is our essential nature and Being. It is the pure Self, the limitless One, the ultimate reality—it is awareness itself. But we have become unaware of the magnificence of our true nature on account of our upbringing, conditioning, and education, which paint a very different picture of who we are, and all of which we believe." – Mooji, spiritual teacher

5 Bazillion Unanswered Emails, Texts, and Voicemails?

With all the constant demands placed on the average human, any additional messages are just one more thing to deal with on a very long list of to-dos. It would be quite tempting to ignore them all, hit the delete button, and go back to sleep. Avoidance of this kind is not recommended, unless, of course, you owe taxes or are in a witness protection program. While you most likely want what's best for humanity, you also have other tasks to consider and a serious lack of time to manage it all.

However, we understand that this waking-up business requires real skills and a proper plan because if you are going to stay awake, it *better be worth it.* Some benefits of becoming self-aware include gaining a fresh outlook on your daily tasks and responsibilities. This new perspective can help you approach your "to-do" list with a renewed sense of purpose and understanding. By embracing self-awareness, you experience a profound shift that can positively impact the way you navigate your day-to-day activities. Additionally, you can stop worrying about always having to respond to everyone, unless you truly want to!

"If you want to awaken all of Humanity, awaken all of yourself." – Lao Tzu

When Staying Woke is No Joke!
Some Tips to Keep Your "Eyeballs" Open

Stretch your body first, then focus on your mind and spirit. Follow up with a nice cold splash of water.

Drink a strong, dark espresso every morning if needed. Ditch the latte (also known as caffe latte according to some *very* particular Italians) because you might need the strong stuff.

Stretch a bit more but don't rush to catch up on Planet Chaos. Avoid the morning news, unless, of course, the Apocalypse has *finally* arrived. If so, you may want to check the weather report in case you need an umbrella.

Take responsibility for your life. You didn't think this was all fun and games, *did you?*

Be open to a change in perception. That's right, now that you are awake we are asking you to stretch yourself mentally and in any other way that will help. It's time to recognize that there is much more beyond what your eyeballs can see, and what your orifices and appendages feel, smell, and hear. You didn't realize all that, did you, while you were basking in your comfy haze of denial?

Have another cup of espresso, or if it is later in the day, maybe some vino would be more appropriate.

Pinch yourself. Yes, you are really awake. Gently pinch the human next to you. *If they're awake, we're all getting somewhere!*

Continue practicing being fully alert, attentive, and conscious in the present moment. **Take a nap when necessary.**

Resist the temptation to go back on auto-pilot or to slip back into the comfy haze of denial.

Release your mental grip on any rigid beliefs, many of which may be based on limited information. Instead, start using observation and experience to comprehend a situation.

Do not ignore any additional messages.

Take a break and indulge in some delectable delights! Staying "awake" requires energy and treats!

"Who looks outside, dreams. Who looks inside, awakens." – Carl Jung

Eyes Wide Open Yet?

The experience of waking up to a new reality can bring about a real awakening, which can differ from human to human and is not always easy to describe. *One minute you are operating from your usual perception of life; the next minute, "boom!", what you thought you knew and believed in is no longer lining up.* For some Earthlings, this awakening is sustained over time but for others, the wake-up is just a momentary glimpse. However, there is no need to despair, as some illumination has likely seeped through. Extra time is sometimes needed to process things.

Awakening on a deeper or higher level is best described as a life-altering event. Okay, maybe that's a bit dramatic, but hey, evolving is dramatic. After this momentous point in time, there is a shift in how one perceives the relationship between themselves and the world. This shift enables one to see through the illusion of separation, which is essentially a false indoctrination.

The process of waking up has its challenges. There will be days when denial seems like a great option and the temptation to hide under the covers will be overwhelming. Like any journey, it is important to pace yourself. Once you get accustomed to being awake, you will find the strength to continue. In the meantime, make sure to get plenty of rest so that you are refreshed and ready to be the best version of yourself!

In essence, awakening is an ongoing process – a personal journey of reconnecting with your inner-self and understanding the interconnection of all things. It is a time of self-discovery that will continuously expand your perception. The urge to return to your familiar comfort zone will gradually diminish.

Transformation and growth can be uncomfortable and sometimes scary, but no one gets anywhere in life by constantly hiding under the covers. There comes a point when there is no choice but to *finally pay attention* to those alarms that have been ignored for far too long!

"A great revolution in just one single individual will help achieve a change in the destiny of a society and further, will enable a change in the destiny of humankind." – Daisaku Ikedo, Japanese Buddhist leader

Thoughts?

Notes

1. A call can be made according to a prior arrangement to wake a person or thing. It sometimes causes someone to become fully alert to an unsatisfactory situation and take action. The words *wake, awake, and woke* typically refer to transitioning from a state of sleep or rest, but can also hold spiritual, mental, and emotional significance. However, the word "woke" has evolved beyond simply being awake in a physical sense; it can imply a state of attentiveness to critical issues, such as those related to racial and social justice. Unfortunately, some humans have deliberately rebranded this word into something negative. These may be the same humans who feel that change is *too scary*, or those who like to keep repeating things without knowing why.
2. Although the typical definition of an apocalypse is the end of the world, it can also refer to a lifting of the veil, a disclosure of something hidden, and a coming to clarity.

7. Paying Attention Yet?

"The first step toward change is awareness. The second step is acceptance." –
Nathaniel Branden, Ph.D., psychotherapist

Leveraging one's *a-wakening* abilities requires more than a passing interest in your existence. By improving your self-awareness skills, it becomes easier to resist the urge to press the snooze button of your life when faced with certain unpleasant realities, although no one said self-growth was easy (that we know of).

Keep in mind that the level of awareness you have at any given moment requires a degree of consistent attention. *Hello, are you paying attention right now?* Of course, you will also need to be somewhat alert to the workings of your innermost mind and the world around you. This becomes easier when you become more perceptive in noticing and observing life without immediately passing judgment.

However, achieving a higher level of clarity may get slowed down if you have a very high opinion of yourself and refuse any sensible reality checks. The downside of having a limited understanding of yourself and unrealistic perceptions is that you may end up spending too much time in self-adoration instead of self-reflection. One upside to seeing yourself clearly and objectively is that it will help *shift you from selfies to self-awareness.*

Awareness is a choice you make to pay attention to what's around and within you.[1] By becoming more aware of yourself in your daily activities, there's a good chance that you may come to realize that, oops, you didn't know yourself as well as you thought you did!

And This Is Important, Why?

According to Dr. Vortex Vulcani, a Galaxy-Renowned Authority on Evolving and Advanced Being Studies, and the President of Universal Universe University (UUU) whose motto is "It's all about YOU," it has been confirmed that "Yes, it's all about YOU!"

Dr. Vulcani asserts that "*multiple intergalactic studies across galaxies verify the importance of understanding how a species' mind works, or in some cases, doesn't – because it is quite possibly the last frontier – and should perhaps be left alone until the Universe expands a little more. In other words, research in quantum evolution has led to the conclusion that most minds shouldn't be touched with a 10-foot laser pole, let alone examined!*

However, it has been demonstrated time and time again that a species can improve its level of awareness by implementing the simple theory of putting into practice the synergistic effect of talking less, being mindful, and closing off all unnecessary orifices. Highly recommended to be done regularly for at least 10 minutes per day until you find your mind."*

Dr. Vulcani emphatically confirmed that he is covered under all Cosmic Intergalactic Conduct Codes and is professionally certified, electrified, and mesmerized through the Council of Cosmic Mind Counseling.

Blocked mindsets and other Earthly impediments that promote rigid, limiting beliefs will require clarity and quite possibly, more than one glass of Chablis. Sometimes, a few concise and clear questions are all that's needed to ignite the burning desire to "know thyself."

The Well-Aware Scale

The following questionnaire has been designed by UUU cosmic professionals with the highest standards for your safety and sanity. No galaxy species or non-species have been harmed, probed, or abducted in developing these highly vetted inquiries into the recesses of inner mind space (and other places we won't mention).

For optimal test taking, grab a nutritious snack, drink plenty of liquids, light a candle, infuse your surroundings with essential oils, and avoid all contact with other Earthlings until you finish. Contemplation and completion may take 5 minutes or 5 hours. Please do not rush the process of providing adequate responses.

1. Are you awake and ready to roll towards awareness and further delights?

__Yes, I am wide awake and well aware! (5 points)

__No, I am not "well aware" at all, and I already have some delights. (10 points)

__Maybe? I think I'm well aware that I need to be more aware. (5.50 points)

2. Are you becoming more aware, maybe even starting to freak out with clarity and ready to change?
__Yes, I can handle some freaking out and I am well aware that it may be necessary! (5 points)

__No, I am not well aware of freaking out or the need to change to become aware. (10 points)

__Maybe? Am I ready to change? Do I really need to change? I'm aware that I don't know. (5.50 points)

3. Are you aware that something needs to be done, but are almost tempted to wait and put it off?
__Yes. I'm well aware that I need more time, but I have to run out and get some more snacks. (10 points)

__No, I do not want to wait. I believe the Apocalypse may be around the corner.   (2 points)

__Maybe? Okay, I admit, I have absolutely no idea and am now worried about the Apocalypse. (5.50 points)

4. Are you aware that things might be tough but are ready to deal with it?

__Yes. I'm well aware of things being tough and I can handle it to some extent. What else is new? (5 points)

__No. I don't want to deal with anything except my Netflix subscription and enough beer in the fridge. (10 points)

__Um, maybe? Do you mean things will get even worse? I'm now aware that *I just want my Mommy!* (5.50 points)

5. Are you aware of what awareness actually is?

__I got it, no worries, no kidding. All clear with awakening my inner awareness ability. (5 points).

__Nope, wasn't paying attention, and I'm not sure I even care. I like being "unaware." (10 points)

__Maybe? I'm completely confused, why do I need awareness? I am more concerned with the upcoming Apocalypse! (5.5 points)

Your Results

0-22 points: You sure are confident! Maybe a little too confident. **Check again and look within.**

23-27.5 points: You're a bit cautious. It's *not* necessary to call Mommy. **Trust yourself.**

28-50 points: You are very relaxed and **perhaps exist in a bubble.** Please don't wait until it pops.

"What is necessary to change a person is to change his awareness of himself." – Abraham Maslow

Let's Have Another Look, Shall We?

Perhaps you are finding that your awareness ability is not as finely tuned as you would like it to be. No worries, you are not alone in that department. Who has the time to take on another project, especially one that involves the inner workings of yourself and possibly the continuation of humanity? Well, you do of course!

Taking a look into the inner workings of your mind is not wasted time, unlike some of the other habits you may have acquired, including but not limited to, consuming copious amounts of mood-altering substances, a dependence on sweet and salty snacks, making dubious entertainment choices that involve extended periods of reclining in a prone position, frequent use of profanity, and having an aversion to bathing and intellectual pursuits. Not all in that order.

Never fear, we are confident that you can find the energy to take charge of your self-improvement regardless of what you may believe about yourself. Once you gain a better understanding of the benefits of awareness, you may pleasantly surprise yourself and realize that like vitamins, a daily dose of awareness can be good for you!

"The better awareness, the better your choices. As you make better choices, you will see better results." – Anonymous

What do you think about on a regular basis?

What are your typical habits and behaviors?

What are your current beliefs?

Why do you believe what you believe?

What habitual thought patterns no longer serve you, or the planet?

Why Can't I Remain Comfortably Numb?

Well, for starters, it hasn't been a great go-to method for Earthling development. Certainly, there are instances where gently numbing oneself may be the only answer at the moment. Unfortunately, the human habit of "checking out" during times of turmoil is most likely about to end. *Unless of course*, you don't mind that there may be a permanent checkout plan in the works. Then, by all means, proceed as usual.

Self-reflection can be an uncomfortable exercise, similar to a human colonoscopy, where sometimes you have no choice but to face your "crap." No wonder some of you would rather put off the process of honest "self-evacuation" as long as possible. *However*, sooner or later, that crap is either going to come out or it will cause some kind of blockage. Constipation of any kind is not fun but neither is non-stop poo-poos! The good news is – and there is good news – that beneath all that crap, most humans are generally okay.

"B.S. can only go so far before it starts to stink." – AB1 & AB2

It's no coincidence that this information confirms the various messages provided by Earthling spiritual masters, gurus, yoga teachers, therapists, and other "mature" humans. Which is a simple one – *that the quest for self-knowledge is a bumpy road.* If this road is taken, however, it will result in GROWTH that will promote the continuation of humanity, a noble cause that we hope more humans will believe in.

Now, if you are ready to *finally* let go of your unhelpful belief systems by becoming mindful of them, then you may be on your way to sustaining awareness. Yes, you will be in that select group that is paying attention to the inner workings and outer machinations of their reality. However, maintaining this state of mind regularly requires practice to sustain it, and sometimes, taking a sanity break will be necessary!

Here's Looking at Your Self!

- Just like a good neighbor, awareness is here for you.

- A heightened level of awareness can completely redefine your concept of well, everything.

- Shifting your perception intercepts your automatic response mode leading you to hit the snooze button less often.

- Paying attention is a personal and unique process. Who knows where it will lead you?

- The advantage of increased awareness is that you become more present with yourself, others, and even with your plants and pets.

- Awareness can lead you to appreciate life, love, and well-being. Who wouldn't want more of that?

- Being aware means you can let go of the past. You can learn from it, but it's over, so there's no need to dwell on it.

- Awakening to awareness involves understanding the connection of all things, both on the planet and beyond, including Advanced Beings, furry friends, insects, microbes, dust, and even Uncle Ed.

- Dive deeper into self-awareness tips to discover what works best for you.[2]

"If you grow in awareness, you will grow in love." – Osho, mystic

What's Next?

Now that there is a real possibility of becoming the best version of yourself, you may feel excited about the need to *hurry up and evolve*. Certainly, world events and various humans have created a sense of urgency around this matter, but we hope that the ultimate goal of being your best is more important than worrying about the end of civilization as you know it.

The next steps in the self-tweaking process rest on the solid foundations of high-order values and principles that embody an evolved human, or any other advanced species. Embracing any or all of the recommended evolving elements acts as a gateway to a higher level of advancement and has been proven to effectively enhance wisdom and intelligence in life forms across the cosmos. Results may vary, and species can experience life-altering changes that span from nanoseconds to eons.

Remember that while reading about different subjects and gathering information certainly expands the mind, *it is the application of that knowledge that is most important*. This is where the "rubber meets the road" or where the spacecraft meets quantum velocity.

Can We Have Your Attention Please?!

Close your eyes and notice your breath. Are you still breathing? Good. Next, notice what you are feeling, both in your body and in your heart. Now notice what you are thinking. If it's crap, put it in the trash. Anything else, simply observe and do not judge any of it!

Open your eyes and notice what you see and hear. This is your "in the moment" experience right in front of you, which many of you may not notice because you are often distracted and unaware of your surroundings. Now, focus on everything around you and *just be present with it!*

Every time you practice this short exercise, you are connecting with awareness, even if only for a minute or so. Hopefully, you will eventually extend your level of awareness for longer, but you have to start somewhere. In any case, this is a way to manage what goes into your autopilot system, which is part of your subconscious mind.

Thoughts?

"Let us not look back in anger or forward in fear, but around in awareness." – James Thurber, cartoonist and playwright

Notes

1. Awareness is the state of being conscious of oneself and one's surroundings. It involves having knowledge or perception of a situation or fact, as well as a well-informed interest in a particular situation.

2. Davis, Ph.D., Tchiki. *What Is Self-Awareness, and How Do You Get It?* Psychology Today, 2019 https://www.psychologytoday.com/us/blog/click-here-happiness/201903/what-is-self-awareness-and-how-do-you-get-it

PART III
STEP FORWARD TO EVOLVING

8. Let the Tweaking Begin!

"It's never something huge that changes everything, but instead the tiniest of details, irrevocably tweaking the balance of the universe while you're busy focusing on the big picture." — Sarah Dessen, novelist

For what seems like eons, humans have been striving to overcome negative behaviors. Alas, many still find themselves stuck in repetitive and self-limiting patterns that they struggle to change.[1]

However, any human who still questions their ability to change should remember that they can start no matter where they are in their development, even if it seems hopeless. When attempting any type of "self-tweaking,"[2] having a roadmap can be very helpful, especially when it comes from guides who are willing to hold your appendages (only in theory, of course) while you get there.

Dr Youpoke Yopraugh, also known as Dr. Yo Yo, M.D.B., is the Director of YO- YO- GA Center for Inter-Galactic Species Development and has this to say:

"Advice communicated in a simplified and thoughtful way helps release certain negative blocks that can keep a species stuck. Pearls of wisdom spoken in plain language, along with appropriate doses of kind and honest feedback, can assist in re-calibrating chakra imbalances and emotional energetic dysfunction. This will provide sufficient positive reinforcement to both the heart AND the brain cells of said species – possibly in combination with sensory stimuli in the form of delectable edibles or liquid reinforcements – that will possibly, with any luck, induce a harmonic tsunami that releases various blockages preventing said species from evolving. Good luck!"

We agree with Dr. Yo Yo's concise analysis because upon reviewing humankind's many wisdom teachings and other general advice, it seems feasible to assume that the conflicting interpretations and instructions regarding the human condition may have inadvertently overwhelmed many humans! It's quite possible that advice (and preaching) from *"well-meaning"* wellness professionals, *"wanna-be"* experts, and *"overly excited"* televangelists, is a misguided approach for the general masses (with some exceptions of course).

Perhaps humans today need another way to self-tweak their inner selves, without all the unnecessary jargon and pomposity that comes from those who proclaim themselves to be oracles of wisdom. With this in mind, we believe that our less complicated and "out of the cosmic box" tweaking approach will clearly (and perhaps, comically) provide a path to your transformation.

"We are all looking for someone to save us." – Cynthia D. Griffin, writer

---

So, What is Required for the Self-Tweaking Process?

First, your *attention.*

Second, some ability *to absorb* information. No major degrees or technical skills are necessary.

Third, a basic level of *commitment.*

Fourth, a *willingness* to keep an open mind to absorb what you read and encounter.

Fifth, the *motivation to reflect and put into action* what resonates with you, even if it's a small step.

Sixth, having a *genuine trust* in the process, which could lead to a collective wave of transformation.

Seventh, *maintaining the motivation to keep a positive vision* of yourself and the world around you.

These basic requirements of absorbing, reflecting, re-absorbing and then taking a little action each day are all it takes. Trust the tweaking process because it will work. Before you know it, you may be singing happy tunes, doing random acts of kindness, helping the Planet, getting involved in a worthy cause, or maybe, even becoming an energy healer to assist other Earthlings in this time of great transformation.

Of course, igniting your better nature and jump-starting the next evolution on Planet Earth is not only a worthwhile effort for you, but for all Earthlings!

And, all this is possible without any probing!

Alien Probing: "To be poked by an alien, and then tested." – Urban Dictionary

We promise that there will be no need to probe you, as you will be tweaked through your own efforts. To clarify, the self-tweaking process *does not* require any probing intervention from us, although we are aware that some humans might actually be interested in this type of activity. The sheer amount of false facts about aliens is staggering, but we are not here to advise the media or various mental health organizations.

Think about it. Why would probing be necessary when there is so much information about the human body available to anyone with a library card or access to the Internet? (Yes, we also have access to your Internet, in case you were wondering.) Whether you are advanced or not, a medical degree is not needed to understand what should or should not be probed.

So, we repeat, no probing because we are not those aliens (the ones with the exam rooms and tools)! Remember, we are Advanced Beings, with emphasis on the *advanced*. However, if you truly desire to be probed, you are welcome to schedule an appointment with your local urologist, or even better, with a highly qualified therapist or healer who we assume would be more than happy to help you with some inner probing (which may lead to self-discovery or healing).

"There are certain bad habits we've groomed our whole life, from personality flaws to fashion faux pas. And it has been the role of parents and friends, outside of some minor tweaking, to reinforce the belief that we're okay just as we are. But it's not enough to just be yourself. You have to be your best self. And that's a tall order if you haven't found your best self yet." – Neil Strauss, author

Cosmic Calibration

To fine-tune your evolution will require leveraging the most beneficial ways to make the most of your experience and efforts. A key step is to properly reflect on the information and new ideas presented, while remaining open to changing your perception of what you can achieve. Before dismissing what you are reading here as "woo-woo"[3] concepts magically pulled out of our orifices, the fact is that there is really nothing wrong with believing that to be true!

Rest assured that the recommended calibrations have been based on analyzing the various behaviors found in the universe. In this case, we have studied humankind in real-time. There is nothing more insightful than observing a species before approaching them with information that would best help them. We have found that although there are many paths to self-growth, for some species it's best to start with the basics (even though they are anything but basic).

It's Elemental, My Dear Human

The **12 areas of self-enhancement** can be focused on separately or as a complete integration. How you approach the process will depend on your commitment to becoming your BEST SELF. We are hopeful that most humans are ready to make this journey because what else is more important than becoming your best self?

Kindness
Emotional Intelligence
Inner Peace
Communication and Connection
Gratitude
Humor
Respect
Non judgment

Generosity
Wisdom
Ethical Consciousness
LOVE

Take your time with each level. Your goal should be an authentic desire to improve and to do that, you will need to assimilate the qualities into your being in a way that becomes a part of you.

We suggest that you follow the listed order for optimal flow in embodying the concepts into your life one step at a time. However, if your intuition is pulling you to a certain chapter, then go for it! This may mean you need to focus on a particular area and that is okay.

You can review all 12 steps to understand the objective, but then you should start from the beginning and work through them.

If you need to stick with one concept for a while, do so. **It takes about 21 days to about 3 months for new habits to become, well, habitual.** This means automatic and on autopilot. Incorporating changes depends on the individual and overall circumstances.

If you are super eager to evolve, you could knock yourself out and just absorb the entire book. Yes, this is possible! Some of you may become so inspired that you will allow for an upload of a new consciousness to spontaneously happen and transform you.

IF FOR SOME REASON, YOU BELIEVE THAT YOU DO NOT NEED TO "EVOLVE" AND THINK YOU ARE GOOD THE WAY YOU ARE, WE HIGHLY RECOMMEND YOU READ THE ENTIRE GUIDE BEFORE YOU MAKE UP YOUR MIND. FOR MOST HUMANS, TWEAKING IS NECESSARY, DON'T KID YOURSELF!

If you only have time for one or two of these components, we would HIGHLY suggest **KINDNESS** and **LOVE.** These two virtues alone are the most important aspects of becoming a better human – and if you changed nothing else, embodying love and kindness would be enough to lead to an inner transformation that would facilitate growth in other areas. Once you commit to setting an intention to change, you start the self-evolving process for yourself, and hopefully, for humanity.

Seems crazy huh? That one little guidebook from the cosmos can change the course of humanity. *Who knew?* Well, we did actually.

Thoughts?

"*What lies behind us, and what lies before us, are tiny matters compared to what lies within us.*" — *Ralph Waldo Emerson*

Notes

1. Self-limiting refers to a belief or behavior, whether physical or mental, that can restrict you from growing. Unfortunately, this mindset is common on Planet Earth. These inflexible thoughts and opinions that one believes to be absolute truth can have a negative impact and prevent humans from progressing, ultimately slowing down the evolutionary process.
2. The term "tweak" is best defined as a verb meaning to "*change something slightly, especially to make it more correct, effective or suitable.*" Our use of this word is not intended to imply anything offensive or encourage any distressing behavior, such as being under the influence of methamphetamine (also known as speed).
3. According to humans, woo-woo means dubiously or outlandishly mystical, supernatural, or unscientific. However, to be clear, we and the Universe *are* mystical, supernatural, AND scientific. In fact, we embody quite a few "*out there*" characteristics and abilities. However, our guidance for humans is based on some very holistically balanced objectives so that you can reach the next level, where *a lot* of woo-woo stuff is happening!

9. Human Kinder

"The next evolutionary step for humankind is to move from human to kind." – Anonymous

Be Kinder

Do you consider yourself to be a kind human? Be honest. Perhaps you think you are and we certainly hope so. However, thinking and being are not always the same thing. If you think you are kind, but don't put it into action regularly, then how kind are you really? Like a tree falling in the forest, does anyone hear or see it? Wouldn't it be better if you shared that kindness with others?

Being kinder means acting in a manner that arises from being considerate, polite, caring, and thoughtful of another's feelings. Of course, maintaining kindness has its challenges, *especially* when other humans are irritating you! However, showing some kindness can be one of the most important tools to use when confronting a particularly difficult human, instead of raiding the liquor cabinet or hitting your head against a wall.

Kindness is not only necessary for individuals, but also for the evolution of the human race in the universe. It is considered a highly ethical characteristic that plays an essential role in a well-functioning society. In fact, just a few unkind words and actions can hinder a human's ability to be kind to others, leading to consequences that can destabilize the moral fabric of civilization. Kindness is really that powerful.

It is not surprising that when a human being is treated unkindly throughout their lifetime, they can become hateful, fearful, and miserable. Those who have repeatedly experienced cruelty, pain, or worse can become wounded and may respond with anger and violence. Without compassion and empathy, a human can become disconnected from their feelings, potentially leading to psychopathic tendencies.[1]

Kindness is a catalyst for genuine, positive change that lays the groundwork for a more harmonious future. It is an essential gateway to other positive attributes that create a wonderful feedback loop. When a human embodies certain traits and qualities, it moves them forward towards a better version of themselves.

There are many ways you can show kindness to other humans, animals, the environment, and the planet. However, cultivating positive behaviors may not always come as easily as you would like. Certainly, some humans are born kinder than others, and it may come more naturally to them, while others have to work harder at it.

Anyone can increase their "kindness factor" through self-reflection, meditation, or by seeking support from a therapist or life coach if necessary. Connecting with your inner emotional and mental state can provide clarity and peace, so that showing kindness to others becomes second nature.

Remember, whether it is just being more courteous to strangers or performing small random acts of kindness, it doesn't have to be complicated. Sometimes, the simplest offerings of kindness are just as appreciated as grand gestures.

Truly, you can become a kinder human if you choose to do so. Well, most of you can, except perhaps for the hard-core cases that may require the assistance of professionals and advanced healers on your planet.

Kindliness Can Be Expressed As...

EMPATHY, compassion, goodwill, affection, warmth, gentleness, tenderness, concern, care, consideration, helpfulness, thoughtfulness, unselfishness, selflessness, altruism, sympathy, understanding, bigheartedness, benevolence, benignity, friendliness, neighborliness, hospitality, amiability, courteousness, generosity, magnanimity, patience, tolerance, charitableness, graciousness, lenience, and humaneness. *Pick any or all of these!*

"If you want others to be happy, practice compassion. If you want to be happy, practice compassion." – Dalai Lama, spiritual leader

Don't Treat Me This Way!

How many times have you heard the saying, "Treat others the way you would like to be treated," or something similar to it? When a saying becomes cliché and overused, it can lead humans to becoming immune to its real meaning and less inclined to live by its truth. Often, the sheer simplicity of a truism gets overlooked or over-analyzed. Nonetheless, treating others as you would like to be treated is clearly how humans should regularly interact with each other unless, of course, you happen to be a deviant with deep emotional and psychological problems.

DING DING!
The real test of kindness is not with your favorite humans, but rather with difficult and unlikable humans, or in some rare cases, unlikable aliens. Maintaining your kindness towards these types can take great effort. No matter how tempting it may be to pick up a two-by-four[2] and temporarily put some humans out of their misery, *violence is never recommended or encouraged.* Instead, try to ignore your rising blood pressure (and don't forget to put down that two-by-four!) and connect with the kindness in your heart.

Sometimes, the most effective way to show kindness to a negative human is to avoid responding with anger, hate, or disgust. Instead, throw a "kindness curve ball" by smiling, telling a quick joke (making sure it's not at their expense), or taking a deep breath and responding as if you were a highly paid psychiatrist. It can go a long way in disarming someone.

Practicing patience and compassion may seem challenging to those uninitiated in the "art of kindness," but it can be effective in defusing a human who is seething with annoyance, irritation, fury, or anger. A kind gesture, like a hug, can sometimes magically turn things around. You can also seal the deal with some chocolate and a cute plush animal.

If none of this works, feel free to excuse yourself from the presence of this ornery Earthling. Sometimes, the kindest thing you can do for someone, and yourself, is to ignore them and let them continue wallowing in whatever they need to wallow in.

Keep in mind that being kind does not mean you should tolerate being pushed around or taken advantage of because of your good nature!

What if unfriendly aliens suddenly arrived on your planet and began behaving in a destructive and unkind manner? That would NOT be great, right? We can all agree that such behavior is ill-mannered and quite inconsiderate. The truth is, no one deserves being treated poorly, whether in the universe or on Planet Earth. Therefore, it shouldn't be hard to imagine that you wouldn't like it at all!

The point is, no matter what life form you happen to be, kindness has the power to create a bond and connection that transcends differences. In most cases in the universe, it leads to positive outcomes, but we can't guarantee it 100% on Earth because humanity is still a work in progress!

"My religion is very simple. My religion is kindness." – Dalai Lama

You're *So* Nice!

While the planet can certainly benefit from nicer humans, there is a distinction between kindness and simply being nice. When the primary motivation for being nice is to be liked above all else, it can unintentionally overshadow genuine kindness. Most of us desire to be liked, even Advanced Beings, but understanding your motivations can truly make a difference.

Maintaining a facade of niceness to get along, either by not speaking up or worrying more about what others may be thinking, is not the essence of real kindness. Sometimes, humans hide behind a facade of being nice when they are anything but nice. Other times, being nice is not enough in a situation where empathy and kindness are required. Intentional kindness is about doing what is right and maintaining a high standard of behavior even when things get difficult. This may not be easy, but showing kindness is *usually* the right thing to do in most situations (admittedly, some situations may require alternative options).

If you are an Earthling who is generally kind but hasn't recently shared your kind nature, then this is a good reminder for you to spread it around more often. Likewise, if you're a decent human who has become cranky over time, there is always the possibility of becoming kinder again. However, don't try to fake kindness, because it can become obvious if you're being phony about it. Real kindness requires a sincere and benevolent nature that can usually be felt from one human to another, whereas a fake attempt at being nice may stem from underlying motivations that have nothing to do with being nice or kind. In other words, you have to genuinely want to be kind, not just in theory but in practice!

"Everything I need to know, I learned in kindergarten." – Robert Fulghum, *author*

Planet *Kinder*Garten, Can You Hear Us?

Yippee! If **Kinder**garten is the official launching pad for evolving, we like it! However, do these rules *only* apply to human children in the land of *Kinder*garten and not to anyone over 5 years old?

We are calling all the little "*Kinder*garten" humans to help Planet Earth and teach cranky adult humans how to be kind! We fully support handing out lollipops, saying "please" and "thank you," using tissues, and sharing toys and snacks. We also enjoyed reading the Earthling book[3] on commonsense rules that are taught during time spent on *Kinder*garten Planet, but were surprised to learn that it was written by an adult human and not a 5-year-old! No matter, the main point is that you're supposed to learn certain positive behaviors in *Kinder*garten and continue them into adulthood.

It's unfortunate that after graduating from Planet *Kinder*garten, adult humans are less inclined to share lollipops, toys, or snacks. Adult manners take a nosedive as well, and to make matters worse, there is a serious decline in using tissues when needed, especially in vehicles where picking and sneezing are rampant. Nap and play times are eliminated from adult human schedules and there's less attention paid to the ritual of snack time. No wonder there's an issue with humans being kind to each other!

Has anyone on Planet Earth begun to investigate the correlation between kindness and what happens *after* one leaves Planet *Kinder*garten? Perhaps serious research is needed into the techniques and methods used by these little humans. Special kudos go out to the adult teachers by the way, as they are likely evolved to some degree.

In any case, do not despair that your days at Planet *Kinder*garten are lost and gone. While the inhabitants of Planet *Kinder*garten may have an evolving edge over most adult humans, the truth is that many adults can still improve themselves. You can re-learn what is important and needed most right now, which is that kindness counts. So we suggest that you start small and begin with the habit of doing one kind thing every day. Make it fun and be sure to include lollipops or some chocolatey delights!

Gaining further insights into how you function is a priority and vital for your growth because it impacts your life here and elsewhere (karma can be humbling).[4] Cultivate your state of mind so that you can fully embrace kindness as a way of being. If nothing else, please try to embody kindness not only as something *you do*, but as something *you are*. Cosmic wisdom and recommendations are meant to kick-start your neurons and heart chakras towards their optimal levels. This simultaneous exchange of energy can be truly transformative.

Master Yogishimi Yami Zami, Author, Teacher, Guruologist AND Director of the *Cudha Shoudha Institute of Being Here But Not There*, highly recommends the following for optimal kindness:

"Each day, connect with yourself through deep breathing and some quiet time, preferably either when you wake up or prior to any morning rituals, so that you can set the tone for the day. This practice can last from 1 min to 1 hour, depending on your schedule. While focusing on your breath, bring your attention and intention to your heart (chakra) and imagine it expanding in kindness, to yourself and others, and especially towards those who cause you extreme aggravation and annoyance. Let any negative emotions and thinking patterns release in your exhale. Keep at it, especially the breathing, and try not to judge what comes up. Yes, yes, release all that judging.

None of this requires you to skip a meal, sit on a pillow for hours or be perfect at it. Just be in the moment. That's it. Now, once you flow out of your meditative state – and the speed, or lack thereof, may depend on the velocity of the calibration of your chakras – you may want to consider setting an intention or affirmation that you can infuse your day with. It's all about inner and outer energetic resonance.

You can meditate on kindness forever, but eventually, you will need to practice it in some (simple) manner that doesn't require a professional mediator or, in some cases, a meditator to help you. With this in mind, an "out of the Cosmic box" approach to elevating your kindness ability is to treat yourself and a cranky human you know to some time together, during which you both enjoy delectable treats while giving each other compliments for 15 minutes non-stop. As you gaze into each other's orbital (eye) orifices, think of things you can say that will uplift the other human. Take turns, so that each of you can enjoy basking in the compliments of kindness while munching or sipping on whatever delights your taste-buds.

The most important insight to understand is that those who are the MOST ANNOYING are actually your greatest teachers in the lesson of kindness.

You may find this MAJOR INSIGHT *illuminating, similar to a light bulb moment, or you may find it incomprehensible that any* DING-DONG[5] who annoys you is trying to teach you kindness, but this is what the UNIVERSE is trying to help you with at this PRESENT MOMENT.[6] *If you are a DING-DONG yourself, wouldn't you rather have others treat you with kindness, rather than responding with anger, outrage, or possibly causing boo-boos? Kindness is so essential that without it, higher life forms cannot evolve to become advanced beings unless they learn this lesson. Without kindness, "love and peace" are merely empty slogans. Cheers!"* – Master Yogishimi Yami Zami.

But I Don't Feel Like It!

There will definitely be times when you may not feel like being nice or kind, and in some cases, it may be justified. When you feel like you just *can't take it anymore*, the best thing to do is to remove yourself from the offending human or situation and retreat into a safe and peaceful environment. After observing the reality show that is life on Planet Earth, we have concluded that those who are motivated to evolve must pace themselves. Please hang in there!

The Art of Kindness Initiation Rites

- Surprise another human or non-human with a random act of kindness.

- Do something nice without expecting anything in return.

- Be friendly and kind whenever the opportunity arises.

- Say "thank you" and show your appreciation to others.

- Smile and offer greetings when appropriate.

- Give a compliment or a hug to another human (always ask before hugging).

- Hold the door open or let someone go ahead of you in line.

- Offer help when needed, even when it's not expected.

- Show appreciation to others whenever possible.

- Try to see the best in others. Everyone is going through something, so avoid jumping to conclusions.

- Have patience and compassion for others.

- Express gratitude to those who have made a difference in your life.

- Donate your time and resources to those in need.

- Send out positive energy to others, wherever you may be.

- Brighten someone's day by giving them an unexpected gift.

- Assist an elderly human or simply spend time with them.

- Sometimes, the kindest thing to do is nothing. Wait until you regain your equilibrium when dealing with difficult humans.

- Consider how others feel when kindness is offered to them. They feel good and so do you.

- Keep tissues, lollipops, or **CHOCOLATE** handy to share with others (and for yourself as well).

- Be considerate of animals, plants, insects, the environment, and Mother Earth.

- Remember, kindness has the power to heal!

"Be kind to yourself as you proceed along this journey. This kindness, in itself, is a means of awakening the spark of love within you and helping others to discover that spark within themselves." – Tsoknyi Rinpoch, Buddhist teacher

Even as you intentionally seek to be kind to others, don't forget to also be kind to yourself. If you are kind to yourself, it's more likely you will be kind to other humans and all life forms, including your planet!

Keep in mind that kindness, like love, is considered a superpower in the universe. In the present timeline, being kind is seen as a courageous act to overcome the pervasive negativity that has taken hold of far too many humans.

Repeat After Us

I am kind to myself and everyone I meet.
I do good deeds whenever possible.
Today I will choose kindness over anger.
I trust myself to choose to be kind over being right.
May all of my words be kind and gentle.
I model kindness in every area of my life.
I am improving both my state of mind and my manners.
The kinder I am, the kinder the world will be around me.

"Seek to do brave and lovely things which are left undone by the majority of people. Give gifts of love and peace to those whom others pass by." – Paramahansa Yogananda, monk and yogi

Thoughts?

"The world needs all of our power and love and energy, and each of us has something to give. The trick is to find it and use it, to find it and give it away, so there will always be more. We can be lights for each other, and through each other's illumination, we will see the way. Each of us is a seed, a silent promise, and it is always spring." — Merle Shain, author and journalist

Notes

1. Certain psycho-pathological conditions include traits such as shallowness, callousness, lack of empathy, and emotional detachment. Often, humans with these disorders exhibit antisocial, criminal, and violent behavior that may be concealed from others.

2. Two-by-four wooden implements are allegedly slightly less than two inches wide and four inches deep and can be cut to various lengths. They are not intended to harm others. According to *Popular Science*, these 2 x 4s are not actually 2x4s: https://www.popsci.com/two-by-four-lumber-measurements-explained/

3. "*All I Really Need To Know I Learned in Kindergarten*," by Robert Fulghum 1989, includes tips that are still relevant, *no matter how old you are now!* Apparently, the author enjoyed his time on Planet *Kinder*garten and probably should have never left. https://www.robertleefulghum.com/

4. A cycle of cause-and-effect, karma is an energy created by willful action, through thoughts, words, and deeds.

5. "Ding-dong" is an informal way of describing a silly or foolish person.

6. The "present moment" simply means "here and now." It can also mean being aware and mindful of what is happening at the moment, being centered in the "here and now," and not getting distracted by the past or worrying about the future. *The UNIVERSE is always in the here and now and very rarely distracted by anything.*

10. Emotion Commotion

"We are dangerous when we are not conscious of our responsibility for how we behave, think, and feel." — Marshall B. Rosenberg[1]

Explosive Outburst Alert!

At any given moment, a very emotional adult human may explode and start yelling, crying, ranting, screaming, or reacting aggressively to whatever sets them off. *Is this describing YOU or someone you know?* While intense emotional commotion can be a bit worrisome for humans who encounter this type of behavior, volatile outbursts are just as problematic, if not more so, for the one who is "blowing their fuse." Repeatedly being stuck in destructive emotional patterns can lead to aggressive behavior, violence, and other negative states of being. It's not a good way to interact with the world, or the universe for that matter!

Therefore, a more beneficial approach to "defusing your fuse" – one that puts you in charge of your emotions instead of losing control of them – is highly recommended. While it certainly helps to have some basic insight into human nature, *what's more important is understanding your own behavior!* At the very least, *try to GET A HOLD OF YOURSELF!*

Understanding how your inner emotional landscape operates can assist in effectively managing highly charged encounters, not only with irritable humans but also with an increasing number of stressed-out species who would prefer to avoid having any encounters with humans![2] Although there are no guarantees when it comes to improving one's emotional equilibrium, it is certainly worth the effort. After all, someone needs to stay calm, and *shouldn't that someone be you!?*

Of course, managing your own emotions may end up taking a back seat due to the tasks and distractions that consume your time. However, you may be more inclined to take charge of your emotional space when you realize that much of what keeps humans busy and stressed often leads to temper tantrums and meltdowns, which *most definitely* interferes with the process of EVOLVING!

Changing your turbulent inner programming to a more enhanced operating system will help you move forward in creating emotional balance.

Adults who frequently experience explosive outbursts and have short fuses should consider asking themselves if some introspection – *or even an intervention* – is needed. Humans should resist the impulse to deflect or blame others for their behavior, which is a common reaction on Planet Earth and is keeping many stuck in repetitive nonsense.

Finding one's inner stability may require additional support to address unruly emotional turbulence. The path to becoming your best self is best navigated with the help of guides who can offer assistance. You may get further on your journey when you tap into the collective wisdom of mental health practitioners, healers, therapists, yoga, and meditation teachers (perhaps even your Mommy) who can help lead you to inner calm and sometimes, even healing.

Fully accepting responsibility for losing your cool and being accountable for your actions is considered a sign of emotional maturity in the Cosmos. Isn't it time for that to be the case on Planet Earth as well?

Human Emotional Explosive Disorder (HEED)[3]

When a human struggles to manage intense and explosive emotions, it often results in unpleasant conduct such as volatile outbursts, difficulties with reasoning, impulsive behaviors, and out-of-control orifices and appendages. To make matters worse, many of these dysfunctional behaviors are also frequently ridiculous, hurtful, annoying, repetitive, and MIND-NUMBING!

Anyone who experiences **HEED** — which from our cosmic perspective is approximately 79.999% of humans — feels emotions intensely and spews them out towards humans standing in their way (or sadly, towards their pets), sometimes for extended periods. **HEED** can occur for any reason, depending on the humans involved.

HEED is especially set off when something or someone disturbs, annoys, or challenges a human, often leading to an intense and usually destructive emotional response that results in a meltdown of some sort. Needless to say, there are numerous examples of **HEED**, many of which are frequently captured on various devices and shared widely with eager audiences.

While emotional meltdowns are distressingly common on Earth, rest assured that they are a rarity in the Galaxy – *and we intend to keep it that way!* To prevent the spread of this condition in the Galaxy, the **HEED** diagnosis has been added to the **Cosmic Behavior Database (CBD)** for further analysis and review. It should concern humankind that their crazy antics are subject to cosmic evaluation, but given the current tumultuous times, we're not counting on it!

In fact, explosive humans typically show little concern for anyone else's perspective – whether human, animal, *or alien* – besides their own. This lack of awareness is unfortunate because a cosmic, non-human perspective on human behavior is precisely what is needed to awaken humankind to how bonkers their civilization appears to others in the galaxy.[4]

With this in mind, the "Cosmic Consensus" is that humanity must quickly *come to its senses* and establish a baseline of acceptable adult emotional behavior, regardless of current habits and conditioning. Holding humans accountable for detrimental dysfunctions can help prevent negative behaviors from becoming normalized and tolerated. This will require emotionally mature adult humans (and perhaps some wise children) to finally take the steering wheel away from "adult toddlers" in order to prevent a further meltdown of your world.

Reaching a higher level of emotional maturity can happen faster with a commitment to evolving. Clear thinking and reasoning should become second nature to humans, along with a full understanding that ongoing dysfunctional behavior is not conducive to the future survival of humankind. Of course, not all humans are able to regulate themselves without support. There may be underlying issues that require further examination to determine exactly what is going on, such as certain brain conditions. Some humans may not realize they are struggling with unmanageable emotions and think it is normal to overreact to minor irritations. Getting help should never be postponed, no matter the reason, as accountability for one's behavior is essential.

Gaining emotional maturity involves acknowledging and recognizing the parts of yourself that may make you feel uncomfortable. Because if you are uncomfortable, it is quite likely that you are making others uncomfortable as well!

SIGNS to HEED

- Overall wretchedness.
- A pessimistic outlook.
- An inability to control one's temper.
- Easily offended by the slightest issue.
- A negative and grumpy attitude.
- A high level of rage, fear, and anger.
- Frequent and uncontrolled emotional outbursts.
- A rigid and inflexible mindset with explosive reactions.
- Intense outbursts of outrage at the slightest provocation.
- A lack of compassion or self-awareness for another.
- Repetitive negative thinking, often not based on reality.
- Harsh and intolerant attitudes towards others.
- Emotional dysfunction that often leads to a meltdown.
- Inability to be civil with those who hold differing opinions.

If you realize that "ugh oh," you have more than one **HEED** symptom, don't despair or become dejected. Having one, several, or all of these symptoms does not necessarily imply you are hopeless or irredeemable. Rather, it usually means that *you really*

---

need to take a good look at yourself and your behavior. If you can do that, you can then begin to do something about it.

Serious self-reflection or a consultation with a professional can help determine whether one's meltdowns are a chronic or short-term condition. At the very least, you may want to engage in some form of a time-out to initiate the soul-searching process.

"Humankind is challenged, as it has never been challenged before, to prove it's maturity and it's mastery, not of nature, but of itself." — Rachel Carson, marine biologist, writer, and conservationist

What Does Your Mind Got to Do with It?

If you answered "nothing," *think again!* There comes a time, which could be now, when it is imperative to understand that losing one's mind and self-control is not only unproductive and harmful, but also gets in the way of self-growth and evolution. In fact, evolving may seem like wishful thinking during this millennium of meltdowns, when even well-meaning humans struggle with maintaining emotional equilibrium.

When ongoing planetary dysfunction becomes the new normal, mindless emotional commotion can erupt at any time during human interactions. Rational and clear thinking becomes difficult during tense encounters with rude humans or when dealing with disturbing world events, such as shortages of favorite goodies or toilet paper, that can lead to further conflict, aggression, and violence.

However, it is exactly when intense emotions go astray, that paying attention to your "head space" is of utmost importance. Thereby, you can dial down the intensity before a total meltdown occurs!

DING DING!

The mind has an important connection to your emotions since it serves as the gateway[5] to your self-control and self-mastery! Perhaps you read something about this concept somewhere on social media, or your yoga instructor mentioned it while you were trying to breathe and release your negative vibes. Essentially, the thoughts that you regularly think about, like those that run on auto-pilot, can influence how you feel, and vice versa.

Why this momentous insight doesn't receive the MAJOR publicity it deserves is incomprehensible, especially since emotional immaturity – and its multitude of negative consequences – continues to cause dysfunction on both a personal and global level!

Just in case you are still confused about who is having emotional tirades, *we're talking about human ADULTS, not children!* Furthermore, it's not just the occasional human in aisle 4 having a meltdown,[6] but a growing number of humans who are losing control both privately and publicly as stress and chaos persist on Planet Earth.

If You're Going To Have A Tantrum, Then At Least Learn From It!

For those who are unable to get a hold of themselves before blowing a fuse, utilizing out-of-the-box cosmic tips may help interrupt the meltdown circuit coursing through your system. The objective is to have a higher level of self-awareness around your adult tantrum.

When you feel your *temper rising*, take a moment to find a mirror and look at yourself. This can be quite illuminating and may even make you laugh! Don't look away, be brave, and just observe.

If mirrors aren't available, make any meltdown moment extra productive by recording yourself. Watch it later and take notes. Just make sure no one else records your "moment" to share with the world, unless of course, you actually want to share it.

If the previous options are not suitable, you can try this: Immediately take a deep breath, count to four, and release slowly. Repeat this at least five times! Alternatively, you can lie down, close your orbitals (eyes), and if possible, take a nap.

Later, when you come to your senses, you should rationally reflect on what happened during your emotional malfunction.

Once you are stabilized, ask yourself these questions:
What set you off and why?
How might you respond differently next time, before a meltdown?
Did you like what you saw in the mirror or on your recording?

Are You Melting?

If you don't want to be pulled into a *mindless vortex of meltdowns* – whether caused by you or another human – then it's essential to become **THE BOSS OF YOUR OWN MIND.** Stay calm and centered so you can make better decisions instead of getting lost in an emotional tirade that could end badly.

As *da* **Boss**, additional benefits include checking in with your inner authority to decide if you need a much-needed break without requiring another's permission to do so, especially when decompression or relaxation is called for. Ultimately, the big bonus is when other humans – and if you're really lucky, your pets – find your enhanced demeanor quite appealing to be around, making you much more popular for the right reasons!

In fact, there's a good chance that your cool composure will be admired when encountering any type of out-of-control meltdown, no matter where it happens. Being in command certainly doesn't mean that one has to become a cold-hearted sociopath, because human feelings are essential for optimal functioning and you wouldn't be considered human without them. The intention isn't to suppress emotions or detach from feelings, but rather to fully experience and work through them.

Without a doubt, taking charge of your head space will require an approach that works best for you. One effective strategy is to learn how to *meditate your mind*, rather than just medicate it. Not surprisingly, meditation is popular in the Cosmos, and hopefully, this will soon be the case on Planet Earth as well! Many advanced beings maintain ongoing equilibrium through mindful meditation practices and enjoy contorting their appendages in Yoga-like positions, while integrating highly developed psychological techniques[7] that promote a healthy emotional state.

Let The Vortex Be With You![8]

Use the method of pausing and breathing whenever you experience an emotional disruption in your vicinity. To enhance the experience, set aside some time to mindfully enjoy a delectable treat, relax in a lavender oil-infused bath, or sip a herbal beverage to further calm your nerves.

Breathe deeply, pause, recenter, and let go of any non-serving emotions.

Connect with your center, which is within you. Keep searching, it's there. Keep breathing deeply.

In this pause, remind yourself that you are more than just your mind and emotions.

Remember, the Vortex is always with you.

"I have noted that the healthy release of emotion is frequently very unhealthy for those closest to you." – Spock, Star Trek: Plato's Stepchildren, 1968[9]

Cosmic Behavioral Expert Dr. Youpoke Yopraugh, affectionately known as Dr. Yo Yo, has spent eons researching multidimensional meltdowns and their related issues.

Upon analyzing the Emotional Commotion Syndrome on Planet Earth, Dr. Yo Yo's initial recommendation was for humanity to continue with a cosmic time-out until further notice from the Universe. However, since an apocalypse may be around the corner, Dr. Yo Yo realizes that time is of the essence when facing a potential meltdown of such magnitude! As a Multidimensional Being, Dr. Yo Yo zooms in on identifying what prevents a species from fully integrating themselves in a holistic, multidimensional manner.

Without a doubt, many humans need to have their chakras (energy vortexes) tuned up and although this is a concerning issue, humanity's lack of control over their mind and body orifices is even more worrying than unbalanced energy vortexes. Furthermore, if explosive human behavior continues to be normalized and accepted, achieving a collective re-calibration process may become increasingly challenging. Stability in any form is at risk when there are frequent implosions, explosions, and meltdowns occurring everywhere. **Dr. Yo Yo has this to impart:**

"Humans are more than capable of overcoming their emotional malfunctions once they face the reality that if they want to continue living on Planet Earth, they have no choice but to grow up as a species! Despite the Earthling belief that some sort of awakening is imminent, the majority of humans aren't quite there yet. Many are still snoozing, but if you're reading this, you can help wake a few of them up.

Paying attention to your inner emotional commotion is one of the first steps to becoming aware of the mental landscape you live in, because to BECOME THE BOSS OF YOURSELF, you will need to change your relationship with yourself – who else?

To do that, you must become aware of acknowledging the issues at hand, which for some humans means accepting their unruly and uncontrollable natures! Therefore, humans must close unnecessary volatile orifices and re-center themselves with whatever is necessary to stabilize further meltdowns, so that the process of mature emotional re-calibration can begin." In Peace – Dr. Yo Yo

Maybe I Need to Decompress?!

When intense emotions and mental overload get the better of even the most composed and calm human, sometimes the best course of action is to stop engaging and instead, start decompressing. This process is as simple as locking your door, shutting down distracting devices, grabbing a comfy blanket to cuddle with cute furballs, and essentially doing whatever else is necessary to ensure that your peace is not disturbed.

A decompression bubble that effectively relaxes your nerves is a serious undertaking and should not be taken lightly. It is important to be adequately prepared in order *to* avoid *any* disturbances to your well-being from the outside world. Whether you are an explosive human or not, there are times when intense reactions are justified, especially during chaotic times on Planet Earth. This is when a safe and proper decompression cycle can do wonders to re-calibrate a human. After all, who doesn't deserve a break from the rest of humanity once in a while?

Making use of decompression strategies can alter the course of one's emotional landscape and at the very least, take the edge off things. In some cases, a break in the meltdown cycle may even lead to the momentous insight that you want OFF from the emotional roller-coaster ride. Once you're on firmer ground, it becomes possible to achieve a more enhanced approach to emotional equilibrium, ultimately bringing you closer to becoming the "Boss of Your Own Mind."

Managing your emotional landscape has numerous benefits, including strengthening your resilience to turbulent circumstances, whether they are your own or someone else's. This can create a positive feedback loop that reinforces emotional stability and helps maintain a calm center. Regularly experiencing a state of equilibrium can make you feel good and leads to having compassion for others.

Self-mastery of your mind and emotions helps prevent anyone or anything from disturbing your inner peace. It is a sign that you are on the way to becoming the boss of yourself. Honestly, there's no better feeling than being in charge and realizing that, '*hello*," that someone is actually YOU!

Cosmic Minds Just Want to Know...

Consider how some humans would react if a spacecraft suddenly landed in their backyard. Would they remain calm, or would they panic and thoughtlessly react before these cosmic visitors had a chance of offering greetings? Confronting unexpected visitors, whether alien or human, can be unsettling and requires composed civility.

I'M THE BOSS OF MY OWN MIND
(Who else would you want it to be?)

1. Recognize and become aware of your emotions

Self-awareness is one of the keys to understanding your emotions and ultimately, yourself. When you feel a strong emotion coming on, take a step back and observe it. This becomes easier the more you practice it. Try not to judge what you are feeling but instead, check in with what you are experiencing. Naming emotions is the first step to being able to manage them.

When you can identify and distinguish specific feelings, you become more familiar with how each emotion presents itself. Perhaps you are mistaking anger for fear, or are simply hungry or exhausted. Don't be too hard on yourself when dealing with uncomfortable emotions. Instead, acknowledge and let them go.

2. Understand what sets you off

Understanding your hot buttons[10] is especially important if there is much that sets you off. When you become aware of what triggers your emotions, you will realize that certain signals or stimuli can cloud your judgment. Notice how different situations or humans push your buttons. Think deeply about how you usually react to them.

3. Manage your reactions

Intense emotions can create the impulse to thoughtlessly react, so learn how to pause *before* you respond. If you tend to lash out too quickly, you may want to *slowly* count to 10 and take deep breaths.

The impulse to react without adequate reflection is precisely why it's imperative to manage your head space. Training your mind to create space for rational thinking *before your emotions hijack your behavior*, and effectively managing your responses and behavior, is a more beneficial way to interact in any situation, with any life form, whether human or not.

4. Connect with your own body

Your body is listening to everything that is happening, so you may want to take that into serious consideration, *especially if you are prone to anger.* Pay attention to how different emotions affect your body by observing your breathing pattern, heart rate and muscle tension. **Do not ignore warning signs**, such as your rising blood pressure or the feeling that your head is about to explode, because these are indications that a potential system overload is imminent!

Learning how to prevent tension in the body is crucial because your body is a sensitive emotional barometer of your well-being. You can keep things running smoothly by pausing and taking a breath BEFORE you react. This can help you avoid creating damaging patterns of thinking and behaving that can lead to a physical meltdown. Stress is a common precursor to many illnesses and in severe cases, can even lead to death.

5. Stay in the Mindful Loop

To get into the mindful loop, you need to *consistently pay attention* to "what's going on in there," not just when you feel like it. There are no shortcuts to better understanding your mind space or learning how to overcome limiting behaviors. Achieving a mindful approach to living is a personal and unique experience based on *how you perceive and react* to the world around you.

Being aware of what is happening inside your head will help you avoid getting sidelined by needlessly repetitive and destructive emotions that keep you from well-being. However, it's easy to fall back into mindless habitual ways of thinking and behaving. Therefore, do not be hard on yourself if that happens, as learning to be patient with yourself and others is an ongoing process.

Staying in the loop is all about constantly fine-tuning your ability to adjust, as no one (*especially not us!*) ever implied that managing your (human) mind would be easy!

"*Any person capable of angering you becomes your master.*" — Epictetus

Mind Half Empty or Half Full?

Quite possibly, some humans want nothing to do with their minds, especially if they see no real benefit in doing so. Staying on auto-pilot and letting emotions run amok may be more convenient than making the effort to deal with them. Certainly, managing your thoughts and mind space is not for the lazy. It is called "a practice" for a reason, because *you have to keep doing it to get better at it!*

Avoidance can only take you so far because your mind belongs to you, and at some point, a lack of attention may end up backfiring in spectacular ways. Besides, if you don't know what is truly going on in your headspace, how can you expect others to understand you? Unless, of course, they possess advanced abilities or are mind readers of some kind. Depending on what's in there, they may choose to keep their insights to themselves!

DING DING!
Making a conscious choice to understand one's thoughts and emotions can lead to a peaceful mind. By acknowledging the power of your mind, YOU become the one who determines whether your emotions will improve your life or instead lead to unintended consequences. In essence, emotions and your mind can either enhance or ruin your life. **In order to make this choice, you must first become aware that it is, in fact, a choice.***

*Certain humans may require more than just awareness, mindfulness, and meditation techniques to effectively manage their emotions. They may need to seek professional support in emotional mastery and healing. This type of assistance is not covered in this chapter, so it is highly advised that

those in need begin looking for appropriate mental health professionals, healers, and spiritual guides to improve their overall well-being.

Rescue Your Emotions

*Identify and manage your own emotions, while also acknowledging the feelings of others.

*Make the best use of emotions by applying them to tasks, such as thinking and problem-solving.

*Understand that constructive emotions can improve a situation, while destructive emotions make it worse.

*Express emotions constructively and take responsibility for them.

*Make an effort to positively re-frame and convey your feelings.

*Mindfully think about the words you use to describe your feelings, rather than impulsively reacting.

Lost Your Mind? No Worries.

Sometimes, losing your mind is unavoidable and perhaps, even necessary to fully understand yourself. Eventually, you may realize that perhaps your mind wasn't lost after all. Losing one's mind is typically rare or temporary, unless, of course, a human has serious psychiatric or mental conditions. When it feels like you're going to lose your mind, it's usually because strong emotions are hijacking your very being and causing a circuit overload.

Keep in mind that when experiencing an emotional tsunami, it can be difficult to think clearly in that moment. During these times, having any actual awareness of losing one's mind is close to impossible until you can return to a more balanced state. However, *try not to panic* when you're in this state. This temporary mindless state can lead to significant growth and be an insightful learning experience. Once the storm passes and the sky clears, hopefully your mind will clear as well.

The Path to Peace*Able*

When you are able to consistently maintain a certain level of inner calm, you will start to experience a more peaceful nature. *Humankind cannot have a peaceful world if humans themselves are not peaceful.* Human thoughts, emotions, and behavior determine the course of life, both personally and collectively. Humans must achieve some level of self-mastery in these areas to maintain a peaceful coexistence with each other. The "millennium of meltdowns" must come to an end or it will be your end. Fortunately, there are paths to becoming peaceable, and one of them is practicing some form of meditation or quieting of the mind.

The purpose of meditation is not to eliminate thoughts but to notice when you are drifting in thought, emotion, or sensation. By recognizing this, you can then bring yourself back to the present moment. Each distraction serves as an opportunity to come back to your breath as your breath is constantly in the present. Once you realize this, you become more mindful of the current moment you are experiencing!

Starting your day with a practice to quiet your mind is ideal, but it can be done at anytime. Alternatively, you can go outside because nature can help to rest your mind. For those who are especially restless, walking mindfully while focusing on your breath can also provide meditative benefits.

- Sit comfortably, with your back upright and your neck comfortably straight.
- Relax your face, mouth, jaw, and any other tight body parts.
- Close your eyes and notice the sounds around you but don't judge or analyze them.
- Move your awareness to your breath but don't try to change or alter it in any way.
- Notice the rise and fall of your breathing with each inhale and exhale.
- You may notice that certain thoughts, sensations, and emotions come up. Do not try to stop thinking or feeling. Simply notice and visualize them floating away.

- Reconnect with your breath, taking deep inhales and exhales.
- Feel and notice the relaxation in your body and mind.
- Just a few minutes is all you need.

Repeat After Us

My mind is my friend.
I observe; I do not react.
I can manage my emotions.
I am aware of my emotions.
I am not defined by my emotions alone.
I am grateful for the present moment.
I welcome a sense of calm into my life.
I recognize that my emotions are temporary.
I am experiencing this moment without judgment.
I allow myself to feel what I feel and then let it go.
I have the power to change my life by changing my thoughts.
I am more than just my mind and emotions. I accept all of myself.

*"Wisdom tells us that the best time for silence is when we are mad or upset." —
John Patrick Hickey, author*

Thoughts?

"A calm mind directly leads to peace of mind." — Dalai Lama

Notes

1. Marshall Rosenberg, Ph.D., developed Nonviolent Communication to resolve conflicts. Wikipedia & https://www.cnvc.org/about/marshall

2. It's not their fault! Nidhi Sharma, NBC News 2023 https://www.nbcnews.com/science/environment/carnivores-attacks-humans-are-becoming-common-climate-change-isnt-help-rcna68998

3. Heed means to pay attention, consider, *and listen.*

4. The viewpoint of an alien or advanced being is a vast subject.

5. Human gateways can malfunction or stop working. Some may stay wide open for too long, while others are closed and sealed shut. Some may simply require maintenance. If your gateway is functioning properly, consider yourself lucky and very special indeed!

6. Is aisle 4 the only aisle where irritated human shoppers are blocking the way? We don't believe so. It seems that numerous aisles are filled with exasperated shoppers. However, any unsuspecting human who happens to go down aisle 4 may find themselves caught in a vortex of meltdowns caused by an alignment of unknown forces that have yet to be understood by humankind.

7. Cosmic counseling and Universal therapy are common practices in nearly all galaxies as psychological well-being is crucial for the full development and potential of any species. Advanced Beings harness highly developed mental abilities and consistently improve the process to ensure that all faculties operate efficiently and smoothly. Humans experiencing complex emotional or mental challenges, whether mild or severe, may want to seek assistance from a qualified professional, because if you think you're going to solve all your problems by yourself, think again.

8. Being in the vortex means being in vibrational alignment with your true self. When you are in this vibrational state, you are also in alignment with the Supreme Source of Energy. Things flow smoothly from this Vortex! If you want to feel more of this energy, go out into nature and simply breathe. You can also experience energy vortexes in specific special places on Earth. Learn more about vortex healing. Institute of Noetic Sciences © 2015 https://noetic.org/wp-content/uploads/2021/01/Vortex-Healing.pdf

9. *Star Trek*, American science fiction television series, third season. https://en.wikipedia.org/wiki/Plato%27s_Stepchildren

10. Hot buttons are behaviors that can upset, anger, or irritate humans and trigger a destructive reaction. Almost all humans have the ability to control these buttons if they choose to do so. Instead of reacting to the hot button, try pressing the cool-down button.

11. Be Chill

"Peace is not a goal to be reached but a way of life to be lived." – Desmond Tutu, Archbishop and Activist

 **Peaceable**: to be disposed to peace: not contentious or quarrelsome: quietly behaved: free from strife or disorder.[1]

For Peace Sake!

If recent world events and other worries are keeping you up at night, then inner peace may seem out of reach due to increased chaos and general craziness. Not surprisingly, the current Earth vibes radiating out into the cosmos reflect a planet that has high stress levels. Although burning copious amounts of sage or smoking an herbal peace pipe would help, a deeper transformation is needed.

Fortunately, the "dawning of the Age of Aquarius" is upon you,[2] which will hopefully move the process of human transformation forward. Didn't see this on your social media feed? No worries, all you essentially need to know is that the Aquarian Age is all about fostering inner growth and personal responsibility to create a more peaceful planet.

"When the moon is in the Seventh House and Jupiter aligns with Mars, then peace will guide the planets and love will steer the stars." – Recorded by the 5th Dimension in 1967 by James Rado, Gerome Ragni and Galt MacDermot

Of course, you may be wondering how peace on Earth is possible when so many agitated humans are still on a rampage. If you're hoping for a cosmic deportation program to remove some of these offending humans, we're sorry to say, "It *ain't gonna happen.*" What can happen – to end the insanity of nonsensical behavior – is to realize that inner turmoil creates the reality of outer turmoil. Consequently, changing your reality relies on solutions that, like many other evolving tips, usually start with YOU putting your MIND TO IT.

Peace becomes possible when humans FULLY accept that maintaining a personal level of inner peace is a universal responsibility for all of humankind. This requires you to become aware of the power of your mindset and its ability to have both positive and negative consequences. When human consciousness can fully embrace that "peace begins within," a collective shift will occur worldwide.

Now, wouldn't a higher level of harmony be nicer than all the craziness currently going on? Humanity continues to struggle with maintaining peace, as it has been prone to aggressive and violent tendencies for centuries. Hostile and confrontational behavior is regularly reflected in culture and has become widespread in film, social media, politics, and music. This further influences human attitudes and behavior, resulting in a negative feedback loop. What's worse is that certain individuals and groups are promoting negative and aggressive rhetoric to manipulate others on a larger scale than ever before!

Fortunately, humanity's quest for peace has not all been in vain. Civilizations have utilized spiritual and practical interventions to foster a more harmonious coexistence. Cultivating a peaceful inner composure results in many benefits, such as lowering blood pressure, reducing heart attacks, and increasing self-control. Furthermore, it can help lessen the urge to lash out or hurl vulgarities at annoying (and sometimes horrible) humans.

Additionally, a relaxed and centered mind enhances self-control, making you better at controlling yourself. This helps you deal with tough times more calmly and clearly. When you feel peaceful inside, you're less bothered by annoyances that can chip away at your patience and goodwill. By reacting thoughtfully, you can prevent bad feelings from spreading and instead, can help create a more kinder and peaceful world, even in small ways. This inner peace becomes a powerful force for collective harmony.

Quite possibly, during this crucial juncture in humanity's attempt to stay relevant in the cosmos, one of the most important benefits of inner and outer peace will be that humankind will CONTINUE TO EXIST – *because inner peace helps with becoming an overall nicer human* – which may in turn, speed up the Aquarius Age of inner chill and *finally* usher in the utopian lifestyle prophesied by ancient oracles of long ago.

The effort to support your understanding of evolved perspectives sometimes requires further clarification about why it is necessary! The Universe knows that some species have a hard time figuring themselves out, especially when ongoing chaos and turmoil interfere with their efforts to create a better future. Further complicating the matter is that certain species have very high opinions of themselves, usually not based on reality. The urgency to evolve is lost on them, which of course, is quite concerning.

The bottom line is this: Being peaceful isn't just a nice idea but a requirement to overcome the mayhem that is overtaking Planet Earth. Humans who want to consider themselves civilized and advanced have to realize that constant agitation, disharmony, and violence *are not pillars of an advanced society*, but rather the shaky foundations of a barbaric lifestyle!

"Peace within, peace without, peace begins, peace throughout. Lover of peace, in mind and soul. All is one and one is all. For it is Truth, Peace is Love." – Star-Ashanumi

---

Dr. Vortex Vulcani, ABA BABA B100, a Galaxy-Renowned Authority on Evolving & Advanced Being Studies and President of Universal Universe University (UUU), truly believes **it's all, *but not all*, about YOU, YOU, YOU** and has this to say:

"To become an evolved and peaceful species of any magnitude, one must reign in one's inner turmoil so that one's sh*t does not spill out into the ether and beyond, because inner turmoil usually foments

---

into outer turmoil, quite possibly disturbing the peaceful vibes of surrounding species and the environment, and which can then lead to some nasty and hostile exchanges. This means you, agitated human in aisle four[3] or wherever you may be right now!

Consequently, paying attention to your inner level of peace is not a one-off event but must be attended to daily. For those especially discombobulated species, who are prone to explosions that shatter any level of serenity, maintaining a specific schedule for inner peace activities is not just recommended but crucial to their existence and the survival of their communities. Disciplining your mind and possibly other areas (such your appendages, if you have them), with time to properly chill out so that you can experience what peacefulness feels like, is a good start. However, each species must create its own plan and put it in place. Better sooner than later for the human species in question.

INNER PEACE is the GOLD STANDARD of an evolved species, as maintaining one's tranquility while chaos and sh*t are flying around is not just a superpower, but is actually a smart thing to do. Why let others disturb your inner sanctum of relaxed and chilling vibes when you can have that opportunity to just step back, breathe in whatever you breathe (if you are a breathing species), tap into your reservoir of tranquil energies, and just allow the meltdown of hostile aggressive activity to commence.

HOWEVER, this does not mean that you should just PUT UP with any "LESS THAN PEACEFUL" species or situations. There are times when inner calmness helps to make decisions in a relaxed manner, which would then take care of volatile and unpleasant situations in the best way possible. **NO ONE** is suggesting that a peaceful entity or species be a PUSHOVER!

Thus, even peaceful and calm species can make decisions, sometimes utilizing some type of benevolent force, that helps the other "snap out of it" in time so that no one gets hurt! IF you absolutely have to, utilizing a 2×4 type enforcer is sometimes *permissible if only as a warning to others (if your planet has them, if not, use an appropriate substitute of some sort). The bottom line is that peace isn't always easy, but it is essential. Peace be with you for sure. Cheers!" – Dr. Vortex Vulcani*

"Peace is more than the absence of war, it is living together with our differences – of sex, race, language, religion or culture while furthering universal respect for justice and human rights on which such coexistence depends." – UNESCO

So *what does this mean for* YOU? It means that in order to achieve Planet ZEN, humankind must place a higher value on maintaining and PROMOTING peace over conflicts and violence. This requires a conscious effort in your personal life, as well as making it a priority throughout society. Furthermore, it is no longer acceptable to simply pay "lip service"[4] to the idea of peace while the use of various weapons of mass destruction continues. Not only are these weapons dangerous, but so is the mental state of agitation and discord that human brains consistently marinate in.

Of course, it's not always easy to stay calm and maintain a serene equilibrium when dealing with assorted ornery humans who seem hell-bent on destroying any inner peace you may have tenuously achieved. The ability to maintain adequate composure while simultaneously dealing with ongoing insanity requires a certain level of inner self-control, among other things! Unfortunately, this ability isn't as common (yet) as it should be, and consequently, consistent inner peace may seem challenging for ordinary human mortals.

Therefore, it's not surprising that many still believe that the only truly peaceful and tranquil humans are those who reside in remote temples[5] far away from the maddening crowd. *Oh sure* (you're probably thinking), of course it would be much more peaceful to have your very own mountaintop retreat with unlimited access to mind-altering substances such as incense, essential oils, and sound bowls. Understandably, a typical human may wonder how they can reach a state of nirvana while dealing with constant stress and agitation, without actually needing to retreat to a mountaintop.

Dealing with stress and anxiety (and we should mention turbulent times) requires developing skills that initially change YOU! One of the first things you can do to make that happen is to understand that you have control over how you choose to respond to stressful situations or upsetting humans — and this response, from you, really matters.

"To find inner peace, search deep inside yourself. Is there a doughnut there? If not, take corrective action." — Anonymous

Look Within

Actually, where else would you look? **Inner peace** is an inside job and starts with the realization that it is a state of calm you feel within yourself, one that *you create and MAINTAIN*. So go on, take a moment to look within. Have you found your "inner doughnut of peacefulness?" While you may think that having a doughnut would help right now, true inner peace usually requires more than just stuffing yourself with various delectable delights. Of course, it may seem easier to finish off an entire box of doughnuts than to work on your inner serenity. However, you will gain more than just empty calories if you put down the doughnut and instead focus on your inner peace!

Unlike a sugar high, an infusion of peaceful vibes can help you experience an emotional, mental, and physical shift that may have long-lasting effects. These altered states are often supported by enthusiastic yoga teachers, spiritual healers, and meditation teachers who may or may not use sound bowls and essential oils to guide you towards a calmer and expanded state of mind. While guides are certainly helpful, rest assured that inner peace is within your reach, whether or not you decide to add a doughnut or sound bowl to your efforts.

However, before you indulge in that last doughnut in the box, there are some important things to consider when seeking inner nirvana. A good starting point is to become aware of your behavior and overall outlook on life. Take time to reflect on your attitudes, conversations, and how you interact with others.

Do you tend to be more peaceful in your encounters, or are you usually angry and aggressive? Are you more likely to avoid conflicts, or are you generally argumentative and prone to knee-jerk outbursts?

Of course, not all arguments escalate into violence, but it is more common for argumentative humans to lack inner peace and become more aggressive. However, it is also important to understand that lacking inner peace doesn't necessarily mean one is aggressive or angry. Many times the struggle for a sense of serenity can result from incessant thoughts, mental turmoil or feelings of discontent, fear, and anxiety.

DING DING!

The increasingly out-of-control events on Planet Earth are adding to the stress that many humans are feeling, making it difficult to live in the Zen Zone. Therefore, providing sufficient support for mental and emotional well-being should be a top priority in any society that is serious about its future. This will ensure that the synergistic efforts that are essential for transformation are put in place! [6]

A Not So Chilled Human may be...

unruly
noisy
easily disturbed
constantly distracted
judgmental and harsh
hostile and aggressive
discontented and dissatisfied
mentally and emotionally unwell
insistent on always having to be right

inclined to dislike others and themselves
struggling with overwhelming and busy thoughts
likely to use weapons of destruction (of any kind)

A Nicely Chilled Human...

walks away from drama
enjoys stillness, nature, and quiet
puts a priority on rest and serenity
is comfortable being themselves
is considerate, compassionate and empathetic
cultivates and embraces patience
enjoys laughing (at themselves) and with others
knows when to let go of whatever needs to be let go of
is not easily drawn into conflicts and confrontations
isn't worried about convincing others to understand them
enjoys their own company and their version of happiness
stands up for what's right in a benevolent manner
loves furballs, shares chocolate and sometimes eats donuts,
without any guilt

"He who lives in harmony with himself lives in harmony with the world." –
Marcus Aurelius, philosopher.

Enter the Zen Zone

In a world full of commotion, there's always the possibility that
encounters between humans can quickly devolve into ranting, yelling,
throwing objects, or even violence. Consequently, properly cultivating
a calmer mindset will help safeguard your inner well-being from these
volatile situations. Before entering your inner sanctum, you may want

to grab some lavender oil or sage to diffuse the negative vibes of any offensive human who has caused disturbance to your equilibrium.

Of course, it is important to remember that lasting inner peace is a journey and a way of living, not just a temporary respite from chaotic shenanigans. Staying in the Zen Zone will require a commitment that goes beyond commonplace platitudes and empty slogans.

Master Yogishimi Yami Zami, Author, Teacher and Guruologist, as well as Director of the *Cudha Shoudha Institute of Being Here But Not There*, has this to say about the highest level of chilling required to become adept at staying calm and peaceful in any galaxy:

"In civilizations that have achieved long-lasting peace, the common denominator is a commitment to utilizing methods that become an integral part of the species' character and general behavior across all its various forms. **In other words, there's gotta be a plan!**

This achievement is made possible without the need for hallucinogenics, medication, or interventions (with rare exceptions, of course). Various techniques are integrated into all aspects of society and are upheld as vital values, which are encouraged and modeled from birth to mature adulthood. **In other words, the plan has to be effective, popular with the natives, and put into place!**

The Cosmic norm is to stay chill and calm. Disruption to inner and outer peace is considered abnormal behavior and is very rare in societies that have adapted their natures to a new setting, one in which all species have the same objective and support in maintaining their level of peaceful composure. This ultimately benefits the entire planet in the evolving process. **In other words, this is a group project and all of you need to work together to get to the good stuff!**

The obvious takeaway is that being "cool, calm, and collected" is an ability that gives you more than just peace of mind; it provides you with tranquility and contentment, which in turn, leads to personal growth without adding stress to your chakras or possibly, to your appendages (if a species has them). **In other words, being a peaceful creature has benefits and it FEELS GOOD!**

Due to the many successful outcomes in the Cosmos, peacefully evolved species have come together to create and promote a multi-galaxy

Cosmic Chill Campaign that has become the deluxe standard in advanced inner peace development. These trainings include self-chill techniques that are comprised of several universal concepts known to balance inner energies without causing anyone to blow a fuse, whether they are on or off the planet or in any galaxy.

In other words, if you want to be part of the COSMIC PLAN, you need to GET WITH THE PROGRAM!" – Be chill, Master Yogishimi Yami Zami

---

COSMIC CHILL-OUT
Don't just enter the Zone. *Be the Zone*

Center Yourself. Step back mentally, emotionally, and physically (if need be). Step away from other humans if necessary or desired, which in many cases, it will be.

Control your breathing. BREATHE IN through your nose (or the orifice that breathes), count to 4, HOLD FOR 5, THEN BREATHE OUT through your mouth (or similar orifice), counting to 6. Explore the best breathing routine that works for you. Refer to further instructions below. If you stopped breathing permanently, you now have no worries and most likely, are a lot calmer than before.

Visualize your personal Zen Zone, your happy place, unlimited delectable delights, and any humans or others (if you're lucky, some very cute felines), who love you.

If you NEED to grab that chocolate (doughnut), or lavender oil, *go ahead and do so NOW!*

Observe and become aware of the source of your turmoil; is it real or a perception? If you need that 2×4, GRAB it NOW otherwise, LET IT GO! (meaning the turmoil; keep the 2×4).

Develop a sense of COMPASSION, for yourself and others. Compassion is possible when you gain empathy for others.

CHILLED BUT NOT SHAKEN

Live in the present and for today. Where else are you going to live? You can visit the past but don't stay there. Dream of the future but don't lose yourself in waiting for tomorrow.

QUIET your MIND – find a quiet place, practice some form of meditation or just become aware of your thoughts and take a deep breath.

Pay attention to feeling alive and enjoy what is around you.

Wisely choose thoughts that bring you peace, instead of those that don't.

Ask yourself, "Who's running the ship or spacecraft? You, or the autopilot?" *The answer should be YOU!*

Accept yourself and live authentically. Let go of who you think you should be.

Learn to be content and simplify your life. Less is more in most cases (except in the case of chocolate, when more is better).

Let go of looking for happiness or peace. Just be a joyful and peaceful person. That's it. You will have it because you are it!

Give up the belief that inner peace is difficult to attain. It is your birthright and once you accept it, you will access it within yourself.

QUICK CHILL FIRST AID

If you feel agitation coming on, immediately BREATHE DEEPLY, slowly in and out. Deep breaths will bring oxygen quickly to your BRAIN (*if you have one*), which it needs when STRESSED. Do not ignore this simple first step, as it is effective.

Proceed to count to 10, close your eyes, and continue to take deep breaths. Resist holding your breath!

Whenever possible, take a break BEFORE you feel any agitation, stress, upset, or anger!

Make this FIRST AID CHILLING RESPONSE your habitual go-to method to help prevent agitation from ruining your day, or perhaps, even your life!

However... There Will Be Moments

– when you will detonate and lose your cool, your sh*t, your supply of breath mints, essential oils, the last chocolate (or doughnut), and even the ability to BREATHE because well, no one is that perfect (except felines we believe). *DO NOT BEAT YOURSELF UP!* Proceed to go back to the Zen Zone and resume normal operations.

Having meltdown moments or even an entire day of commotion doesn't necessarily mean that you're done with achieving inner peace, or "*Universe forbid,*" evolving! It just means there will be hiccups along the way. Dust yourself off, take a deep breath, have some more chocolate, and remember, humanity and Planet Earth need you to stay the course.

Promote Peace

If you are advocating for something that goes against peace, YOU NEED TO STOP. Humans who use violent aggression to express themselves and dominate others are dangerous to the world. Hatred and hostility are particularly destructive, especially when weapons of any type are used against fellow humans. Violence and aggressive conflicts hinder real cooperation and instead, create the possibility of an apocalypse. By promoting divisiveness and fear, certain groups are embracing this possibility of "end times" and are not interested in living in harmony with each other.

The calmer you are, the better you can stay in control to manage human hotheads that come your way. Learning how to maintain a peaceful demeanor while tempers flare can help prevent terrible outcomes, and depends on properly assessing the situation for everyone's safety.[7]

Reducing conflict should be a top priority because unfortunately, many humans are still struggling with basic needs and live in areas where violent conflict is common. It may seem difficult to imagine a peaceful planet when there is so much discord and chaos. Understanding the underlying causes of how different perspectives can lead to violence, conflicts, and wars will better enable humankind to develop synergistic solutions for sustainable peace efforts.

However, maintaining a level of peace doesn't necessarily mean an end to all conflicts because disagreements are to be expected. Humans just need to learn how to AGREE TO DISAGREE. A healthy society encourages differing views through civility, logic, and nonviolent discourse. What isn't healthy is the normalization of violence and war as solutions to problems, especially when those problems can be solved through other means.

Peace can have different meanings depending on the culture, so ideally, an integrative approach will include social, community, and personal dimensions. Peace is essentially a perspective that can have various meanings and frameworks that reflect the individual or one's society and culture.

Consequently, like all other steps to evolving, the ability to create a more peaceful planet will primarily depend on those who can positively affect and advance society for its highest good.

Positive sayings such as *"Peace be with you"*[8] can sometimes use a little tweak. *"May Peace be within Me, and You"* might better convey the idea that inner peace is always available to you when you intentionally choose it.

"For peace to reign on earth, humans must evolve into new beings who have learned to see the whole first." – Immanuel Kant, philosopher

Keep the Peace

Humankind needs to find a way to live with each other, regardless of whether they get along or not. It should be clear that fighting amongst yourselves has no positive outcome. Peace isn't just about meditation, essential oils, sound bowls, and feeling groovy; it's a practical way to move humanity forward. Who doesn't want that? Let's see, maybe the ones who benefit from chaos and destruction? Well, once humankind moves along on the peace train to resolve differences, many of these types will become irrelevant.

Progress is being made by an increasing number of international peace-building organizations, meditation centers, and other spiritual (and non-spiritual) groups that are providing support and guidance.[9] It's also encouraging to see that there are areas on your planet where peaceful living exists.[10] In these places, humans have created peaceful cultures that can be emulated by the rest of your planet. The wheel doesn't have to be reinvented because these societies have methods that everyone can learn from.

There are many ways to achieve personal and collective peacekeeping that take into consideration the unique factors of each human and culture. In order to bring about this change, humanity must continue it's ongoing efforts to evolve so that eventually, angry and hostile humans will finally be outnumbered.

There is little doubt in the Universe that the reality of worldwide harmony would occur more quickly if there were a collective change in consciousness.

When peace becomes a common part of daily life, it generates positive energy that can ultimately transform your planet. When it is fully understood that *peace resides within you*, it becomes a natural way of being that elevates your potential towards a better future. This will cause a shift in consciousness towards an evolved and peaceful nature that becomes encoded into your DNA. Once this transformation occurs, humanity will fully enter into the Age of Aquarius.

DING DING!

Humans often worry about aggressive aliens invading and destroying humankind. While it's easy to imagine aliens wielding powerful, advanced weapons, the real concern should be on human weapons, not alien ones! Humans already have the capability to wipe themselves out without any assistance from extraterrestrials. This is all the more reason to take human evolution seriously, as powerful technology and advanced weapons can lead to a doomsday scenario all on your own.

Humanly Harmonic

Explore yoga and sound meditation.
Quiet your mind and connect with calm.
Take time for stillness throughout your daily life.
Immerse yourself in nature, as it is healing.
Choose uplifting and positive messages.
Visit a spiritual setting to absorb peaceful energy.
Commit to non-violence in thought, speech, and action.
Make mindful choices in how you think, respond, and live.
Approach conflicts with resilience and compassion.
Stay on the path to self-awareness and transformation.
Take a break from distractions and technology consumption.
Connect with others who share and prioritize peaceful values.
Create a peaceful routine, as serenity changes how you interact with the world.

"Do not let the behavior of others destroy your inner peace." – Dalai Lama[11]

"Peace is reverence for life. Peace is the most precious possession of humanity. Peace is more than the end of armed conflict. Peace is a mode of behavior. Peace is a deep-rooted commitment to the principles of liberty, justice, equality and solidarity among all human beings. Peace is also a harmonious partnership of humankind with the environment. Today, on the eve of the twenty-first century, peace is within our reach." – Yamoussoukro Declaration [12]

Thoughts?

"In other words, peace is not just an absence of violence and war, but also people and groups getting along pro-socially with each other: the cooperation, sharing, and kindness that we see in everyday society. Sustaining peace happens through positive reciprocity: I show you a kindness and you do me a favor in return, multiplied throughout the social world a million times over." – Peter T. Coleman, Douglas P. Fry [13]

Notes

1. https://www.merriam-webster.com/dictionary/peaceable

2. Don't just sit there, *do something*! "Humanity and our planet need your Light more than ever during the next four years. Are you ready to participate in the evolutionary leap that is our planet's destiny? Will you accept the opportunity to help usher in the Age of Aquarius – the Golden Age of Light? The choice is yours." Susan Trout, Ph.D. https://www.showanotherway.org/susans-blog/Ride-the-Waves-of-Destiny-into-the-Fifth-Dimension

3. Agitated humans are found in both public and private spaces, and tend to be especially agitated when procuring supplies.

4. Giving lip service means saying you agree with something without taking action to support it.

5. Some very nice remote temples are located in Meteora Greece. https://visitmeteora.travel/varlaam-monastery/

6. A reminder that certain human behaviors require professional assistance that is beyond the scope of this chapter or book.

7. Some particularly volatile humans would benefit from learning anger management skills or scheduling an appointment with a professional therapist. In certain cases, inner peace is secondary to preventing harm to oneself or others. These interventions are necessary as psychological and mental issues are sometimes at the root of certain behaviors.

8. "Peace be with you" seems to be a common refrain in some human religious gatherings. However, when these same humans are outside of their houses of worship, they may revert to behaving in ways that are less than peaceful, both in their words and actions. Using spiritual truths as mere slogans is hypocritical and can have negative ramifications. Remember, the Universe is watching.

9. The One Earth Future Foundation provides support to help enterprises thrive in conflict-affected areas. https://oneearthfuture.org/theory-peace

10. The Global Peace Index report measures global peacefulness. The Vision of Humanity Institute studies peace and offers research, facts, articles, and evaluations about the world. https://www.visionofhumanity.org/maps/#/

11. His Holiness the 14th Dalai Lama, Buddhist monk and spiritual leader of Tibet, is an advocate of world peace. https://www.dalailama.com/messages/world-peace/a-human-approach-to-world-peace

12. UNESCO is a special part of the United Nations. It works to bring humans together by supporting education, science, culture, and sharing information. The idea of a culture of peace, as UNESCO sees it, grew out of efforts that started with the Yamoussoukro Declaration. This

declaration came from an international meeting about peace held in Yamoussoukro (Côte d'Ivoire) in 1989, which was organized together by the government of Côte d'Ivoire and UNESCO. https://www.culture-of-peace.info/history/Yamoussoukro.pdf

13. The Earth Institute at Columbia University's "Sustaining Peace Project" is exploring new ways to understand, build and sustain peace. http://sustainingpeaceproject.com/

12. And You're Saying This Why..?

"Half the world is composed of people who have something to say and can't, and the other half who have nothing to say and keep on saying it." – Robert Frost, poet.

The verbal or non-verbal act and process of using words, sounds, signs, or gestures to express or exchange information, or to convey ideas, thoughts and feelings to another human (or to another species, *and if lucky*, to an advanced one) is defined as communication on Planet Earth!

Communication, like respect, is considered one of the essential foundations for relationships and interactions between humans (and other species). However, due to a lag in human development that hasn't kept pace with the accessibility of technical advancements, communication continues to be an ongoing challenge on Planet Earth.

While there are various ways[1] to communicate, talking and writing are typically the most popular methods of connecting. Listening and comprehending are also crucial parts of communication, but they often do not receive the necessary attention, unless one is a human mental health professional or an exceptionally good listener.

Many humans believe that what they are doing regularly is communicating, but in reality, they are often just automatically expressing their thoughts, *usually without much thought!* This lack of awareness can lead to ineffective communication, which essentially, becomes a form of blabbering.[2]

Oftentimes, relentless blabbering can hinder constructive communication and lead to numerous misunderstandings, especially when it is done through technology. Modern communication doesn't always ensure better understanding and in some cases, can sometimes escalate arguments, division, and confusion.

Are *You* a Blabber Mouth?

While we daydream of the tranquility of deep space, our telepathic and auditory receptors remain focused on sorting through the constant "cacophony of human blabbering." Despite our auditory circuits occasionally snapping and sizzling, we persist in deciphering human conversations about preferred foods, top binge-worthy shows, the WEATHER, recent celebrity gossip, and the daily escapades of numerous dysfunctional leaders. Additionally, there is a significant amount of chatter surrounding current global events, disasters, wars, infectious diseases, and other urgent matters of the day.

A great deal of this blabbering, whether intelligent or not, is being carried out on assorted devices shared on various media or held directly with another human, orifice to orifice.[3] This incessant racket of mostly nonsensical babbling has led to auditory overload on Planet Earth, causing quite a spike in stress symptoms!

Understanding why you communicate is just as important as how you communicate.

Unfortunately, a LOT of this "talking" devolves into yelling and arguing, frequently accompanied by harsh profanity and a nasty undertone. Using profanity[4] as an emotional outlet to "blow off steam" can sometimes be justified in certain situations when used appropriately. Similar to using the right amount of spices in food, profanity should be used selectively, at the appropriate time, and in moderation. Overdoing anything can often lead to either ruining a meal or a conversation.

The frequent use of angry words and profanity in everyday conversations may be a sign of certain underlying issues, such as emotional dysfunction or problems with rage. Interactions with irate humans using crude words and obscene gestures can turn ugly and pose a threat to those nearby. Unfortunately, this could also harm innocent animals and plant life that are in the vicinity of such explosions!

Other notable forms of blabbering include humans talking or muttering to themselves, which can sometimes turn into one-way arguments, especially when it involves the activity of watching and listening to other humans. The level of yelling and blood pressure increases when certain illustrious humans and other self-important types monopolize the airwaves with *incoherent gibberish or idiotic blathering.*

In this highly charged atmosphere of "hyper-communication chaos," there is a real lack of coherent dialogue, discussion, and flow of information, despite the speed of technology or the availability of an optimal cell phone plan. Interestingly, we found that humans have the best conversations with their pets, who, in their wisdom, simply listen quietly or offer some form of soothing, sympathetic response. Not surprisingly, the most logical response to human nonsense comes from the advanced feline race, whose general attitude and policy is to ignore humans when necessary. Which is often the case from what we observe!

Spewing non-stop drivel from your orifice isn't beneficial when you're trying to have a meaningful discussion, nor does it reflect courtesy or intelligence. Boring monologues that cause others to fall into a semi-comatose state within minutes, or worse, screeching tirades that can shrivel orifices no matter where they are located, are certainly obstacles in maintaining civil and enjoyable conversations with each other.

In summary, the current human talking spree[5] is unlike anything we have personally encountered in this galaxy or the next. We assume that this increase in human blabbering is possibly due to those who confuse talking with genuine communication.

"If people would only talk about what they understood, Earth would be a very quiet place." — Albert Einstein

Privacy Disclaimer: The Cosmic Health Intergalactic Privacy Standards and The Domain In Personal Secrecy (CHIPS and DIPS) protect species who do not wish to expose their personal information in the galaxy. Some species are actually embarrassed by their lack of progress in evolution (hint hint). In order to maintain their confidentiality, alternative names are selected to best describe a planet and its species.

Planet Blabbverton illustrates the severe consequences of a planetary communication meltdown. Hopefully, humanity will recognize the similarities and avoid a comparable situation on Earth.

Dr. Yangoorish Yinish and Dr. Zoopa Zip, the esteemed founders of the Advanced Being Behavioral Association (ABBA), have conducted numerous studies on species that faced challenges in evolutionary development. They have come to the MOMENTOUS conclusion that *"talking without thinking is a common denominator in lunacy throughout the cosmos!"*

Investigative research by Dr. Yinish and Dr. Zip confirmed that Planet Blabbverton involuntarily imploded sometime in the last century due to high concentrations of illogical miscommunication, resulting in erroneous information and general misunderstanding between the two major species inhabiting the planet. The lack of connection and comprehension of basic facts and planetary laws caused various factors to congeal in the most unfortunate ways, leading to several disasters that were detrimental to the planet and its various species.

These higher life forms, the Blabberians and the Introvertarians, shared their planet with plants, animal-like beings, and various other species. The Blabberians regularly conversed and communicated using multiple orifices, either selectively or in unison. Communications were primarily based on a certain set of beliefs, viewpoints, and influential biases, making them quite opinionated on all subjects.

The Introvertarians mainly used two orifices for communication, which was more than enough since their primary method of communicating utilized mind meld and telepathy. However, their communications with the Blabberians typically involved orifice-to-orifice conversation. Telepathy was rarely used because a frenzied orifice usually indicates a disordered mind, leading to less-than-optimal telepathy.

Since the Introvertarians were more inclined to inner reflection, they used their orifices intentionally and with forethought in communications. This was based on a combination of knowledge, compassion, highly adept listening skills, superior control over managing their orifices, and a sacred belief that in order to advance, *species must share a common inner connection to a higher vision.*

Prior to the development of advanced communicative technology, these two species got along amicably by taking the necessary time to understand each other. This was possible because properly communicating with each other requires a higher level of effort, one that is sometimes lost through instant virtual communication. Their interactions were usually mutually beneficial because enough attention was given to *both the message going out, and the message coming in.*

As time went by, however, communications became more impersonal and less productive due to the misuse of advanced technology. This was an unfortunate outcome because the Introvertarian's main goal in developing these sophisticated tools was to conveniently share information, not to replace thinking or the exchange of ideas. These technological devices were given to the Blabberians in good faith and with the best of intentions and were not intended to replace direct contact with each other.

The Blabberians regrettably became highly dependent on technology, with little self-control in how they were using it. It quickly became apparent that they were losing the ability to communicate effectively or discern genuine messages from gibberish or idiocy. They started believing that the tools they used allowed them to express anything they pleased, without regard for the message or its consequences. Rather than prioritizing the true purpose of communication – to connect, learn and comprehend – they chose to simply *blabber without self-awareness*.

Unfortunately, many Blabberians *intentionally misused* communication technology to further their own agendas and goals because negativity spreads faster than positivity. This resulted in numerous misunderstandings, propaganda, intentional chaos, gossip, and lies, ultimately leading to divisiveness, angry rhetoric, and overall craziness. The situation became so noisy and chaotic that systems and structures rapidly began to unravel. Civility and commonsense seemed to go out the "orifice window!"

Blabberians everywhere believed in everything and nothing at all and since everyone was overloading the airwaves, it was nearly impossible to sort things out. To make matters worse, the constant noise from orifices blabbering at all hours sent reverberations throughout the planet, causing the natural environment to destabilize from the negative vibrations and extra chemical vapors emitted into the atmosphere.

While this destructive discord of a tsunami was gaining momentum, the Introvertarians became alarmed and tried to warn the Blabberians. However, their attempts to convey logic and truth were *lost in the noise*. Since their concerns were dismissed, they decided through **group telepathy** to relocate to another planet as soon as possible. The consensus was that there comes a point when there is absolutely nothing one can say or do in response to uncontrolled blabbering from orifices that are tightly shut to all reason.

Above all, the Introvertarians understood the **Grand Evolved Theory and Cosmic Law of Universal Energetic Harmony (also known as GET A CLUEH).** This theory is based on the fundamental principle of unifying communication through mutually aligned intentions and vibrations, whether through spoken word or telepathy. In other words, if there is no comprehensive connection to what one is expressing or listening to, then all bets are off. You might as well be talking to a cosmic wall.

In conclusion, Planet Blabbverton created a systematic implosion of its civilization through its misuse of communication technology and a lack of evolved articulation and comprehension skills. Their orifices were simultaneously opened and closed, which caused further destruction of common knowledge and cultural wisdom. The majority of Blabberians proceeded to make really bad decisions, leading to chaos, violence, and lots of boo-boos.

Not all was lost, however, as the planet is currently inhabited primarily by cute furry creatures, peaceful plants, and industrious insects that communicate respectfully with each other. The remaining Blabberians have been relocated to a remote area without internet service and the most basic communication resources. Not surprisingly, they are rather content and have taken up "letter writing" as a more conducive way of communicating with each other.

The Blabberian saga should serve as a cautionary tale for any species that are not sufficiently evolved and mistakenly believe that technology is more important than effective communication skills. Do not follow in the footsteps of the Blabberians!

"For the human race to properly evolve requires high level communication skills, along with an ethical mindset to connect, comprehend and collaborate with each other. Humanity must choose to communicate with each other in a positive manner in order to reduce the damage caused by those who negatively influence others and cause harm on a large scale. There may be humans who are very good communicators, but that doesn't necessarily mean they are the best humans." – **Dr. Youpoke Yopraugh,** M.D.B., Director and Founder of YO- YO- GA Center for Inter-Galactic Species Development

The Art of Conversation

Whether written or spoken, words have the power to be used wisely or destructively. Words that spill out are hard to put back in, whether it's directly from human to human or through other methods, such as technology. Humans should carefully consider what they want to say *before they say it*, being mindful to avoid any misunderstandings when communicating. Unfortunately, this awareness is often lacking in those who need it the most – humans who impulsively talk, text, or tweet highly charged opinions and questionable rhetoric, that are best described in cosmic terms as *pungent word vomit.*[6]

What's a human to do when their orifices don't behave as they should?

Well, one suggestion is to recognize that there is an "art to conversing" and yes, it can be effective in reducing unwanted verbal vomit. Wouldn't it be lovely to have pleasant and dignified discussions with each other rather than being subjected to detrimental explosions shooting out from various orifices?

When one's thoughts and speech reflect respect, civility, and truth, *and include* attentive listening, conversing becomes enhanced. Yes, fortifying communication with an improved approach can even make you a better human, which is a worthwhile goal. This skill may come in handy during moments when the urge to fling verbal vomit at another human is overpowering!

However, in no way does any of this imply that you should be boring or suppress everything you say. Verbally self-monitoring yourself is a good habit but that doesn't mean it has to become a full-time censoring job. Reading the room and understanding your audience is important, as talking is more than just expressing your thoughts.

In some ways, becoming an adept communicator requires a certain level of charm and finesse. Having a good sense of humor and tossing in a good joke or saying something funny is highly recommended to get your points across. Of course, developing any skill requires various levels of engagement, creativity, and perseverance. Without improving these skills, humans will continue to *talk at each other,* thereby continuing the epidemic of verbal vomit currently in vogue.

The Honorable Dr. Vortex Vulcani, ABA BABA B100, a Galaxy-Renowned Authority on Evolving and Advanced Being Studies and President of Universal Universe University (UUU), has this to say about evolved communications:

"Expressing yourself on any level, including telepathy, is a wonderful thing when you "know thyself," have empathy, lots of patience, compassion, HUMILITY, a normal healthy ego, sufficient supplies of breath mints, a highly evolved sense of HUMOR, and most importantly, have something WORTHWHILE to say. It is also important to possess the ability to control any and all orifices while keeping a direct connection to your mind and brain, and to be willing to consider other points of view, rather than just your own.

Before sputtering out something without giving it any thought, it is highly advisable in many instances to put an appendage over your orifice and remove yourself from any and all living beings or objects – including, but not limited to, gadgets, assorted technology, devices, or if you are going retro, pen and paper – and then quickly find a quiet place to calm your mind, ingest some delectable treats (inhale them if that works better) and proceed to take the necessary time to think through your thought processes.

HOWEVER, as a RENOWNED Professional dealing with assorted BEINGS, there are important times when blurting out your honest opinions and thoughts, and ignoring orifice control, is the only recourse in reaction to others who cannot or will not communicate properly. Just make sure you are prepared for the possibility of a thermonuclear type of "blow back" from the orifices and appendages of whoever or whatever you are attempting to communicate and connect with."

Dr. Vortex Vulcani's Not-So-Quick Tips

When you feel the need to express yourself and connect with another human, a furry friend, plants, or possibly an advanced being, you may want to consider some *cosmically time-tested* strategies that have worked wonders for many in the galaxy. This is especially helpful for those who tend to *talk first and listen later.*

Take time to carefully consider what you want to say.

This may seem challenging at first, especially if you are prone to pontificating[7] on many subjects. Allow yourself some verbal space and time to think (rather than pretending to think), *before* speaking or writing. Simply doing this could prevent more than half of disagreements and heated arguments that may escalate into incoherent outbursts, verbal vomit, or the urge to commit boo-boos.

Communicating with others should ideally involve equal time for both listening and talking. However, since there is usually one in every crowd who "monopolizes the airwaves and doesn't come up for air (*for what can feel like an eternity*)," both sides will need to check in with each other. At regular intervals, you may want to confirm that you are listening but also indicate when you are ready to get a word in. If you find yourself monopolizing the conversation, you should ensure that the other human is still listening (and breathing).

Create an essential backup plan to block out verbal vomit. Breath mints, high-quality essential oils, and orifice plugs are essential. Another favorite go-to method is to use the *nodding technique*, along with regular statements of "*I understand.*" These effective strategies are used by both human mental health professionals and Advanced Beings in the Cosmos – NOT *a coincidence!* This will hopefully give you enough time to formulate an exit strategy in case of possible verbal vomit explosions or implosions from the offending party.

"If you can't dazzle them with brilliance, baffle them with bullshit." —
W.C. Fields, actor, comedian

The Power of Pondering

To ponder is to consider, evaluate, think and reflect. If you haven't
tried pondering, now is the time! The decline in civil dialogue, debate,
and critical thinking skills, combined with the misguided human
notion that *all opinions need to be expressed*, has created a worldwide
"theater of the absurd." This is not to imply that censorship of any kind
should be condoned, or that the expression of one's views should be
repressed.

*However, if there was ever a time to reconsider what comes out of your
orifices, it is right now. The modern speed of communication has
uncovered the sad fact that despite your fun and sophisticated tools,
most of you don't know what you are talking about!*

Pondering has been known for eons (at least in the cosmos) to improve
your ability to converse AND enable you to control your orifices
without too much effort. Simply by taking the appropriate time to
ponder, many humans could avoid causing or experiencing pointless
conversations that end up sizzling the auditory orifices.

Time spent in reflection can be enhanced by adding a glass or two of
your favorite concoction, or nibbling on a delicious chocolatey delight
so that the experience of ruminating without speaking becomes an
activity one can look forward to! Indeed, the "power of pondering"
should be the new go-to method of responding to any rambunctious
rantings and ravings that are hurled from one human to another.

Pondering can enhance critical thinking skills and possibly even
intelligence, ultimately raising the standard of civil debates that are
essential for maintaining a civilized society. Living in a civilized society
requires a certain level of cooperation and dedication to the common
good. Without this commitment, the fabric of society can unravel,
leading to division and conflict. The foundations of a thriving society
- trust, empathy and mutual respect- are eroded. It is definitely
something to ponder on for sure.

Pondering is beneficial for the mind, body, and soul (if you still have one) and the benefits outweigh the time required for this valuable and underrated skill. It would be wise for more humans to ponder on a variety of subjects that can enhance their intellect and mind. While gossiping and engaging in negative conversations may be enjoyable for some, it should not become a regular habit as there can be consequences for this type of behavior.

Pondering on a variety of subjects can come in handy in conversations and debates, especially when socializing! Think of how you can dazzle your audience with a well-thought-out conversation that doesn't depend on a quick dip into the social media quagmire of questionable opinions and general verbal vomit.

In any case, effortlessly maintaining the art of conversation usually requires some level of skill, one of which is the ability to form complete sentences while effectively managing diverse thoughts simultaneously. Your pondering efforts will help manage this challenge and more. Without a doubt, words can influence the outcome of any situation, either positively or negatively, and can reveal attitudes and beliefs that reflect who you are (which may or may not be a good thing!).

All the more reason to consider the power of pondering; because time spent properly pondering encourages the underrated activity of reflection, which helps prevent carelessly expressing anything that might be better left unsaid.

"The great thing is to know when to speak and when to keep quiet." – Seneca, statesman and philosopher of Ancient Rome

Points to Ponder

Delve deeper into the reasons behind your words and thoughts. Do you feel confident that you absolutely know what you are talking about? Are you sometimes spouting nonsensical drivel based on highly charged emotions? Is the majority of what you say based solely on your personal opinion? Do you possess a solid grasp of factual information and genuine knowledge, or are you spreading ideas rooted in unexamined beliefs and hearsay?

What is your goal or purpose when talking, debating, conversing, or even yelling? Take a moment to thoroughly examine your reasons so that you are truthful to yourself in how and what you communicate. Carefully think through what you want to share, ideally before sharing it, especially if it's a hot topic that can trigger emotional outbursts.

Take time to reflect, contemplate and deliberately examine your ideas, opinions, and thought patterns. The point here is to examine your thoughts through an inner process. Some form of quiet processing or meditation will help, and we do recommend this often throughout our messaging. Regular inner self-examining will help you gain clarity around why you think the way you do.

Acknowledge that there may be value and truth in other viewpoints, even if you don't agree. Change the attitude that you know everything! Genuinely try to understand why other humans differ in their thinking and beliefs. There's a chance you may gain a new insight or if not, you will become better at learning to agree to disagree. Sometimes, that is not only the best option, but the only option!

Proper pondering requires an open mind or at least one that is willing to explore new territory without relying on outdated mental scripts that reinforce rigidity.

Keep asking the question, *"And I'm saying this, why?"*

Talk. Not too much. Mostly from the Heart.

When it comes down to it, most things can be transformed when you start from a place of kindness. This is why the initial step to evolving requires kindness as its main foundation. Once this becomes your default setting, it can change your interactions and relationships with others, and ultimately, your life.

When you speak from your heart with kindness, it fosters empathy in others. Other living beings may respond accordingly and like you more for it, which can possibly transform how you relate with each other. Having a heart-centered approach to communicating fosters understanding of yourself and others. The effort of connecting positively with those who are NOT EXACTLY LIKE YOU, however, is not always an easy task and is sometimes complicated by language barriers, cultural differences, and the subjective reality of an individual human. This can mean that occasionally, you may have to put up with some challenging humans, whether they mean to be or not.

Fortunately, speaking from the heart doesn't require therapy (although it helps), the latest technology, or a degree in communications. When the intent is to find common ground through kindness and respect, it allows some form of connection whether you completely understand each other or not.

Transforming communication is possible through empathetic listening and being fully present while respecting another human's feelings. This shouldn't be as difficult as it sounds, especially once you get used to talking less and listening more. It may also include subtle body language, direct orbital (eye) contact, and any other non-verbal methods available to you (just don't cross any lines that are borderline offensive!).

Coming from a place of kindness and patience also means you are less likely to anxiously count the minutes until it's your turn to talk while ignoring what's being said. The benefits of staying engaged (and awake) will hopefully promote a better understanding with your fellow Earthlings! HOWEVER, there may be times when it's impossible to avoid nodding off because you're seriously sleep-deprived or just bored. Remember to be kind and patient with yourself too!

Lost in Translation?

If many humans struggle to communicate with each other in the same language, then it's not surprising that communication between different nations speaking different languages is even more challenging. Certainly, things can get complicated due to the unique nuances in languages, which can lead to misunderstandings when being translated. Linguistic and cultural barriers can create obstacles, as nations and societies differ in ideologies and lifestyles. Despite these and other challenges, all cultures must prioritize effective communication.

Certainly, language interpreters and technology help to translate for those who do not speak the same language. However, it is imperative to consider any improvements to global communication, as this would help in reducing misunderstandings caused by translation errors.

When words and information are not accurately translated from one language to another, an entire message can fall apart and lead to serious consequences. Until humans become proficient at communicating with empathy, their abilities in translation and interpretation may have limited effectiveness.

This does not mean that human cultures should discard their unique languages, as that is not the real issue when it comes to interacting with each other. There are instances when humans may not understand the language being spoken, yet a connection is still established despite the language barrier.

Language is a tool for communication, but it is not the only tool. As humanity progresses and evolves, communication will also evolve alongside you, potentially including telepathy.

Technological and other modern advancements have enabled humanity to communicate beyond just language. The ability to leverage visuals, music, and translation technologies is a step toward bridging barriers. Effective communication requires humans to first develop themselves so that, regardless of how they communicate, it will be done in the best manner possible.

"Seek first to understand then to be understood." — Steven Covey, author

Communication is the process of conveying information to share ideas, opinions, facts, values, and more. It involves sharing thoughts and feelings with the intention of being understood.

Comprehension is the skill of not only hearing what is being said, but also understanding it and being able to relate to it in some way.

Conversation is the exchange of words, a discussion, and ideally, a connection.

Connection occurs when there is an effort to understand new information and the perspective of the other human delivering the message. When done correctly and with genuine intentions, it can establish a strong bond.

"Most of the time, communication gets confused with conversation. In fact, the two are distinctly different." – Dr. A.P.J. Abdul Kalam, scientist

---

Let's Chat Someday

Conversing with extraterrestrials seems unrealistic given the current state of affairs on Planet Earth. If you are struggling to communicate with each other, how can you expect to converse with beings from another Galaxy? An evolved mindset is necessary when communicating with life forms that are vastly different, many of which humanity cannot comprehend at this time.

In other words, *not all Advanced Beings are like us!* Telepathy and other non-verbal forms of communication are preferred methods used by many Advanced Beings and extraterrestrials. *However, not everyone utilizes telepathy with empathy.* Unless there are enough humans with telepathic skills or other forms of advanced communication, finding common ground may be tricky at best. Let's hope that when the time comes for a "cosmic meet and greet," humans will be truly ready.

Talk This Way!

Be a good listener.
Choose your words wisely.
Smile with a genuine feeling.
Pay attention to your tone of voice.
Manage your emotions effectively.
Strive to create a positive exchange.
Avoid constantly interrupting others.
Make others feel comfortable and at ease.
When you talk, remember it's not all about you.
It's okay to disagree and have differing opinions.
Focus on building connections and understanding.
Acknowledge when you understand, and communicate when you need further clarification.
When expressing yourself, ensure that it is truthful, helpful, inspiring, and above all, KIND.

"Sometimes, it's better to be kind than to be right." — Anne Lamott, *writer*

Mindfulness, good intentions, and kindness can transform how you relate to each other.

Repeat After Us

I listen more and speak less.
I think before I say something.
I am respectful and listen before I speak.
I make an effort to empathize with others.
I carefully consider my words before speaking.
I try to understand and respect another's point of view.
I listen to learn instead of just waiting for my turn to talk.
I strive to express myself without dismissing someone else's feelings.

"We speak not only to tell other people what we think, but to tell ourselves what we think. Speech is a part of thought." – Oliver Sacks, neurologist

Thoughts?

"Whatever words we utter should be chosen with care, for people will hear them and be influenced by them for good or ill." – Buddha

Notes

1. **Verbal communication** consists of speaking, either in person or through devices and technology. **Non-verbal communication** includes facial expressions, posture, eye contact, hand movements, and touch. **Listening** is a crucial skill and when utilized properly, can effectively enhance understanding. **Written communication** was once common and involved using paper, quills, pens, and pencils to correspond with others. Technology has now replaced these tools with emails, social media posts, and texts. Regardless of the method used, communication can be negatively impacted by poor writing skills, angry rhetoric, and misinformation. **Visual communication** has evolved from primitive cave art to magnificent artwork and modern digital technologies, such as AI, film, social media, videos, and images that can inspire, motivate, and entertain. Images have the power to convey meaning and are sometimes more impactful than words.

2. Blabbering is the act of talking enthusiastically and excessively, or uttering meaningless or unintelligible sounds, sometimes in an incoherent or repetitious manner. Babbling is often considered charming in human babies, but not as much in adult humans.

3. Orifice: An opening or hole, especially one in the body, such as the mouth (and other areas of a human).

4. Human profanity includes foul words, swearing, obscene gestures, and sometimes risque jokes that are typically enjoyed by like-minded humans. Some humans simply enjoy vulgarity and cursing as a common way to converse, often unaware that it may indicate a deficiency in verbal adequacy. Humans seem to feel much better when spewing profanity, especially when they are irritated, frustrated, angry, or annoyed. HOWEVER, "spicy" words should be used in moderation, although at times it can assist in dealing with intense emotions that even mental health professionals may find challenging to address.

5. Spree is a period, spell, or bout of indulgence, such as a specific wish, craving, or an intense burst of activity.

6. Pungent word vomit is a potent mix of unintelligible words, grunts, vulgarities, idiocy, and other toxic expressions, usually spewed by agitated humans that can cause recipients to recoil in disgust, concern, horror, annoyance, dismay, and a range of other negative emotions. Make sure to avoid this type of verbal vomit, or at the very least, arm yourself with protection.

7. To pontificate is to speak or express opinions in a pompous or dogmatic way, as if you know everything and only your opinion is correct.

13. Thanks A Lot!

"True happiness is to enjoy the present, without anxious dependence upon the future, not to amuse ourselves with either hopes or fears but to rest satisfied with what we have, which is sufficient, for he that is so wants nothing." – Seneca

It's Not Too Late. Until It Is.

If saying "thank you" is no longer a priority – *unless you happen to be a Kindergartener*[1] – then you may want to keep in mind that ingratitude often leads to regrets or worse, a life-altering reckoning. The difficult lesson of not appreciating your life is often learned during times of upheaval and misfortune, and in many cases, after you've left the planet for good.

When life is upended and what you had is lost, you may finally come to realize that "you don't know what you've got until it's gone." What's worse is that when it's gone, *it may also be too late.* Learning this the hard way can be filled with remorse and quite a lot of tears. One way to avoid this sad scenario is to simply appreciate what you already have. If done regularly, this practice will create a beneficial feedback loop that improves your well-being and capacity to manage adversity. This is especially useful when stressful circumstances challenge your ability to feel thankful for anything.

Sometimes, reflecting on your personal life or past human history can help you become aware of just how good you have it. This is especially true when you consider human life long ago, such as in the Middle Ages (also known as the Dark Middle Ages).[2] This period shouldn't be confused with the "middle ages" of the 20th century, which while having some *nerve-wracking* challenges of its own, doesn't quite compare to the Dark Ages.

One would assume that the hardships of pestilence, plague, and personal hygiene dysfunction would put most humans in a bad mood. However, that is not always the case, as some humans find a "bright side to life" no matter how gloomy things may become.[3] In fact, this era gave humankind the ever-popular (and sanitized) modern version of the Renaissance Fair!

After your deep dive into human history, you will hopefully begin to appreciate your *much-improved* living standards, such as indoor plumbing and WiFi, because truthfully, most of you are living a pretty good life! While it may not be a "Wonderful Life," [4] it's probably better than you give it credit for, especially when it comes to personal hygiene and TOILET PAPER.[5]

Are You Entitled?

Okay, perhaps you're not purposely unappreciative but rather cluelessly self-absorbed and spoiled. Whether intentional or not, the consequences of living in an affluent world have led to privileged behavior that has, ironically, resulted in less contentment *despite* material prosperity. Often, this dissatisfaction is reflected in grievances and complaints from humans who feel they cannot get any satisfaction regardless of how much they possess. Let the whining commence!

Overly entitled humans see nothing wrong with believing that they have the right to be self-centered and demanding, even when it's at the expense of others. This type of behavior has become common in a "selfie culture" that reinforces mindless consumption, which may ultimately lead to having nothing left to consume. This stands in stark contrast to those who are experiencing poverty, hunger, and scarcity but still find a way to be grateful, *confirming that having more doesn't necessarily correlate with happiness.*

Ingratitude often fails to acknowledge the kindness or generosity of other humans, or even other life forms! Humans who rarely give thanks to others and expect special favors and privileges are usually narcissistic, or at the very least, spoiled rotten. Consequently, deep-rooted ingratitude can become a character defect.

"He who dies with the most toys wins."
(Attributed to Malcom Forbes, Billionaire Publisher)

Wins what actually?

We wonder if Mr. Forbes still believes in his theory of "winning with the most toys" now that he has exited Earth and is in another dimension, possibly even in another galaxy. Hopefully, it's now evident to him that you cannot take your toys with you to the next dimension, and that maybe the race to accumulate things may not be the best way to approach life or the "afterlife."

Real winning in the next dimension has very little to do with the acquiring of earthly material goods. What's more, your material world is not that "material" after all (quantum physics and so on) and should be a sign to focus on more important matters, such as your vital task of evolving!

Are You Appreciating or Depreciating?

Making choices based on a feeling of lack or not having enough can lead to resentment, anger and sometimes, even criminal behavior. The pursuit of happiness, especially through acquiring material possessions, often leads to greater unhappiness because **happiness isn't something to be found, but something that you become.**

Unfortunately, when a society primarily focuses its efforts on acquiring money, humans are more likely to become sidetracked. The constant need to accumulate material goods becomes the ultimate goal for marking one's status in life. However, a never-ending quest for more may reflect a lack of inner self-worth. Using material goods or money to fill emptiness or soothe feelings may initially feel good, but they are only temporary solutions to bottomless voids.

However, there are times when seeking certain comforts can be more than just a superficial remedy. Treating yourself to lovely gifts or spending a day shopping for scarves and delectable delights can be considered well-deserved self-care, as enjoying things with gratitude is very different from mindless self-gratification.

Authentic wealth does not rely on external gratification; rather, it is an inner experience that reflects an appreciation for one's life and being. The Universe is abundant and generous, rendering greed and senseless accumulation irrelevant.

"A grateful outlook does not require a life full of material comforts but rather an interior attitude of thankfulness regardless of life circumstances." – Robert Emmons and Charles Shelton, Handbook of Positive Psychology.

Gratitude is an action you take.

Give thanks for something every day, even if it's just one thing.

Thank someone and let them know how much you appreciate them.

Do something nice without being asked. Many will be grateful that you did.

Practice small acts of kindness to cultivate gratitude.

Acknowledge and pay forward kindness with a thankful heart.

Keep a gratitude list to reinforce positive thoughts. You can do this in a journal, on a device, or if you're more visually oriented, as a collage.

Consider keeping a physical symbol of gratitude, such as a smooth stone, crystal, or another meaningful item.

A tangible reminder can help you stay focused on gratitude throughout the day, especially when your mind wanders. Your token is a reminder to stop, breathe, and truly feel grateful.

Creating a thankful community depends on spreading the positive energy of gratitude outward, which will ultimately impact all those who encounter it. The more you actively seek out moments of gratitude, the easier they will come and the more impactful they will be.

"When you appreciate, you don't depreciate." – Sirius

Sirius Lee Cosmic, the Founder of the Planetary Artists Group, Creator of the Groovy Civilizations and Legends Series, and Bestselling Author of "What's Your Galaxy Vision," "Create with the Cosmos," and "Atlantis Gone But Not Forgotten," has compiled a list of totally groovy civilizations that could serve as inspiration and has this to share about his most recent visit:

"While bouncing around the Cosmos recently, I came across a minuscule planet on the outskirts of the third Galaxy to the left of the second black hole, beyond the Quantum Galaxy and behind the North Star. Generally, I seek out little "out-of-the-way planets" that give off a cool vibe and that may have gotten lost in the shuffle while the drama in the Universe plays out. Anyway, I dropped in (quite literally, as I have less than stellar de-materialization abilities) and got met with a warm welcome from some real chill beings, who were quite cool and kinda cute. Imagine Earthling Furballs with large orbitals, big ears, and a very round shape.

Now, I usually give off a very CHILLING vibe, which helps calm the residents of certain planets. Normally, I bring along some (ahem) "supplies" just in case they are needed to provide further chilling, for both me and the locals! Anyway, the reason I'm visiting this planet is first, they had really cool colors that are visible from space, and second, the planet is surrounded by a particular vapor that seemed quite interesting to me cause it reminded me of something familiar.

In any case, upon materializing on their planet after several tries (listen, I'm not certified yet), I felt even more chilled than usual. I'm wondering, what the heck is going on here on this planet? I wanted to know like, right away but hey, I didn't want to be rude, you know. While I usually get welcomed in friendly ways, some locals can be a bit uptight at times. BUT, nope, all was mellow. So the head honcho "FURBALL" tells me telepathically (thank the Universe I speak fluent Empathatian) that "Hey, want to see our chilling community?" Sure, I nod (just in case).

So, just to speed up this story, we zip (like literally really zip) straight up to the main complex in this city that looks like a ginormous freaking crystal castle, with rainbow colors shooting out in all directions, passing wild scenery that made my orbitals pop and feeling major "full-on warm all over" sensations (so sweet) and an aroma that was so PLEASANT that I almost passed out from overwhelming delight. I'm not going to get into what this kinda felt like, cause the planet would attract way too many visitors, and who needs that when they're doing just fine on their own?

Anyway, it turns out that these groovy and very chill FURBALLS know how to PARTAY and needless to say, or should I say it, they are living the life. Not only have they created a totally AMAZING civilization (and believe me, it's AMAZING) but they are one of the nicest and most gracious species I've had the pleasure, and I mean pleasure, of meeting. So of course, I'm wondering, besides the secret sauce of the vapors chilling out the planet, what exactly is the other secret here that is keeping their planet oh so super cosmically chilled?

So Major FURBALL, who is picking up my radar, is telepathing to me that (drum roll now...) "it's all about being grateful and appreciating LIFE." I'm like WHAT? That's it?? He, She, They say "Yep, just chill, say thank you, be grateful and just roll with things cause you never know when it can be gone so enjoy and appreciate it while you can." Now that little pearl of wisdom was a bit MIND-BLOWING in some way to me, cause just in case you haven't quite read my credentials, I'm originally from a planet that was once called Atlantis and yes, things got out of hand, even though we thought we were so groovy and living the dream. But honestly, we weren't that chill toward the end, when the major mind-blowing happened.

And, if there's one thing I know, it's all about mind-altering, as my very own planet literally blew its mind due to some serious problems with entitlement issues and a lack of gratitude for well, just about everything. Look, it happens to some life forms – things become too easy and BAM – nothing really matters anymore. It's all just one big blur of things and more things and easy cheesy living. Hey, not saying we didn't like it on my previous planet, but by the time we figured out that the sh*t was gonna hit the fan, it was beyond repair. OOPS for sure...

In any case, this little planet, which I am NOT going to identify, is well off the charts in living the good life. Wish my buddies and I had gotten the memo that savoring, cherishing, and appreciating (with sufficient chilling), is the way to well, stay in the groove. When things aren't taken for granted and there's a real appreciation for life, there's gonna be very little impetus for greediness, nastiness, violence, or shenanigans, cause well, everyone will simply be enjoying life!

While I was decompressing from the vapors and getting ready to de-materialize (so I could get back to zipping around the galaxy), Major FURBALL gave me another peek into Her, His, Their, super powerful insights. It turns out that the super special secret sauce for maintaining good vibes, with or without vapors, does more than just keep residents cool and chill. It also provides additional benefits for your cells and chakra energy. Well dang, that must be one of the reasons why the colors on this planet are so vibrant and, of course, that extra positivity puts you in the cosmic zone (without needing to leave your planet!).

This is where you want to be folks – in the groove of the Universe, which beneficially impacts your ENTIRE Being. Cherish your cosmic self, because when you appreciate, the Universe appreciates with you! Stay cool!" – Sirius L.C.

Fake it until you make it?

Um, no. You need to be grateful for the right reasons. The true spirit of generosity is more important than simply going through the motions of being thankful. It requires you to be authentic and honest with yourself and others. Otherwise, you run the risk of appearing fake and shallow.

Changing your thoughts can change your life, so instead of grumbling about whatever it is you usually grumble about, try being grateful for what you already have. When you do this, and we hope you will do it often, it will move your mindset from negative to positive. When you can turn almost any situation into a learning experience and see it as a gift, you shift into an attitude of gratitude!

When life sucks, give thanks anyway.

Be grateful for your existence, because if you're still breathing and alive, it's probably a good day!

Thank those who love and care about you, including your furry friends.

Be thankful for good health and well-being.

Be grateful for NATURE'S beauty: flowers, trees, mountains, lakes, waterfalls, clouds, sunsets, sunrises, birds, snow, butterflies, dolphins, horses... the list is long.

Appreciate kittens, puppies, bunnies, and cuddly stuffed talismans.

Give thanks for food, water, CHOCOLATE, online ordering and takeout.

Express gratitude for band-aids, modern medical care, hospitals, dentists, and emergency services.

Be thankful for a stable Wi-Fi connection.

Appreciate the GAZILLION entertainment choices available to you.

Be grateful for electricity, heat, AC, and indoor plumbing!

Appreciate you comfy bed, your favorite blanky and pillow.

Be thankful for the LIBRARY (FREE), beaches, parks (usually FREE), and museums (sometimes FREE).

Express gratitude to anyone – including non-humans – who can make you laugh and feel good.

Give thanks to the Universe, to Advanced Beings, to Cosmic Dust and Eco Glitter! Think of SOMETHING, *anything*!

During those times when it's hard to feel grateful for anything, *even your underwear*, that's when you should make the effort to do so! Sure, it's easier to feel grateful when times are good and your day is filled with lots of goodies. But when really bad things happen, feeling grateful usually becomes low on the totem pole. It's much easier to complain and share your grievances on social media. Certainly, it's not easy to look at the positive side of life when things are going downhill fast.

HOWEVER, tough times can be real opportunities for reflecting on how to turn a disaster into a stepping stone for growth.

Yes, you read that correctly. If you can accept that life involves some level of suffering, you can then be much more grateful for the opposite experience. In other words, sometimes pain and loss[6] are trying to teach you something, and whatever that lesson is, learn it. If you do, you will be more appreciative of the good things in life *while you still have them!*

Although you should not deny or ignore whatever calamity is happening, try to remember that once the storm passes, you will see more clearly and may better appreciate the lessons it has to offer. Being more aware helps you live a richer, more thoughtful, and happier life, even when things get tough. You can better appreciate the inner strength you've found, those who have helped you, and especially the important things you've learned. You'll start to enjoy the small things, cherish meaningful relationships, and feel thankful every day.

Without a doubt, it may NOT be easy to see the silver lining when doomsday attitudes are prevalent, especially when reading a book downloaded by Advanced Beings warning about possible apocalyptic scenarios because humankind seems to be in *no hurry to EVOLVE!*

Holding onto the silver lining in any doomsday scenario requires a different skill set than those needed to survive when you've lost your connection to Wi-Fi for a few minutes. Overcoming adversity usually requires an ability to stay hopeful while practicing gratitude, turning obstacles into opportunities, and shifting negativity into a positive mindset. Even during tough times, it's possible to be thankful for something, no matter how small.

However, it's not enough to simply plaster on a grin-and-bear-it smile and utter superficial clichés like "count your blessings," as that can do more harm than good in the long run. Processing life experiences through forced gratefulness won't be effective, as it can breed resentment and even hostility.

True healing and resilience come not from denying negative emotions, but from acknowledging and learning from them. It means feeling sadness, anger, and fear, while also trying to find things to be hopeful and thankful about. This balance helps you get through tough times. The key lies not in acting like everything is fine, but finding the strength to keep going, even when things are not.

Regardless, some may find it challenging to feel grateful, whether they are in difficult situations or not, simply because they are inherently ungrateful. If you don't see yourself as one of those humans, be grateful for that.

Adversity can be a tough teacher, one that may not be appreciated at the time. However, the lessons you learn from it are usually the ones you end up being thankful for. Remember, when YOU appreciate, the Universe appreciates with you!

"Be content with what you have; rejoice in the way things are. When you realize there is nothing lacking, the whole world belongs to you." – Lao Tzu, philosopher

"The secret to happiness is not in acquiring more, but in appreciating what we already have." – Manly Hall

Thoughts?

"Gratitude changes everything." – Anonymous

Notes

1. Cosmic research has shown that on Planet *Kinder*garten, over 95% of human children regularly say "please" and "thank you" approximately 5-8 times per day. Human adults should visit this planet more often to relearn the basics.

2. The Dark Ages is a term often used synonymously with the Middle Ages, which lasted for 900 years in Europe from the 5th through 14th centuries, beginning after the fall of the Roman Empire (bummer). This period eventually led to the Italian Renaissance and the Age of Discovery. There is ongoing debate about whether the Middle Ages were truly dark and if the term "Dark Ages" accurately describes this era. Spalding, Dr. Katie, *How "Dark" Were The Dark Ages, Really?* IFLScience (2023) https://www.iflscience.com/how-dark-were-the-dark-ages-really-71724

3. Pruitt, Sarah, "*6 Reasons the Dark Ages Weren't So Dark.*" (2024) https://www.history.com/news/6-reasons-the-dark-ages-werent-so-dark

4. "*It's a Wonderful Life,*" an American film by Frank Capra released in 1946, is widely considered one of the most inspirational and beloved movies in American cinema. It has become synonymous with Christmas, when it is frequently televised. https://dailyillini.com/opinions-stories/2019/12/25/opinion-its-a-wonderful-life-shows-psychological-underpinnings-of-gratitude/

5. Ponti, Crystal, "*All the Ways We've Wiped: The History of Toilet Paper and What Came Before.*" (2023) https://www.history.com/news/toilet-paper-hygiene-ancient-rome-china

6. An excerpt on grieving from the book, *Bearing the Unbearable* by Joanne Cacciatore, can help you understand how grief, gratefulness, and other emotions can be felt at the same time. Wisdom Publications is the leading publisher of books and online courses about modern and classic Buddhism, mindfulness, and meditation. Wisdom is a nonprofit charitable organization that supports authors and instructors worldwide, helping people find methods for living thoughtfully and kindly. https://wisdomexperience.org/wisdom-article/how-to-grieve/

14. Who's Joking Now?

"The human race has only one really effective weapon and that is laughter." – *Mark Twain*

Grim and Bear It?

Without a doubt, humans living on Planet Earth need to have a good sense of humor[1] to cope with the various *idiotic sh*t-storm scenarios* playing out regularly. However, while humor helps to relieve stress, there may be times when it becomes challenging to find anything to laugh about. To be better prepared, you may want to consider having additional coping methods to take the edge off, such as extra chocolate (or whatever), because if you don't, your head might explode.

Now, whether or not your head actually explodes is probably not the most serious matter of the day, *believe it or not!* What's more important is figuring out why so many humans still cannot laugh about anything, including themselves! It's not as if there isn't enough material to work with. Besides, everyone else is laughing – sometimes at them – so why haven't they joined in on the fun? Is it constipation, hemorrhoids, or what? Theories and conspiracies abound for sure. Could these miserable humans be the true lizard people that certain serious oracles have prophesied about in recent times? *Are we joking?* Maybe.

If you have a hard time laughing, you need to find out what's getting in the way of your "funny bone"[2] because it's a necessary skill for living on Planet Earth. Finding humor in your world may require a conscious effort. However, the rewards are well worth it, as it can lead to a more resilient, joyful and connected existence. While some humans may have valid reasons for being humorless, it wouldn't hurt to do some *inner self-probing* to discover what's happened to your own funny bone.

To start, ask yourself a few simple questions.

Are you a mildly dreary or boring human who needs to better appreciate the absurd, or are you genuinely miserable for a valid reason (and not feeling like laughing right now)? However, if you are consistently miserable, and overall wretchedness is your usual state of mind, then you have more serious issues to worry about than just wondering what happened to your funny bone!

Sometimes, *so-called boring* humans are misunderstood and may actually just be shy or have a quirky sense of humor. Boredom can have its upsides, as it can spark creativity and new ideas. It does not always signify laziness or a lack of purpose. In fact, taking a break can provide much-needed rest, especially when it's necessary to step back from the constant busyness that often keeps humans from experiencing moments of peace and stillness of any kind.

Laughing and enjoying something funny are essential for life on Earth – *and beyond!* Humor is not only necessary for maintaining one's sanity, but it is also an authentic reflection of the ability to see beyond hatred, anger, and other negativity. It is a universal language that transcends all nationalities and *even intergalactic species!* Using humor in our messaging is not meant to ridicule or mock humankind, but rather to shed light on your situation. Frankly, if you can't laugh, you may want to ask yourself why.

"Laughter is the language of the angels. Laughter is the conductor of peace and unity. It is not only universal but effects worlds in all dimensions. Tears of compassion create a more compassionate world. Laughter brings harmony and merges with the musical spheres of Heaven. It is that which creates inspiration, for the vibration of this is powerful and touches all with memories of home, where the infinite dwells, infinite love, infinite consolation, infinite inspiration." – Anonymous

Are you truly miserable, or are you just an average, non-miserable boring human? There is a distinction.

The Truly Miserable Ones

Are humorless and have trouble even smiling.
Are overly critical of almost everything in life.
Often blame everyone else, except themselves.
Are quite unconcerned about being miserable.
Maintain a consistently gloomy outlook on life.
Have inflexible mindsets and cling to a life of re-runs.
Have something uncomfortable stuck in their orifices.
Complain and look on the dark side, usually all the time.
Often frown with a pinched and tight expression.
Are unable to laugh at themselves but like to make fun of others.
Are fed up with life but make no effort to make things better.
Have extremely negative thoughts, even about positive things!
Hold beliefs based on nonsense, falsehoods, or hateful biases.
Believe they are smarter than everyone else but can't prove it, although they do try.

Miserable energy can be draining, especially for those who are exposed to it. In addition to feeling miserable, these humans may also be depressed, which is a serious matter and should not be taken lightly.

"All the acts of the drama of world history were performed before a chorus of the laughing people." – Mikhail Bakhtin, philosopher and scholar

The Somewhat Tedious, Boring Ones

Love to hear themselves talk, often for what feels like an eternity.
May seem confused about whether to laugh at your jokes.
Put others into a "coma" with their uninspiring and uninteresting viewpoints.
Have overly high opinions of themselves with no correlation to any reality, whether on or off the planet.
Have no interests outside of themselves, which of course, is automatically boring.

Note: Sometimes, a human can be both extremely miserable and very boring *at the same time!*

"*The point is seeing that THIS — the immediate, everyday and present experience — is IT, the entire and ultimate point for the existence of a universe. I believe that if this state of consciousness could become more universal, the pretentious nonsense which passes for the serious business of the world would dissolve in laughter.*" — Alan Watts, writer

Can You Lighten Up?

Laughter has been proven to improve your overall mental, physical, and spiritual well-being, and can be considered healing medicine. When you laugh, smile, or chuckle, your energy shifts and your heart – if a species has one – becomes less burdened with troubles. Your essence may take on a new glow, and life becomes cheerful and carefree, even if it's just for a few minutes. The ability to laugh and find humor in any situation is a form of resilience. It also keeps one humble, especially if you can poke fun at yourself.

Humor brings humans together, *and possibly even alien species*, fostering understanding, camaraderie, and sometimes just pure silliness. Never underestimate the power of a genuine smile, along with a really good joke. This can come in handy when dealing with miserable and angry humans who, by some miracle, may find themselves laughing when you catch them off guard with your levity.

Perhaps your finely honed skills in the absurd, and keen insights into hilarity, will break through the barrier of rigid misery and soften the pinched energy expressed through facial expressions and tight orifices. One can only hope.

Are we implying that humans should engage in silly, non-stop ridiculous behavior or make lighthearted fun of someone (*when they deserve it*)? Um, yes. Kidding. Not kidding. Like most things, there should be a balance when using humor in certain situations. However, if you can't laugh at yourself or with others – or even with us – then you're missing out on a certain level of joy. Undoubtedly, having a sense of humor can help unhappy and grumpy humans avoid making some idiotic decisions and choices, which ultimately benefits the rest of humanity!

Unquestionably, there are significant issues affecting your world, and it's not all fun and games. But when has taking a completely serious approach ever been able to totally transform your world?

There are times when certain tasks require a high level of seriousness because extreme absurdity can be detrimental if it borders on lunacy. Certainly, a raving, laughing lunatic[3] would not be helpful during surgery or in stressful times like the Apocalypse.

The "cosmical" consensus, however, is that overly serious humans are often very overrated (usually by their own inflated opinions of themselves) and could benefit from some *serious loosening of orifices*. Achieving this unwinding requires taking a more lighthearted approach to situations. It also involves knowing when it is necessary to be serious, and when it is appropriate to be humorous. Many advanced species utilize this balancing skill to avoid the possibility of tight orifices and pinched energy!

"God is a comedian playing to an audience too afraid to laugh." –
Voltaire, writer, philosopher, satirist, and historian.

Laughter is *Universal*

Dr. Yangoorish Yinish and Dr. Zoopa Zip, authors of *"Theories of Inter-Galactic Humor to Expand Cosmic Relations"* and *"If You Can't Laugh, You're Boring"* have this to impart:

"Advanced Beings most definitely have a highly developed sense of humor and enjoy laughing and finding the absurd in most things. After all, we're here helping you, aren't we? Anyway, Cosmic Comedy is quite popular in the galaxy. Fortunately, our attention doesn't always have to be solely on the expansion of galaxies or offering coaching services to species that need an upgrade in their development, thank goodness! We're allowed to take breaks! Perhaps some overly serious minded species may find this concerning, but there's quite a bit of absurdity in the galaxy, all of the highest order and quite necessary.

To fully develop as a Cosmic Comical Being, one must have the ability to see things from all perspectives, and humor is one of the most important qualities. It's not only about laughing, but about having an evolved sense of humor. Consider this: if the Universe didn't have a sense of humor, it wouldn't have created it. Get it? If not, please keep trying, because the ability to expand requires it. Without having this capability, a species will doom themselves to misery and very tight orifices, all of which can be avoided with levity (and perhaps, some loose clothing). Cheerfulness, joyfulness, optimism, and more are all part of this ability to bring out the best in oneself and others.

We may sound a bit too serious on occasion, but rest assured, there is always some hilarity going on behind the scenes. Once in a while, we may even seem pompous, but it doesn't last very long and we end up laughing at ourselves. As we should, since humor keeps us on track for continuous expansion. The ability to laugh is essential because the alternative, intense seriousness, can lead to total miserableness, which *can push you into the dark void. Not a place you want to be by the way. Nothing happening there in the void, and especially nothing funny.*

Once humans understand that the Universe wants you in on the Cosmic Joke, you will discover that laughing and evolving are one and the same. Loosen up those orifices! Cheers!" – Drs. Y and Z

Hilariously Healthy

Laughter is an immune booster.
Laughter is contagious in a good way.
Laughter improves optimism and self-esteem.
Laughter can help reduce anxiety and depression.
Laughing burns calories (should be used in some marketing).
Laughter and smiling are intended as a message of goodwill.

The physical act of laughing releases endorphins in the brain, causing a feeling of happiness. Humor improves your likeability! Think about it. Which human is preferable, the MISERABLE ONE or the one that makes everyone feel better?

"Humor is tragedy plus time." – Mark Twain

You Don't Have to be a Comedian

Performing as a comedian is tough, so unless you really have a talent for it, keep your day job! Your task as a light-hearted human is more about connecting with others through laughter. No one should feel that it's necessary to tell jokes or be constantly funny in order to win others over. While it's not always easy to find things funny all the time, nor should it be, it's to your benefit to find a way to laugh as much as possible.

However, laughter should never be at the expense of others. Humor is very personal and what one finds funny, someone else doesn't. It requires a level of respect and empathy, especially when someone thinks they are being funny, but are not. Laughing cruelly at someone or maliciously poking fun is considered hostile, negative behavior, and is typically a sign of bullying and aggression.

Self-enhancing humor feels good, while self-defeating or aggressive humor does not. A good sense of humor means being considerate and should not be offensive. Recognizing the difference between what is funny and what isn't is about understanding the line between being genuinely amusing and being rudely sarcastic.

Developing a good sense of humor[4] stems from noticing everyday life and giving it a *comic or cosmic twist*. In ordinary situations, humor may not be evident unless it's pointed out. Although you don't have to be in a good mood all the time, try to be open to the possibility of laughter or humor whenever it's appropriate.

It is a Laughing Matter

Nurture playfulness and joy.
Learn to laugh at yourself.
Enjoy being silly or goofy once in a while.
Be joyful like the inhabitants of Planet *Kinder*garten.
Read, watch, or listen to something that makes you laugh.
Play some music and dance, even if you're not a great dancer.
Smile more, but don't fake it. A forced smile is called a grimace.
Spend time with animals, they're usually easy to be around.
Share a good joke or even a bad one, but know your audience!
Practice laughing and finding humor in your day whenever you can.

Share your life stories, they often contain humor, but only if they won't bring you down.

Continue reading this guide to cosmically lighten up!

"I have never once in my life seen a fanatic with a sense of humor, nor have I ever seen a person with a sense of humor become a fanatic, unless he or she has lost that sense of humor. Fanatics are often sarcastic. Some of them have a very pointed sense of sarcasm, but no humor." — Amos Oz, novelist

Having fun yet?

Don't wait too long to "let the good times roll," because humor will be needed to help evolve your civilization. Now is the time to crack each other up instead of making each other cry. The Cosmic Comical Collective confirms that any species that can laugh at themselves are 99.1% more likely to save themselves from losing their minds, and potentially their future. Farfetched? Not at all. The universe is full of uninhabited planets where the dominant species not only lost their sense of humor but also ended up losing their civilization.

When you're laughing, you're less likely to be violent, angry, or mean.

CRACKING the "Human Laughter Code" should be a priority before Planet Earth is entirely overrun by miserable humans who have no sense of humor or joy. Humans who lack a funny bone may already be in your neighborhood and are spreading their miserableness. It doesn't take much to imagine what type of world it will become if nasty and grumpy humans become the norm. When you're laughing, there's still hope.

Unfortunately, some humans have unrealistic expectations and are easily offended, which can be a roadblock to understanding each other. However, during times of challenges and troubles, *the ability to maintain a sense of lightheartedness is crucial.* It's not just about humor but about survival! Having the key to your laughter codes could truly make a difference in how humankind manages their serious "grim and bear it" challenges.

The Universe prefers to approach serious subjects with a *touch of humor.* Therefore, the message to encourage humanity's EVOLUTION can only be effectively conveyed through *LIGHT HEARTEDNESS*. If you can understand how cosmic mirth is seen as evolved humor and wisdom, then you may be on the same wavelength!

"A sense of humor is the only divine quality of man." — *Arthur Schopenhauer, philosopher*

Repeat After Us

I am cheerful.
I enjoy humor.
I am joyful and lighthearted.
I always find a reason to smile.
I welcome more fun into my life.
I bring the gift of laughter to others.
I nurture cheerfulness throughout my day.
My laughter releases all tension and stress.
I lift my spirits by thinking positive thoughts.
I lighten the atmosphere with my sense of humor.
I find it easy to laugh at myself in almost any situation.

Alien jokes...

What's the difference between UFOs and an honest politician?
It is possible that UFOs exist.
https://www.jokes.best/space-jokes

Q: What did the (advanced) alien say to the cat?
A: Take me to your leader.

The Universe decides to send Advanced (Alien) Beings to help out
humans on Planet Earth. Once again.
Since previous attempts were not exactly successful, they decide to
download cosmic coaching advice as a guidebook.
The book becomes popular but humans think it is a joke.
The Universe decides it's a joke as well.
– The B.O.S.S.

An Alien walks into a human bar.
The bartender leans over and asks,"What are you drinking?"
The Alien points to the human crowd and says,
"Whatever Kool-Aide they're having. Just make mine a double."
– AB1 & AB2

"Total absence of humor renders life impossible." — Colette, French author

Thoughts?

"What soap is to the body, laughter is to the soul." — Yiddish Proverb

Notes

1. Long ago, it was believed that the human body was made up of four fluids or "humours" that determined one's temperament. For example, humans who easily became angry were thought to have more choler, while calm humans were believed to have more phlegm. The word "humour" came to mean disposition, thus leading to the term "good-humored." As time passed, the term also began to be used to describe a sense of the ridiculous, being ready to be amused or finding things amusing.

2. A sensitive spot near the elbow bone that is very tender to the touch. https://idioms.thefreedictionary.com/funny+bone

3. Whether you feel a bit loony or not, try to enjoy having a good laugh. https://soundbible.com/1129-Maniacal-Witches-Laugh.html

4. Fessell, M.D. David, *How to Create More Humor, Lightness, and Brightness.* Psychology Today, (2021) https://www.skillsyouneed.com/ps/developing-humour.html

15. Behavior Unbecoming

"Civilization is not inherited; it has to be learned and earned by each generation anew; if the transmission should be interrupted for one century, civilization would die, and we should be savages again." — Will Durant, historian

Shouldn't Humans Be Embarrassed?!

The wearing down of basic civility due to ill-mannered and rude behavior has caused serious consequences on Planet Earth. Unlike a takeover by zombies (or aliens), where there might be a push-back from the population, the takeover by rude humans has been incredibly successful across the board. If you are a rude human who loudly shouts opinions with vulgar abandonment, perhaps accompanied with inappropriate gestures from your appendages, you may mistakenly believe that such behavior is acceptable. However, you would be wrong to think so.

Modern barbaric behavior[1] should not be idolized or encouraged, not only because it is annoying, intrusive, and sometimes dangerous, but because it is *also incompatible with civilized life*. Do most well-mannered humans really want crude and rude humans taking over what is currently considered modern civilized culture? Many humans today are taking for granted[2] that a civilized society is a given. *It is not.*

No society is immune to the destructive potential of humans who would rather tear down the fabric of society (and sometimes even their own garments) because of their anger and need for vengeance over imagined wrongs, while reveling in a mob mentality that is fueled by the incoherent rantings of lawless carnival barkers disguised as leaders, experts and other conniving humans getting into the act.[3]

You may be wondering what this has to do with you at this moment. Well, we're here to inform you that it has everything to do with you, regardless of whether your consider yourself civilized or not!

Vulgarians, barbarians, and just plain rude people throw stones at the walls of civilization in every century. In some regions of the world, humans are facing increasing levels of rudeness[4] which is having a detrimental effect on many of its inhabitants. As a result, there have been numerous disruptions that have undermined the fundamental principles of rule and order, both of which are essential for sustaining a functional society.

A civilized society must remain vigilant about certain unacceptable behaviors that could lead to wild and primitive beings wreaking havoc on humanity. If the human race wishes to remain civilized (an important prerequisite to properly EVOLVING!), then they must place a higher value on acceptable cultural norms rather than tolerating detrimental behavior. The bottom line is that regressive antisocial behavior is incompatible with civilized life.

How can Earthlings be respectful to any Advanced Being if they are not respectful to each other?

An evolved civilization values civility in all its forms. It is *not a coincidence* that "civil" is in the word "civilization." The trend toward normalizing and accepting offensive behavior does not bode well for humans who want to be considered advanced. Bad manners, like stupidity, should not be worn as a badge of honor. There is very little that is appealing about a foul-mouthed ding-dong or a screeching harridan[5] ranting on social media or *"wherever."* The constant spewing of demeaning and crude words is a reflection of humans who have lost a sense of DIGNITY, which may seem like a relic of the past, but shouldn't be. SELF RESPECT is always relevant!

The cosmic view is that we observe many rude people who do not respect themselves or others. There is nothing admirable about angry and foul-mouthed human bullies spewing out their obnoxious attitudes, often in public and on the internet. To be clear, *it is usually adult humans who are exhibiting these behaviors, not children.*

Keep in mind that the toxic and unhealthy vibes emanating from your planet are shriveling follicles and causing the involuntary retraction of sensitive appendages of innocent galaxy travelers, possibly even affecting a few sensitive humans! Toxicity has consequences that reverberate in the energy field. Despite these alarming circumstances, there is hope that enough humans will **make manners great again** to encourage a new level of dignity and decency.

The vulgarians have been unleashed, and while some humans may believe that crass idiocy makes for good entertainment, it does not make for a good society.

Good manners are essential no matter which planet you call home or wherever in the galaxy you happen to be. Politeness is the gateway to creating respectful relationships based on common courtesy[6] and a high regard for others. This requires a certain level of empathy and concern for others, not just for yourself. It is an especially useful skill when interacting with a species different from your own, although humans are still working on this with each other, so it may take some time.

Earthlings should keep in mind that "certifiably advanced life forms" in the Cosmos do not obnoxiously travel through the universe in their spacecrafts oblivious to others along the way. Rarely do they use their sonic boosters carelessly to bypass slower moving spacecraft that might be preventing them from quickly zooming into the next galaxy. Even when it's justified, they seldom resort to using appendages or orifices offensively. However, it can be quite tempting to do so when encountering certain species *that are in absolutely no hurry to evolve!*

Cosmic Behavioral Expert Dr. Youpoke Yopraugh (Dr. Yo Yo), is a renowned researcher on galactic species evolution and has this to say about good manners and losing the RUDE ATTITUDE:

"Rudeness and barbaric attitudes are not a good look for any species, especially humans. Orifices spewing and emitting odors, uncontrolled appendages flailing about, shrill yelling and obnoxious noises blaring nonsensical verbiage and general ill-mannered behavior, all without any snappy scarves to alleviate the overall discomfort of others, do not bode well for the human race. In our experience, species that revert to this type of behavior, or heaven forbid, haven't emerged from it and are wallowing in it still, are considered to be backward beings. This is not a judgment, but a verified opinion based on empirical research, and it is a basic fact.

When rudeness becomes a regular autopilot reaction of a being, it can infect and saturate that being, causing an ill-mannered state of mind, and quite possibly affecting appendages or orifices, which then may result in increasingly rude and offensive behaviors that ultimately corrupts not only the stated being, but also those around them. It is not pleasant at all and like so many other negative habits, takes down the mission of evolving as a species.

Now, we are not talking about isolated instances of rudeness, where occasionally, a form of snark or firm response may be called for. What we are talking about here is a systematic breakdown of species interactions that impact large populations, like a wave that turns into a tsunami before you know it has reached your shores. Too many humans are under the impression that manners are not necessary or that good grooming, body management and orifice control are outdated and passe, because why should anyone care that you need to pass gas or burp up your last meal. We are stating, unequivocally and with the utmost civility, that you would be MISTAKEN to think that. The Universe holds high standards for civility for obvious reasons, and if you wish to progress and evolve, you will need to pay attention to this matter.

Since we realize many humans prefer things to be concise and brief, let's make it even simpler. Do not be rude. It can make you offensive. Loud mouths and obnoxious humans are BORING, ANNOYING and sometimes, they don't even have breath mints or use deodorant. Barbarian behavior is not only unwise, it is EMBARRASSING or should be. In the extreme end of uncivil barbarianism, it is DAMAGING. Remember, respectful manners will make humans greater.

If you feel like you have succumbed to barbarian-like behaviors, immediately seek help and close all orifices until you get things under control. A big THANK YOU from the Cosmos. Cheers!" – Dr. Yo Yo

"After our ages-long journey from savagery to civility, let's hope we haven't bought a round-trip ticket." – Cullen Hightower, Author

Health Hazards of Uncivilized Behavior

It should come as no surprise that living with a constant barrage of insults and nastiness takes a significant toll on human health and well-being over time. Not only is there a possibility of GINORMOUS stress due to annoying and inconsiderate ill-bred knuckleheads causing commotion (and the potential breakdown of civilization), but there are also real health risks when humans are exposed to rude and offensive behavior. In addition to the possibility of your head exploding, these obnoxious behaviors can negatively impact your emotional, psychological, and physical well-being. Perhaps it is time to post warnings to properly inform the public of this human health hazard!

We assume that most humans would want to live and work in civil and friendly communities, where respectful interactions are expected.[7] This may require establishing certain boundaries and a commitment to not allowing bad behavior to become popular and acceptable, both on a personal and collective level. There is nothing healthy about a rude and disrespectful human, especially when it comes to the overall well-being of society. Tolerating ill-treatment from another human is usually not ideal, as it can not only harm you but also lead to poor decisions being made by the offensive human.

So who or what is to blame for this human condition of uncivilized ridiculousness? Humans of course, but specifically those who have let things slide, don't care, or haven't given this subject the attention it deserves. It's not us for sure. Since the beginning of human civilization, rudeness, and arrogance were common among certain humans, but not on the scale it is today. Technology and accessible communication didn't cause modern barbarism, it only allowed it to spread and become worse on a wider level. Unfortunately, incivility needs to be politely denounced and condemned as the health hazard it is!

"All of civility depends on being able to contain the rage of individuals." – Joshua Lederberg, molecular biologist

Lose the Rude!

Respect personal space and boundaries.
Avoid using excessive sarcasm or put-downs.
Do not be inconsiderate of another's feelings.
Do not prioritize gadgets over human connections.
Do not insult others, either directly or indirectly.
Do not pick at orifices without proper sanitary supplies.
Stop harassing others with bullying or annoying opinions.
Do not constantly interrupt someone when they are speaking.
Avoid making gross discharges and other repellent behaviors.
Learn to control your emotions and avoid lashing out.
Do not yell loudly or make aggressive demands.
Do not intentionally humiliate, embarrass, or belittle others.
Refrain from using foul expletives, with or without appendages.
Do not behave discourteously or obnoxiously towards humans or animals.

"Manners are a sensitive awareness of the feelings of others. If you have that awareness, you have good manners, no matter what fork you use." – Emily Post, etiquette author and socialite

Polite Humans Matter

While all humans matter, polite people need to advocate for themselves because they often do not receive the attention or respect they deserve. Furthermore, considerate humans tend to experience a higher level of discomfort due to constant discourteous behavior. This may be attributed to their innate sensitive nature, but it is also because being around someone who is extremely rude or ill-mannered can be uncomfortable.

Rebranding good manners and fostering a culture of courtesy is long overdue to emphasize how important civility is to beneficial communication and relationships. Utilizing social media effectively to showcase how polite humans handle various forms of ill-mannered behavior may help raise awareness of why it matters. It makes no sense that angry, rude, and ill-bred humans are often rewarded with fame and riches, while those who are more deserving are not. Unfortunately, current cultural norms appear to favor those who shout, complain, and whine the loudest, *rather than* those who demonstrate courtesy and good manners!

Furthermore, it's quite perplexing that good manners and respectful behavior are required in Planet *Kinder*garten but become less important in the adult world. Exhibiting positive behavior should be a cause for celebration and put into practice as they do on Planet *Kinder*garten. Pass out the chocolates, give a gold star, and share something delightful to acknowledge the polite humans in your presence.

Respect and dignity are truly important for evolution, *regardless of age*. Everyone is responsible for encouraging politeness and making manners a common priority, not just the little humans on Planet *Kinder*garten. Certainly, becoming a more civilized human may take extra effort, but it is worth it. Just ask any human child on Planet *Kinder*garten!

Like many things that seem to get lost in all the noise on Planet Earth, decency isn't trending as it should be.

Make Common Courtesy *Common* Again

Treat others as you would like to be treated, with basic courtesy, kindness, compassion, dignity, and civility. Remember to also respect yourself, because if you don't, who will?

Practice courtesy by treating others with kindness and tact.

Make it a habit to say "hello" and "goodbye" and "thank you." Put effort into being patient, helpful and respectful with others.

Use polite language instead of foul words and vile comments. Speak the way you want to be spoken to. Watch your tone, because your tone conveys your emotions just as much as your words do. Use sufficient breath mints and do not shout into another human's face.

Be reasonable and open-minded towards views that differ from your own. Try to understand or at least respond respectfully. Look for common ground and keep it civil. However, if hateful and violent opinions are expressed, you are not obligated to tolerate them.

Make an effort to find points of shared understanding. Commit to explaining your positions respectfully and thoughtfully. Try to speak less, listen more, and avoid interrupting until the other human finishes talking. Learn from each other.

Develop positive human interpersonal skills and connections by engaging in conversations without looking at screens or being distracted by other types of technology. Be courteous to the humans in your presence instead of ignoring them. Paying attention is a way of showing courtesy.

Promote decency in all that you do. This means refraining from making references to private body parts and appendages, bodily waste, and other vulgar topics. *Invest in your dignity!*

Make polite requests, not demands. Most humans are more willing to do something if asked nicely, rather than being told in a demanding way. If you are rude to prove your point, you may end up alienating the other person. Replace the need to be right with respect. Others will respond better. Think about it. When have angry demands ever inspired you to do something willingly?

"Civility costs nothing, and buys everything." – Mary Wortley Montagu, writer

Good Manners CAN Save Civilization

If that sounds outlandish, great! So far, humans haven't come up with better solutions to worldwide problems, so give it a chance along with the other things we recommend to become better humans. The serious business of saving humanity rests on the foundation of civility and respect. However, a civilized person doesn't just prioritize manners; they also possess a variety of traits, habits, and behaviors that are crucial for a well-functioning society. Civility is not solely or primarily about manners.

What constitutes a civilized society may vary among humans and even other beings, but typically, an advanced civilized society includes highly developed forms of government, culture, industry, food security, and common social norms. Do you believe that barbarians would care about any of these? Enlightened social norms are built on the pillars of civil behavior, but without these standards, humankind can slide backward into barbaric behavior.

Having high standards doesn't mean that disagreements will disappear. Without some disagreement, the possibility of tyranny and authoritarian behavior can arise. A highly civilized culture understands this and fosters respect for the views of others. When there's understanding and connection, it usually leads to positive outcomes.

The bottom line is that respect is an essential component in all interactions of life. Self-respect and respect for others are two sides of the same coin. It is hard to have one without the other. This is important to remember in your daily interactions. While you may not be a rude human, there is a good chance that you are surrounded by a few who are, or may encounter them at some point during your daily activities. You can make a difference in stemming the tide of disrespect by responding with graciousness, compassion, and courtesy. It may not always be easy, but you will be doing your part to keep the barbarians from taking over. Who knows, it may even prevent the Apocalypse from happening.

This is a good time to be reminded once again that in order to change a behavior or habit, one must first be aware of the need to do so.

Repeat After Us

I respect myself.
I am courteous to all that I meet.
I speak kind words about others.
I treat all life forms with kindness and courtesy.
I live my life in thoughtful harmony with all things.
My relationships are filled with love, respect, and trust.
I speak to others the way I want to be spoken to.
I choose my words carefully even when my temper is tested.
I behave politely so others will feel valued and respected by me.
I make an effort to show consideration and civility to all beings.
I use the word "please" so that others know it is not a command, but a request.

"*Courtesy is the foundation for handling people and situations. It is the guideline for human relationships and the benchmark for ethical conduct. When we behave courteously, it is easier for us to maintain appropriate and harmonious relationships. Therefore, courtesy is a basic condition in getting along with others, and it must be cultivated from a young age. From our parents and teachers, we learn the proper manners between old and young, senior and junior. Having courtesy, we should always abide by these manners, so as not to err in dealing with people and situations.*" — Master Hsing Yun, teacher

Thoughts?

"Sick cultures show a complex of symptoms such as you have named ... but a dying culture invariably exhibits personal rudeness. Bad manners. Lack of consideration for others in minor matters. A loss of politeness, of gentle manners, is more significant than is a riot." — Robert A. Heinlein, writer.*"*

Notes

1. A "modern barbarian" is one who usually lacks manners and displays uncivilized behavior that is often characterized by aggression and disrespect toward others. In the past, barbarians were from foreign lands who were perceived as uncultured and violent. However, not all barbarians were necessarily ill-mannered or violent, as the label was often based on cultural biases and historical context.

2. As our *"Taken For Granted"* chapter advised, *"You don't know what you've got until it's gone"* and sometimes, when it's gone, it's too late.

3. In the past, carnival barkers usually referred to humans who would stand outside an entertainment venue, shouting and encouraging others to enter. Nowadays, it is used to describe loud and often very rude "blabbermouths" who constantly talk in an attempt to influence others for their own gain. Entertainment is often part of their tactics.

4. Rudeness is defined as behavior that violates social or organizational norms. Keep in mind that what is acceptable in one area of the planet, may be considered rude in another and vice versa.

5. A "Ding-Dong" typically refers to a silly, foolish and not-too-bright human, prone to idiocy. In some cases, it can signify the sound of bells ringing. A "harridan" is often described as a *shrieking human* who is bad-tempered, unpleasant, angry, and sharp-tongued. While historically associated with females, the term can now be applied to any gender.

6. Courtesy means exhibiting polite behavior and a gracious manner, or simply having some manners. Respect means being deferential and showing high regard or esteem.

7. British psychologist Robin Dunbar claims that human brains have a capacity for 150 relationships, and once that limit is exceeded, things can break down. Dunbar, R., The Conversation (2021) https://theconversation.com/dunbars-number-why-my-theory-that-humans-can-only-maintain-150-friendships-has-withstood-30-years-of-scrutiny-160676

16. Don't Throw Stones!

"Don't throw stones at your neighbors if your own windows are glass." –
Benjamin Franklin

Do *You* Throw Stones?

Human stone throwers tend to make quick assumptions based on biased opinions or a negative state of mind, rather than evaluating or understanding another human or situation. If this describes you in any way, it is time to address and understand yourself so that when you form a judgment or opinion, you do it in a manner that is based on evidence, logic, and kindness!

Fortunately, we are not made of glass, so if a few stones come our way we will be able to withstand them. However, many humans continue to hurl stones at others in their rush to self-righteousness, sometimes causing harm in the process. Before picking up any stone, real or symbolic, it may be a good idea to avoid jumping to conclusions, because sometimes, erroneous assumptions can come back to haunt you.

Utilizing deep breathing and pausing strategies would be helpful to many humans on Earth in order to avoid making snap judgments. However, humans are often making rash proclamations, usually of a negative nature, which are then typically followed by a rant on social media and shared with those who have a similar *group-think* mentality.[1]

Of course, sometimes it's easy to believe that you are smarter or know more than someone you are judging, even though your views may be potentially harmful. Why would you concern yourself with discernment, checking facts, or holding off on conclusions when judgment is easier than taking the necessary time to understand?

Unsurprisingly, hypercritical humans tend to believe they are the ultimate authority on knowledge, morals, and truth. There is no "meeting in the middle" with them because they think they know better than anyone else. Some are skilled manipulators of communication and share condemning beliefs with fellow humans who are just as judgmental as they are. The issue with *fault-finding* humans is their tendency to add unnecessary negativity to situations that don't require any further provocation.

But before we proceed any further, are you harshly judging someone, yourself, or even us right now?

Hopefully, you haven't misinterpreted our slightly sassy tone as harsh criticism because our intention isn't to denigrate humans. Using constructive criticism is sometimes necessary to assist species that need a nice cold splash of reality. While we share our opinions and advice, we try not to have a holier-than-thou attitude because that isn't the best way to win hearts and minds. ABs have compassion for clueless human stone-throwers!

A harsh and self-righteous attitude can create a negative reaction that impedes connection or understanding. If you make snap judgments more than you should, it is time to let go of this knee-jerk habit. Instead, utilize critical thinking skills to understand and assess a situation more fully.

Gaining clarity will assist in avoiding premature conclusions, and hopefully, will expand your viewpoint. This will make it easier to put down your stones.

By being more considerate and understanding, you will be less likely to jump to conclusions. When you are able to feel empathy you are better able to form stronger and more genuine connections. Shifting from judging to trying to understand another point of view will not just improve your relationships; it will also broaden your perspective and help you navigate the complexities of life more effectively.

No one wants others to judge them wrongly or make them feel less than worthy. Most humans want to feel understood and respected. Negative assumptions can damage the human spirit. Taking the time to *notice, reflect, and observe* will help you resist being pulled into the chaos and confusion of *mindless condemnation*. The ability to think clearly and rationally reduces the possibility of jumping to negative conclusions.

"Judging others makes us blind, whereas love is illuminating." – Dietrich Bonhoeffer, pastor and theologian

However, sometimes a quick assessment is necessary, especially during emergencies or dangerous situations. Occasionally, this may even include family gatherings where consuming certain beverages can lead to strong opinions and heated conversations, particularly with certain relatives like Uncle Ed,[2] who while inebriated, enjoys spouting the most nonsensical proclamations that only confirm your opinion that he is a ding-dong[3] of the highest order.

Fortunately for Uncle Ed, you have taken sufficient time to properly ponder over dessert and have come to the conclusion that certain delightful concoctions may have constricted Uncle Ed's blood flow (and possibly other fluids), thereby causing a temporary "disconnect from the intellect." Upon further reflection, you were able to adjust your initial judgment that perhaps Uncle Ed *may not be that ding-donged after all*, although the jury may still be out on the subject.

Wait! Get More Information!

Beneficial judgment is information that leads to an opinion or decision based on thoughts, feelings, and evidence. This can help you decide on a course of action that is helpful. When you can perceive things as they are, rather than how you think they ought to be, you will have achieved a level of discernment. Critical thinking and discernment go hand in hand in situations where it is imperative to make the best possible decisions.

Sometimes, making the best decisions requires quick thinking and action. During these times, the inclination to judge quickly, which is hard-wired into human brains, is a survival mechanism to avoid danger (and sometimes, certain family members). It certainly came in handy long ago when it was necessary to avoid being eaten by something dangerous.

However, this innate impulse to judge isn't always necessary in most situations. Instead, humans should take their brains off automatic pilot mode and shift them into pause mode to gain some perspective. When gathering more information, try to distinguish what is important or true, from what is not. Eventually, as you reflect on your beliefs and why you think the way you do, you improve your ability to understand inner qualities and relationships. Essentially, your days of stone-throwing will be over.

In this ding-dong era of disparagement, many things can go wrong when closed minds are influenced by negative thinking patterns that continue to divide humans. This sad state of affairs has been further complicated by the widespread availability of communication technology and a serious lack of accountability from a *new version of human ding-dongs*!

That's Harsh Coming From You!

Indoctrinated negative opinions, conscious or unconscious, are often ingrained through human family and cultural upbringing. These opinions can often can lead to feelings of anger and hatred, which are low emotional energies that create barriers and division based on misconceptions. False beliefs can arise from cultural biases, feelings of superiority, and religious intolerance, ultimately leading to extreme mindsets. Unfortunately, these beliefs often lead humans to feel superior over others, resulting in suffering and conflicts.

Perceiving reality through your biases can lead to negative consequences. When you are unable to distinguish between your opinions and actual reality, you may start believing that your thoughts and opinions are facts. Understanding universal reality can be tricky if you fail to see things as they truly are, as viewing the world solely through the lens of your human mind can be limiting. This means that some humans keep insisting that their negative judgments are correct and true!

Certainly, it's easier to be less judgmental when you're in a zone of happy thoughts. However, when humans feel threatened, rational thinking tends to go out the window. Criticism has the power to quickly shut down the ability to think, triggering the "primitive brain" to react as a protector and causing a lock-down to emergency mode. In these moments, it is difficult to remain open to new ideas or feel connected with the human who is providing feedback.

To avoid this possibility, it is more effective to show positivity and focus on strengths. This approach can help prevent the human(s) involved from reacting defensively, which can hinder productive conversation. When humans collaborate, they share their experiences and work towards finding common ground, and hopefully, engage in a two-way discussion.

The evidence of harsh judgments is apparent throughout society, causing many humans to be wrongly judged in some way. The constant emphasis on harsh proclamations encourages more humans to negatively use judgment as a tool to control and manipulate others. Self-righteous judgment and harsh opinions do not enlighten but rather, denigrate other humans.

Since innate judgment is a part of the human experience, a good question to ask is "How and why do I judge?" The practice of non-judgment requires developing the habit of evaluating with empathy so that you reach out in connection instead of negative criticism.

When more humans drop their hurtful stones, moral judgments about right or wrong will be based on empathy, compassion, and respect. These are not only necessary components for the progress and continuation of civilization, but also vital for congenial friend and family gatherings!

Harmful Judging Is...

- When you are not grateful.
- When you are being self-centered.
- When you don't understand the situation.
- When you believe you are superior to others.
- When you have unrealistic expectations of others.
- When you close off the process of learning from others.
- When you don't understand what another person is going through.

"Everyone has untold stories of pain and sadness that make them love and live a little differently than you do. Stop judging, instead try to understand." – Anonymous

---

The "How Evolved Are You?" Cosmic Reality Show*

Let's imagine that you, an Earthling, are invited to be on a show that selects and evaluates the best and most evolved species. You say yes, because of course you are excited about space travel and this is what you dreamed of for so long. You get to the next galaxy, and there you are with the other (worldly) contestants, sizing them up out of the corner of your eyeballs. Hmm, you think, this is going to be easy. One contestant resembles a glob of glue-like substance, with a bunch of worm-like appendages jutting out, while the other is a small cube of metal with tiny little feet and two big eyeballs on top.

This is a cinch you think, as obviously, these two don't even look like they have brains, never mind any evolving ability. Actually, you

---

think you remember seeing an Earthling film about some dumb E.T.s who sort of resembled these two. They were squashed by superior Earthlings dressed mostly in black with large tools for exterminating.

Anyway, you're the first one to get up and do your *"human' thing,"* which is to impress them with your advanced intelligence of random facts and figures garnered from the internet, your quantum knowledge of celebrity news, and an encyclopedic ability to retrieve mundane trivia. You notice that the judges seem absolutely impressed with you as they are staring at you with something close to wonder and awe. This is in the bag you are thinking, and confidently walk off the stage after they give you an appendage up, which you, of course, are assuming is a good thing.

Next in line is the little box with eyeballs, who proceeds to inform (in a language unknown to you, but as luck would have it, there are subtitles in your human language) about how *"the galaxy is expanding at warp speed and how their civilization is developing ways to counteract over-expansion, so that no species are harmed or left behind."* Additionally, the little box proudly explains that their planet *"has the longest recorded time of peace, lasting eons, of all galaxies known to Advanced Beings. Plus, they have universal healthcare and access to free Inter-space Internet."* Appendages are clapping and orifices are whistling. You see no upturned appendages and assume that you still have the lead.

Next comes the glue-ball worm thingy, who emits a few gurgles that are translated as follows: *"We love unconditionally, share our wisdom with others on and off our planet, focus on how to enjoy beauty and the arts, and have met the needs of all species currently living on the planet. Spiritual growth and understanding are the priorities of our species and we are tolerant of all beings on our planet and in the galaxy. And, we are committed to our evolving on all levels."*

Appendages are once again clapping, orifices are whistling and balloon-like substances are released into space. Okay, you're thinking, Mr. Squishy was good, but had nothing on you with your facts, figures and handle on all the gossip. Plus, you are certainly better looking than those two!

Well, Mr. Squishy and Ms. Eyeball Box *both won* first place, because well, this is an evolved show and when there's advanced evolving concerned, everyone wins who deserves it. You, however, were unfortunately eliminated and sent back to Earth. After a proper evaluation, you were deemed *"low on the Evolving meter,"* which is what you were told. You were not even close to coming into second place, or even third! You were also kindly admonished to *"not judge a species by their cover"* and were reminded that *"non-judgment is a prerequisite to evolving."*

Little did you know that the intergalactic judges could read minds through telepathy, so they were able to observe your "not so nice judging" of the other contestants, which basically disqualified you almost immediately, but since they had compassion and knew you came from a long distance, they let you finish your *"performance."*

So, how would you feel if you were Mr. Squishy or Ms. Eyeball Box, being judged immediately on how you look? And if you were the human who "lost," how would you feel knowing that your preconceived opinions and judgments were evaluated to be a low-level behavioral response? Would you consider this feedback helpful in fostering your compassion and personal growth?

If Planet Hollywood is interested in this show, please contact Lady CZ so that your humans can get in touch with our beings. Please refer to the Cosmic Copyright Codes for further clarification.

Proclamations from the Podium!

It is not surprising that some human spiritual leaders (and others pretending to be) preach about non-judgment, only to turn around and negatively judge those whose religion, spirituality, or beliefs differ from their own. This is the ultimate hypocrisy of using judgment as spiritual ammunition. *Newsflash!* Holier-than-thou attitudes are not welcome in the Cosmos and beyond. Harsh bombastic rhetoric and angry proclamations that criticize and tear down others are not considered spiritually advanced behavior in any universe we know of.

What's more, it is morally hypocritical to pass "Godly" judgment on those who do not follow your doctrines while also promoting intolerance towards them. Pointing appendages from a podium and making harsh accusations, while ignoring or condoning negative behaviors in yourself or other humans that you feel are somehow exempt from moral behavior, is especially naughty and will lead to the Universe having no choice but to "evaluate" the situation on a higher level.

Highly developed spiritual humans understand the importance of looking within themselves before hastily passing judgment on others. The essence of karma and spiritual integrity lies in self-realization, rather than judgment. For those seeking enlightenment or greater wisdom, introspection and self-awareness are good starting points!

"Judge not, and you will not be judged; condemn not, and you will not be condemned; forgive, and you will be forgiven." – Luke 6:37, evangelist and writer of the third Gospel.

There's Something About Non-Judgment

Non-judgment is a way of accepting those with whom you may disagree. This isn't easy by the way, especially if it includes your parents and other close members of your human family, or anyone else you may have differences of opinion with (whether you like them or not). However, when you learn to evaluate and use critical thinking skills, you become much more open-minded and fair, which helps with maintaining a non-judgmental attitude. Adding mindfulness and meditation to your repertoire of highly evolved talents is also very much recommended.

While being unbiased and impartial is a worthy goal, it's important to recognize that completely eliminating judgments from ever arising is nearly impossible to do. Instead, try shifting your perspective on your judgments and acknowledging that they are fleeting thoughts. Although the human mind is prone to judge, you don't need to be swept away by thoughts just because they arise in your mind! *Consequently, maintaining a non-judgmental approach can transform human relationships and perhaps, even cosmic ones!*

I'M GOOD WITH YOU, AND I'M GOOD WITH ME

Practice noticing with compassion. Explore what it is that you're judging. Maintain a sense of humor when you catch yourself being overly judgmental.

"Do not be the judge of people; do not make assumptions about others. A person is destroyed by holding judgments about others." — Buddha

I Wanna Talk to the Manager!

Your mind needs someone to be in charge, especially if there is an expectation for further expansion into a new mindset. That person is you, and these tasks cannot be delegated to others. You must strive to balance being open-minded while also avoiding being overly closed-minded. Some of you may feel like quitting before even starting, but know that you can rise to the challenge!

While the path to adopting a new mindset may not always be easy, you are capable of overcoming resistance and roadblocks. Just remember that your mind truly wants to expand! Tap into your inner resources, as doing so will lead you to a deeper understanding of yourself and the world around you. The rewards of being in charge of your own mind are immeasurable and lead to positive changes.

Positive mental habits will enable you to manage your *"judgy"* mental thoughts and sharpen your thinking processes. The key is to train yourself to recognize the difference between normal opinions and negative judgments. While it may be easier said than done, *where there is a mind, there is a way!*

- **Be aware of your thought patterns.** Start noticing the automatic thoughts you have about others that tend to be overly critical. Observe when you're being too judgmental. Don't beat yourself up, though.

- **Work on accepting differences**, whether in people, mindsets, lifestyles, or cultures. You don't have to like it, just be open-minded and tolerant.

- **Work on your compassion.** Breaking the pattern of negative judgments can lead to positive, kind, and caring thoughts and behavior.

- **Try to understand others without trying to change them.** Either deal and accept it, or don't. Instead of judging, put yourself in their place and consider another viewpoint. Imagine what may have led them to their present situation.

- **Turn unnecessary judgment into constructive criticism,** as there are certain instances where constructive criticism and evaluation are beneficial and necessary in determining what is best for you or others.

More Tips For The Manager

- When evaluating another human's actions, consider their history and perspective.
- Recognize the negative impact of making judgmental comments. They can be harmful, not beneficial.
- Judge the specific issue, not the human involved.
- Before making harsh judgments, ask yourself, *"Why does this matter to me? How does it affect my life?"*

- If you never acknowledge when you are wrong or are unwilling to change some of your opinions, then you are not evolving.

On a final note, ask yourself, "How evolved do you think you are right now?" We're not judging, just asking questions! Don't be too hard on yourself if you feel you aren't quite there yet. Humans can be their own harshest critics. Just keep working on increasing your self-awareness with compassion and kindness.

When humanity can release self-defeating behaviors and thought forms, the eon will come when you will finally be ready for the "How Evolved Are You" cosmic reality show. However, no matter what happens, the ultimate judgment of how things will turn out will be less important than the fact that you made a sincere effort.

Repeat After Us

I accept myself and am accepting of others.
I choose to love rather than judge.
I am a tolerant and compassionate human.
I release my tendency to judge others or myself.
I let go of judgment with love and understanding.
I release the need to have other humans act in a certain way.
I am curious instead of judgmental about other people and their stories.

"Let him who is without sin cast the first stone." – Jesus, Jewish preacher

Thoughts?

"If you judge people you have no time to love them." – Mother Teresa

Notes

1. Group-think is a type of thinking in which humans can reach extreme, unwise, or unrealistic decisions. This often involves ignoring alternative perspectives and information that do not align with their chosen worldview. It can also lead to expressing disapproval towards anyone who dares to disagree.

2. We are not singling out the Uncle Eds of Planet Earth for any specific reason, other than the fact that we simply like the name. If you happen to know or have an Uncle Ed, please be kind.

3. Just a reminder that "ding-dong" can refer to a silly, foolish, or not-too-bright human. There is also a packaged dessert cake called Ding Dongs.

17. Here, You Can Have It

"The value of a man resides in what he gives and not in what he is capable of receiving." — Albert Einstein

The practice of cultivating generosity requires giving to others freely and abundantly from an open mind and an open heart. It means changing the relationship you have with your possessions so that they don't take precedence over humans, animals, and other species. Putting this into effect may include sharing one's fortunes, letting go of possessions that would better help others, or offering services that benefit a group or a cause without expecting anything in return. Simply put, generosity flows from an abundant heartspace that can share love and compassion.

There are many opportunities to show goodwill, such as doing something special for someone when they least expect it, especially if they are feeling grumpy and having a bad day. The point is not to force someone to be generous if they are not ready, but to sincerely give out of a genuine spirit of generosity. Letting go of excessive selfishness, based on false beliefs and habitual behaviors that have become ingrained over time, is not always easy. It requires detaching from the hold of deep-rooted patterns that have caused an over-reliance on materialism. This will enable you to better improve your awareness of how to change your relationship with what you have and what you actually need.

All humans should strive to be as generous as possible because the Universe responds to the energy of kindness and giving.

The phrase, *"Here, you can have it"* will take on new meaning when you realize there are many upsides to being generous beyond just being appreciated for your good heart. It can lead to a longer life (if you see that as a benefit), healthier behaviors, a stronger immune system, and reduced stress. *"Live long and prosper"* may lead to a new perspective because when humans act with generosity, something magical happens. Positive vibes stimulate areas of the brain associated with happiness, social connection, and trust.[1] Hearts expand, hugs are shared, and good vibes are spread to those nearby, and possibly even beyond.

In most cases, big-hearted and benevolent humans are more pleasant to be around. They readily share their time and generosity, often surprising others with gifts or delectable delights just when needed. They also tend to be cheerful and make the most of what they have because it's not about how much you have, but what you do with it that truly matters. Their positive energy can uplift your own, creating a wonderful atmosphere all around.

Greedy, tightwad humans, on the other hand, are usually not fun to be around unless you happen to be one and enjoy your own company. More often than not, they have very little to share with you because their energy and heart space are all twisted up in feelings of lack and fear. These types of humans have a tendency to grab everything before anyone else, avoid paying for things (even if they have enough money), and are self-absorbed in their selfishness. You can try to share your generous spirit with them, but shriveled energy takes a while to unravel, so be prepared for push-back if you plan to engage. Some may eventually change their ways, but don't hold your breath waiting for it.

However, you keep generously "doing you," which will not only keep your energy positive and elevated but will hopefully inspire a *pay-it-forward* response that creates a ripple effect of generosity toward others. This may encourage more humans to recognize that luxuries and possessions can become unfulfilling without others to share them with. In order to create a better world, humans must consider the "cost" of consumerism on both themselves personally and collectively. This means not ignoring their conscience or denying what is at stake.

"The point is, ladies and gentlemen, that greed, for lack of a better word, is good. Greed is right, greed works. Greed clarifies, cuts through, and captures the essence of the evolutionary spirit. Greed, in all of its forms; greed for life, for money, for love, knowledge has marked the upward surge of mankind." – Gordon Gekko from the film, Wall Street (1987)[2]

The upward surge of mankind?

Look around your planet. Does it seem like there has been an upward surge in what matters the most? Humankind has advanced, but still grapples with insatiable materialistic tendencies that are no longer serving them well. Materialism, excess and selfishness are not aligned with an evolutionary spirit, regardless of how humans try to rationalize it. Mindless consumption and the constant desire for more are negatively impacting life on your planet!

So how did humans end up in this predicament, where unbridled greed has led to a consumer frenzy turning your planet into one massive plastic-filled garbage dump?[3] Are humans truly okay with planetary resources being completely DEPLETED? Did this occur because some of you wanted that extra cookie in Earth school, which then released a negative force field that compelled you to grab everything and anything you could? Are humans inherently inclined towards greed and indifferent to consequences? Well, what do you think?

These questions, and more, are important but time is running out to figure it all out. The days of leisurely analyzing maladjusted behavior or perusing the history of greedy ding-dongs *are* OVER! Planet Earth, along with some very worried humans, is losing patience with lackadaisical attitudes when there is a *real possibility of an apocalypse!*[4]

Sadly, many humans are still operating from a "gimme gimme gimme" mindset that ignores the reality that there may soon be a point of no return. The obsessive worship of money and uncontrolled selfish gratification are destructive and often lead to disastrous consequences. Greedy behavior can range from hoarding food and supplies during shortages to unethically making money, which can ultimately lead to criminal behavior.

When greed is unchecked and widespread in society, it is no longer acceptable to defend materialism as unquestionable progress!

Of course, some humans may not even think of themselves as greedy because modern culture promotes and encourages it as normal behavior. Society constantly pushes humans to feel unsatisfied and want more, regardless of how much they already have. Promoting a skewed version of consumption as beneficial to society is usually based on mercenary motives that increase wealth for a certain few. Those few are always trying to get into your wallet and perhaps, even into other places we won't mention.

In order to break the cycle of mindless and excessive materialism, humanity must first acknowledge that it is an outdated concept. At the very least, there needs to be an understanding that unethical marketing and advertising are akin to casting a spell over unsuspecting humans who are unaware of being influenced. Rampant consumerism in its current form, along with an obsession with money, is not only unsustainable but also *morally* WRONG as it perpetuates a cycle of violence, crime, and chaos. Continuously taking without regard for limits will eventually deplete both human wallets and the planet,[5] leading to disastrous consequences and NO MORE goodies! There are limits to all systems, not just monetary ones.

Maybe You Didn't Realize...

For some, greed and selfish tendencies may seem normal, but humans are hard-wired to be generous. Generosity is a natural survival instinct and has been necessary for your continued existence. Having a generous nature came in handy when it was vital to share food or shelter with others in order to help each other survive. If the human race were a completely overwhelmingly selfish species, they would have likely gone extinct long ago. However, extinction is now more of a possibility than ever before because humankind's selfish ways have a much larger impact and are no longer sustainable.

Material consumption as the measure of a successful civilization is truly outdated thinking and one that is no longer in line with humanity's future. Wealth gained dishonestly or unethically disregards the needs and legitimate concerns of others. On the other hand, genuine abundance and wealth have the power to benefit both individual humans and society.

Fairly allocating resources, money, material goods, knowledge and wealth is necessary to encourage and develop a new vision for an advanced society. This requires a radical shift towards a new paradigm of generosity that fosters cooperation. Such a shift will be necessary for progress and the continuation of civilization, as unchecked greed now poses a threat to your future.

I Am Plenteous

Imagine a new world vision of cooperative sharing based on helping each other survive in this century and beyond — one that takes into account providing basic living necessities while respecting the planet's resources and natural environment.

Achieving this will require stepping away from the previous operating manual you've been using. Why limit yourself to just being a consumer when you can instead be a creative contributor and a generous giver who finds fulfillment on a higher level? Pass out delectables, enjoy free Wi-Fi, and share those cookies!

When humans align their hearts, minds, and spirits for the highest good, they can *re-imagine* the limited boundaries they have created for themselves and allow the upward surge of "plenteous" to commence.

"The love of possessions is a sickness with them." – Chief Joseph of the Nez Perce tribe.

When Enough is Well, Really Enough

It's never too late to reject meaningless accumulation and mindless materialism. Making a shift towards living more ethically means taking responsibility for your actions and their impact on Planet Earth and future generations. Maybe you're already feeling motivated and have started de-cluttering, donated to those in need, or have committed to sustainable living.

Every little bit helps, no matter how insignificant it may seem. Because when things start to pile up, like the plastic waste forming into floating islands in the oceans,[6] the consequences will be far greater than just a cluttered closet or overflowing dumpster. If humanity surpasses the danger zone, it will be much more difficult to get things under control.

Throughout human history, there has always been a level of anxiety about having enough food, shelter, and other essentials. The desire for security can often lead to intense feelings of lack and deprivation, leading to an unhealthy fixation on wealth or money. However, humans now possess the resources to provide for the needs of the majority of the world's population. Now is the time to overcome deep-seated feelings of insecurity about scarcity.

While an excessive focus on wealth can be damaging if self-worth is primarily based on money, it is equally harmful not to have a healthy relationship with abundance. An unbalanced view of money and wealth hinders the sharing of resources and impedes the advancement of civilization. The inability to find the right balance between sustainable wealth and unlimited greed is holding humans back from addressing more pressing concerns, such as your evolving project *to keep humanity a part of the Universe!*

Creating a fair system that provides a basic level of security for the needs of the majority makes sense. It is promising that in some parts of the world, humans are already implementing sensible solutions. When humans share and allocate resources of all types, it becomes possible to work together to solve problems and achieve so much more. It should be quite clear that when your future existence and survival are in question, *being a greedy human is definitely not an advantage.*

"We make a living by what we get. We make a life by what we give." — *Winston Churchill*

Dr. Vortex Vulcani, ABA BABA B100, President of UUU, insists that there's more to YOU, YOU, YOU!

"To become truly evolved, or at least improved, a species must simultaneously understand that although it's ALL about YOU, it's not ONLY just about YOU, but about all the OTHER "YOUS(e)" as well, and that all the "YOUS(e)" are connected as one big YOU. So it isn't, in fact, all about YOU all the time. For some humans, this may be EARTH SHATTERING! However, this upending and truly deep insight will be easier to understand once YOU recognize that whatever YOU do to another will have some sort of impact, and if it is a positive action or thought, it will then enable YOU to EVOLVE – which then, wallah, advances all of YOU in one big cascading positive energy exchange. Whoopee!

So what this actually means to ALL of YOU is that effectively, when YOU do vile, selfish, and very mean things to each other, many of YOU will suffer and eventually, it all comes back in a big Karmic wave to whichever one of YOU dished out that crap to everyone else. However, when YOU do nice things, such as giving, sharing, loving, and helping, the rest of YOU will benefit. When that happens, if all goes according to the PLAN – which is not just a slogan but a UNIVERSAL LAW and CONCEPT – then your world becomes a much happier and EVOLVED place to develop all the wonderful expansive aspects of ALL of YOU!

So you see, the great Cosmic Mystery, although it's not that much of a Mystery among those "in the know," is that it is all about YOU, AND at the very same time, it is not all about YOU. Both are true. Once this little nugget is completely absorbed into the inner sanctum of your essence, it will allow humankind to truly understand the truth that yes, "YOU can have it all" because YOU already have it!

Bottom line: *Generosity isn't just a gift you give to others. It's a gift you give to yourself, confirming that YOU are ENOUGH. Cheers!"*

The point is that abundance and authentic wealth are a reflection of *You* and are manifested in the experience of harmony, or balance, in all areas of your life: physical, financial, emotional, and spiritual. Humanity is now at a turning point, where it must let go of self-destructive behaviors and become better versions of themselves.

I Feel Good in the Loop!

When you give, you are also receiving and create a loop — the quantum dimensional feedback loop – that initiates an upward spiral of well-being. Imagine if this was the overall atmosphere on Planet Earth. Everyone gives and everyone gets, and humans are feeling "*oh so loopy*" in a good way. This wonderful energy flow could likely turbo charge your vibes and realign the vortex of planet Earth, ultimately saving humankind. Farfetched? Not really.

Understanding loops and possibly sacred circle symbols[7] may not come naturally to many human folk. If you have been stuck in your own world for too long, don't despair because you can learn to expand your mind and connect with others. *Really!*

Once you feel comfortable being in the loop, share your new vibe with your favorite, and even some not-so-favorite, humans. Do it with charm, grace, and a genuine sense of generosity. It may surprise you how quickly it resonates with others. Kindness and appreciation are not only positive behaviors, but also a way to have a good time.

If we are giving you the impression that the path to evolution is all fun and games, well, yes, it certainly can be! Once you create the intention for positive change in how you see the world and the Cosmos, it enables YOU (and all the other "YOUSe") to realize the potential to live long and prosper. Good times will commence.

"It is in giving that we receive." – St. Francis of Assisi, mystic

It's Mutual, We're Sure!

- Share your gifts, talents, money, and skills. Everyone has something to share, even a smile.

- Donate or volunteer for a specific cause, such as shelters, animal rescue or environmental groups.

- Give to those who have less than you. Even small amounts of currency can make a big difference in the world.

- Sponsor a child who lives in poverty or offer assistance to a child or adult who needs help.

- Show patience because it's a great quality to share in almost any situation.

- Give the gift of your attention, time, and care to another being.

- Helping others succeed and giving them your support is a very generous thing to do.

- Give compliments or words of encouragement by offering helpful comments. It costs nothing to be genuinely pleasant and can mean everything to someone else.

- Mindfully listening without rushing or being impatient, is a generous gift of caring.

- Buy a meal or a surprise gift for those who least expect it, such as postal service workers, trash haulers, the LIBRARIAN, etc.

- Be generous in the way you treat others and don't be quick to judge. Show kindness.

- If you are a very prosperous individual, company, or organization, *you have the power to positively change many lives and the Planet* by sharing your resources, knowledge, tools, and money.

Your smile is a gift!

Being cheerful and joyful means you are giving from the right frame of mind and heart. However, if you feel pressured to share, it can lead to resentment and anger, so it's best to hold off until you genuinely feel ready. There's no point in prying your debit card or possessions from your appendages if you are not yet ready to let go! You can't fake a generous nature by simply plastering on a grin-and-bear-it smile while handing out free cupcakes or other delectables that *you would prefer eating yourself!*

Instead, start with small steps like whistling a little tune when making a donation, genuinely smiling when you give that big tip, and being cheerful while signing over your fortune to save the world. Yep, it's that easy to be joyful and if you wear a snappy scarf, you will feel even better. Generosity isn't just about giving money or goods to others; it's about sharing happiness from the heart.

Be a giver of peace, kindness, and happiness as that kind of generosity can inspire more acts of kindness and generosity, spreading positivity like a wonderful feedback loop. Never underestimate the power of the loop!

"Nothing in Nature lives for itself. Rivers don't drink their own water. Trees don't eat their own fruits. The sun doesn't shine for itself. A flower's fragrance is not for itself. Living for each other is Nature's rule."
– Anonymous.

Your Generous Earth

Planet Earth is a bountiful giver. Are you grateful for what you receive?

Fortunately, the gifts that sustain life have been freely provided by Planet Earth. Nature supplies all of your necessities for food, water, materials, and numerous resources without presenting humankind with a hefty bill. In addition to all of these free offerings from your planet, nature continues to bestow gifts of breathtaking beauty simply by existing. If the natural beauty of mountains, forests, oceans, flowers, trees, and wildlife fails to inspire awe in you, then you are not appreciating as you should. Perhaps your senses are closed off or your heart has shut down.

However, your planet is currently struggling and may not be able to continue providing because many humans have taken advantage for far too long. It is now clear that humans will need to become active participants in the future of Earth's well-being, rather than just passive recipients. Taking these natural gifts for granted is no longer acceptable or sustainable. In case you missed the latest newsflash, Mother Earth is not very happy with humankind at the moment.

An advanced civilization is obligated to address greed because it is both logical and moral to eliminate the negative behaviors it causes in society. Once the limitations to meeting basic needs are removed, humans will reach a higher level of consciousness, creativity and potential. This will result in a new paradigm of humans living in harmony with each other, nature, and all life forms on Planet Earth.

"The next step in our cultural evolution, if we are to persist as a species on this beautiful planet, is to expand our protocols for gratitude to the living Earth. Gratitude is most powerful as a response to the Earth because it provides an opening to reciprocity, to the act of giving back." — Dr. Robin W. Kimmerer, Professor at SUNY College of Environmental Science and Forestry.

Generosity is a true state of consciousness that aligns with the universal energy of creative manifestation and abundance. In other words, Planet Earth is a gift from the Universe. You're welcome!

"Generosity is the most natural outward expression of an inner attitude of compassion and loving-kindness." — The Dalai Lama

Thoughts?

"Money should not be used as a pacifier." – AB1 & AB2

Notes

1. Studies suggest that humans are biologically wired for generosity. Acting generously activates the same reward pathway as sex and food, a correlation that explains why giving and helping feel good. This also provides further evidence that pro-social activity has been an important evolutionary adaptation. John Templeton Foundation at UC Berkeley. https://ggsc.berkeley.edu/images/uploads/GGSC-JTF_White_Paper-Generosity-FINAL.pdf)

2. Justifying greed exists in reality and in movies. https://en.wikipedia.org/wiki/Wall_Street_(1987_film)

3. Will humans be able to change their behavior before it is too late? BBC, May 2021 https://www.bbc.com/future/article/20210520-could-humans-really-destroy-all-life-on-earth

4. Just a reminder that an apocalypse is a serious event resulting in great destruction. The potential for devastation is a real possibility due to ecological collapse, modern warfare, worldwide pandemics, runaway bacteria, renegade asteroids, and perhaps, even some unfriendly aliens lacking coaching experience or patience, who may decide to put humans out of their misery (just kidding!).

5. Drought is becoming increasingly severe due to climate disruption. Without addressing this planetary crisis, the lack of water will have a significant impact by the year 2050. World Economic Forum, 2022 https://www.weforum.org/agenda/2022/08/drought-water-climate-un/

6. The Great Pacific Garbage Patch is the largest ocean waste repository in the world, containing 1.8 billion pieces of floating plastic and is estimated to be around 620,000 sq. miles, killing thousands of marine animals each year. Wetzel, C. (2021) Smithsonian Magazine, https://www.smithsonianmag.com/smart-news/this-new-installation-just-pulled-20000-pounds-of-plastic-from-the-great-pacific-garbage-patch-180978895/ and Ocean Conservancy, a nonprofit advocacy group https://oceanconservancy.org/trash-free-seas/plastics-in-the-ocean/

7. Circles have deep symbolic importance in many cultures and belief systems. Rose, Sophia, *Spiritual Symbolism of a Circle: The Shape of Infinity.* (2024) https://wisdomofthespirit.com/spiritual-symbolism-of-a-circle/

18. Wise Up

"Knowing yourself is the beginning of all wisdom." — Aristotle

Earth School of Hard Knocks

For those of you who thought you were done with learning a long time ago, we're here to inform you that you thought wrong. If you've dropped out or missed a few lessons at the *Earth School of Hard Knocks*, this serves as a reminder that your ongoing attendance is required to advance to the next grade level. An important part of your curriculum is *how to become a wiser version of yourself.*

Given that humans evolve differently, you may need to reassess how you approach thinking, learning, and solving problems in order to make the most of your learning experience. Most humans have likely encountered hardships of some sort and hopefully learned something from them. Repeating the same mistakes without gaining insight is not the ideal way to live. Understanding the lessons that life teaches you while on Earth requires introspection, and may take a lifetime, or even multiple lifetimes, to fully comprehend.

However, any insight you acquire will lead you towards self-awareness and personal growth, which is one of the goals of this guide. Now, before you start thinking that this isn't what you signed up for in this dimension — after all, you're busy with errands, your social life, and countless other urgent matters to attend to – you may want to consider that learning about yourself is a real priority, even if it's not on your current to-do list!

Keeping an open mind and letting go of limiting beliefs opens the door to your inner wisdom. *It's up to you to walk through that door!* While you can seek guidance for enlightenment from a teacher or spiritual mentor, the ability to unlock your potential is already within your reach.

Lesson 1: Need to Know Basics

Intellect encompasses the capacity to reason, think and understand.

Knowledge is what you use to expand your intelligence through learning. However, facts and information alone do not necessarily make one knowledgeable.

Wisdom primarily comes from the heart, not the head. It synthesizes experience, deep insights, and intuitive understanding of others and situations. Wisdom is the act of applying knowledge by evaluating which aspects are true and relevant. It often involves gaining insight into the reasons behind certain things and requires honesty with yourself and others. Wise humans are often kind but may not be book-smart. Intelligence doesn't guarantee wisdom[1] and vice versa.

Insight is a deeper level of knowing that involves a more intuitive understanding of life, knowledge, and wisdom. It offers a clearer insight into how things are interconnected.

In summary:
Intelligence helps us to comprehend, knowledge enables us to learn from others, and wisdom offers insights to assist others. Although they are related, they are not interchangeable. It is possible to possess one without the others.

"I cannot teach anyone anything, I can only make them think." – Socrates

Taking on the assignment of self-discovery is not always easy, but developing your own personal path to inner wisdom will reap benefits for your future and potentially, for humankind. Giving self-introspection the priority it deserves is necessary because without it, you run the risk of your mind staying stuck on autopilot instead of moving forward. Evidently, closed minds must be open in order to function properly.

Master Yogishimi Yami Zami, Author, Teacher and Guruologist, Director of the *Cudha Shoudha Institute of Being Here But Not There,* has this to say about self-knowledge, wising up and the long and bumpy road to understanding oneself.

"The path to knowing yourself in any way is complicated by a major factor, which is **YOU.** *Self-reflection and the quest to get to know yourself, so that you can function as best as possible, is an ongoing mission that should be taken on like any project that needs your full attention. Make sure you have plenty of snacks! It's probably not going to be easy for everyone, and that's okay because the whole point is to learn something and then go on from there. However, if you're not interested in yourself, then that can be a problem because you need to have some motivation to understand parts of yourself, even if you take things slowly at first. Actually, why wouldn't you be interested, or at least curious, in what makes you tick?*

Many of you are operating without a manual or instructions on how best to conduct yourself. How do you expect that to turn out? Well, it is obvious how it is all turning out just about now, isn't it? Human appendages flaring and snapping at others, orifices blowing out smoke and other vapors, opinions and statements based on a ginormous lack of self-reflection or baseline knowledge – with a prevailing attitude that everyone knows everything, but in actuality, no one really knows much of anything – which pretty much leads one to the conclusion that very few humans have any idea how to properly function in the world!

With all that being said, and it is a lot but just the tip of the iceberg so to speak, your mission to self-understanding will open the door to knowledge, wisdom and wising up in an evolved manner appropriate to your level. No one gets this one hundred percent perfectly, except for the upper echelons — S.D.S, the B.O.S.S., and some other high-level beings. Not even Advanced Beings completely and unequivocally KNOW THEMSELVES, because we are all still a work in progress. Some of us simply study a little more, spend more time in self-reflection, and then, step by step, continue evolving.

So begin wising up, because you were meant to learn lessons, not constantly repeat them!" — With Lightness, Master Yogishimi Yami Zami.

"You know nothing and you know everything." – Master YYZ

Who Knew?

While trying to understand yourself, you may be surprised to discover that you don't have a full grasp of yourself after all. This is because knowing oneself is a never-ending process of *"Oops, is that really me? Holy sh*t!"* moments. Don't let those moments hold you back though!

- **Be willing to question what you think you know!** The key to true wisdom lies in acknowledging what you don't know. It's not about having all the answers, but rather recognizing that there are many unanswered questions.
- **Recognize the limits of your understanding.** This means understanding the differences between what you already truly know and what you have yet to learn.
- **Once you acknowledge your limitations** and identify what you need to learn, you will realize your potential for growth by utilizing your strengths and abilities.
- **Ultimately, understanding oneself involves embracing your inner truth and authenticity,** along with the possibility of some more *"holy sh*t!"* moments.
- **Recognize that you are more than your ego** and that your innermost being is limitless and deep, constantly changing like the shifting tides and sometimes, beyond understanding.

Truth, self-awareness, and kindness keep you on your path.

The journey of self-knowledge[2] is about discovery, but it can also be filled with feelings of doubt and insecurity that may lead to avoiding taking responsibility for your personal growth. This can also cause you to believe that others are more knowledgeable or wiser than you. However, outsourcing your well-being to others increases the risk of encountering a fraud disguised as a teacher or guru. While wisdom can certainly be gained from highly evolved spiritual leaders and guides, connecting with your inner guidance is the best way to determine your unique pathway.

"The highest form of wisdom is kindness." – *The Talmud, the central text of Rabbinic Judaism*

Lesson 2: How Do You Know?

Utilize your intelligence for learning, reasoning, problem-solving, and planning. Make the most of your unique intelligence.[3]

Listen and learn from others but don't blindly follow what others say. Learn how to distinguish truth from lies and think for yourself. Those who you surround yourself with can influence your behavior, thoughts, and mindset, either positively or negatively. Be open to other viewpoints with respect.

Seek out and learn from new experiences, ideas, and different ways of thinking. Remain curious and maintain an inquisitive mindset. Step outside of your comfort zone and challenge yourself to expand your horizons by learning new skills and habits. Strive to learn one new thing every day. Life and the UNIVERSE *are constantly teaching you lessons!* Every human, animal or life form

---

you come into contact with, whether good or bad, serves as a lesson in living.

Acquire knowledge but don't mindlessly accept everything you read or hear. Just because something is written or published by a human doesn't mean their knowledge is infallible (unless they are an Advanced Being with access to continually evolving advice). Not all information is created equal, especially if it's on the INTERNET, so it's better to look for verified experts in their respective fields. Confirm and evaluate the accuracy of information by conducting further research on the same topic or by seeking guidance from someone with experience in the subject. Avoid relying on biased opinions or nonsensical ramblings of random humans on social media or other platforms.

Explore wisdom teachings, philosophy, delve into history, and engage with insightful literature. Use these timeless teachings to create your own valuable resources. Seek out a knowledgeable mentor or continue studying this guidebook.

Cultivate understanding and knowledge by exploring the world around you. If you can't do that at least go to the library! Enhance your mind with new insights and recognize that it is okay to change your beliefs about a subject that you thought you understood, but actually did not.

"Knowing others is wisdom, knowing yourself is Enlightenment." – Lao Tzu

Know It All?

Unless you are born as a wise old soul, there are no shortcuts to becoming wiser. In certain civilizations, initiates into wisdom traditions had to go through certain steps to become *a real know-it-*

all. Nowadays, the widespread availability of information has led some to believe that they can bypass these steps. Unfortunately, this flawed assumption has brought about an increase in humans pretending to be something that they are not.

Information overload, which includes false information, has given rise to a *new type of know-it-all human.* With easier access to information in virtually any field, some humans are able to sound smarter than they actually are. Certain types loudly declare themselves as experts, when in reality, they are simply memorizing a few key points or regurgitating slogans and opinions. Some don't even bother with facts or resources, but instead, insist that they *just know*[4] and refuse to consider another viewpoint. It's probably best not to argue with these types! Sadly, human history has a long record of damage caused by *questionable know-it-all humans* who claimed to know everything but lacked wisdom, resulting in some unfortunate consequences.

It is possible that the sheer amount of information available today, including articles, images, podcasts, blogs, and more, has become too much for human brains to handle, leading to burnout and an inability to learn or function properly. While technology has its benefits, one of the downsides is that it has allowed *self-proclaimed know-it-all experts* to promote themselves and their agenda to a gullible audience without taking responsibility for their claims. Remember, simply having information is not the same as knowing how to use it, and it's important to be wary of those with questionable motives.

Knowledge can exist without wisdom, but not the other way around. Wisdom synthesizes knowledge and experiences to form insights that enhances one's understanding of relationships and situations. Knowledge is like a tool, while wisdom is the craft that uses that tool to create a masterpiece.

"Sometimes I wonder whether the world is being run by smart people who are putting us on, or by imbeciles who really mean it." – Mark Twain

Cult of Ignorance and Stupidity![5]

A priority for humankind should be to set higher standards for themselves if they hope to advance further. Valuing wisdom and emotional intelligence isn't just some outdated notion but a critical component in any well-functioning society. It should be alarming that a particular type of stupidity and foolishness is now considered to be a status symbol and a cause for celebration.

To make matters worse, there is a disturbing trend of *declining intelligence*, as evidenced by recent research![6] When ignorance, idiocy, anti-intellectualism and apathy take priority over acquiring wisdom, it can move humanity closer to the abyss. And folks, that abyss is expanding every day.

Sure, non-stop ignorance and wacky antics that border on imbecile behavior may seem like fun to humans who constantly like to be entertained, but who will have the last laugh when it becomes widespread?

While some may find idiocy amusing, there are unfortunately those who are truly ignorant or intentionally stupid and condone this type of foolish behavior. It seems that some humans lack self-awareness regarding their ignorance, while others have questionable tastes in entertainment. Regardless of the reason, it is hard to understand the appeal of loud-mouthed, appendage-pointing humans who believe their opinions are reflective of appropriate brain activity.

Those who choose to remain ignorant and struggle to think for themselves are easy targets for manipulation by those who promote harmful stupidity for their own reasons. Ironically, these are the same humans who need self-awareness but are unable to achieve it because they have not yet awakened. They may be in danger of being left behind!

The reality is that ignorance can breed fear, fuel prejudice, and ultimately empower those who seek to exploit and oppress. It is up to humans to reject simplistic narratives, cultivate healthy skepticism and actively engage in the difficult but vital work of thinking for themselves. This will require individual responsibility, a commitment to critical self-reflection and an unwavering pursuit of truth. Yes, this will require you to change your inner channels once again.

Elevating idiocy over reason, intelligence and common decency *does not bode well* for a civilized society.[7] There is a purpose to holding others back from becoming knowledgeable and wiser, which is why devious humans try to keep others as ignorant as possible. In this case, ignorance is not bliss, and it is up to you to think for yourself!

At this point, you may be questioning whether the subjects of intelligence and wisdom even apply to you. Judging by the state of affairs on Planet Earth, some humans seem to believe that thinking is highly overrated compared to other activities that do not demand much of it. It appears that joining a cult of ignorance and stupidity is easier than learning how to think in new ways! While some may find comfort in ignorance, the Universe holds a different belief. This is because those who purposefully spread ignorance and falsehoods, instead of knowledge and truth, are not aiding in the progress of humanity.

Wouldn't You Know It?

The UNIVERSE has granted nearly every human the potential to increase their intelligence by using their brain, mind and heart space effectively. Your efforts to become wiser ultimately depend on you coming out of your self-imposed bubble to improve your thinking skills and gain insight. This will require acknowledging your unique capabilities and your willingness to expand your worldview.

Additionally, by keeping an open mind and learning from life lessons, you can avoid repeating the same mistakes. This will increase your wisdom and improve your ability to handle life's uncertainties and challenges. Like most worthwhile endeavors, this requires effort on your part instead of relying on others to do the thinking for you. The road to wisdom may have bumps and setbacks, but do not let that discourage you, as these can serve as learning opportunities. Granted, while not all experiences lead to wisdom, some are worth reflecting on in order to help you attain it.

Wisdom isn't the exclusive territory of monks on mountaintops, spiritual gurus, philosophers, or other visionary leaders, whether human or not. It is accessible to all of you when you are willing to nurture and align yourselves properly with your inner source. You do not need to become a holier-than-thou oracle who spouts one-liners to loyal followers, unless, of course, you are the real deal!

Remember, your main lesson is about recognizing the various paths to wisdom and self-awareness. Choose one and commit to it. Keep in mind that during your time at the *Earth School of Hard Knocks*, any progress you make in your personal growth may help you avoid repeating painful lessons, allowing you to graduate with evolving honors!

Ding Ding!

If you have just read all of the above and are worried that you are not even close to developing any learning or "wising-up" ability whatsoever, do not despair and **DO NOT GIVE UP!** This guide has been created with the Cosmic belief that humanity can truly evolve once they believe, and think, that they can!

"By three methods we may learn wisdom: First, by reflection, which is noblest; second, by imitation, which is easiest; and third by experience, which is the bitterest." — Confucius

Lesson 3: I'm In the Know

Getting to know yourself better will help you understand your habitual ways of responding to the world around you, which is beneficial both personally and collectively. Additionally, self-reflection can improve relationships, careers, and overall well-being. It may even help you secure a good table at your favorite restaurant, but most importantly, it will help shape the future of humanity, hopefully for the better!

1. Set aside a designated peaceful time (begin with 5-10 minutes) to reflect without interruption.

---

2. Consider what defines your true self, not the persona you project to the world.

3. Recognize that your thoughts are only a small part of you and may not reflect your authentic self.

4. Listen to what your heart is trying to tell you. If you are ignoring that little voice, then you may be disregarding important aspects of your inner wisdom.

5. Evaluate your willingness to accept new concepts and ideas.

6. Ask yourself: Who are you? Why are you here? Where are you going and how will you get there? These may be challenging questions, but no one said self-discovery was simple!

"You don't have to burn books to destroy a culture. Just get people to stop reading them." – Ray Bradbury, author

Libraries Make Life Matter!

Where else but the library can a human tap into a vast reservoir of knowledge and enhance their thinking skills— and access to this temple of wisdom only requires obtaining a library card! This is why ALL libraries matter, regardless of size, as they play a crucial role in nurturing the ability to learn, think, and grow. Our research on the current lack of respect for learning and the absurd movement to close certain libraries, has led us to the conclusion that some humans fail to recognize how ridiculous they are. Libraries are an essential part of any community, particularly because they are free and accessible to all humans, even those who may not fully appreciate them.

However, if you choose not to go to a library, that's your choice because no one's forcing you (unless you have a parent who is an avid reader and has been regularly taking you to the library since you were a wee toddler, which luckily for you, included a snack). Why ruin things for others just because *you think you know it all* and want to force others to think like you do? If you are going to have such a closed mindset, then close all your orifices and reign in your appendages because closed minds, without any regulation and a serious lack of self-reflection, can create havoc for innocent bystanders! Simply put, stay home and stop bothering other humans who just want to READ and enjoy the library!

It is quite distressing that some humans have no idea what their libraries offer or worse, don't care. Well, more of you should care, because libraries are sacred institutions of knowledge. We highly encourage you to get a library card if you don't already have one and start using it, because if you haven't been to your library recently, then you are certainly missing out! In addition to a variety of reading materials, there are classes, events, crafts, gatherings, BOOKS, and even cafes, where you can nibble on some delectable delights while you peruse your multitude of options. We have discovered that adding chocolate delicacies to our intellectual pursuits has dramatically enhanced our experience while also expanding our minds!

A love of learning is more than just acquiring knowledge; it is a way of living that expands your worldview. With the arrival of technology, expanding your knowledge has many options. However, as with all tools, it is important to know which ones to use and when. Not everyone is utilizing it properly and options like the Internet can be helpful, but it doesn't THINK for you, which is a crucial skill. Your local library can be a great help in this matter, as many librarians are trained to think critically and would be more than happy to assist and guide you in the right direction. Combining the power of technology with the vast resources of libraries can provide everyone the access to knowledge and information that, not so long ago, was only available to a select few.

Spending more time at a library can enhance your ability to express witty pearls of wisdom at dinner gatherings and, potentially, **start a trend that makes intelligence sexy again!** We wholeheartedly "approve this message," as we are wise-cracking, scarf-wearing geeks from the Universe ourselves. Our wisdom didn't come from reading planetary tabloids or posting on social media while waiting in grocery lines. Instead, it came from visiting libraries and knowledge centers across the cosmos that offer a wealth of teachings compiled throughout the ages and galaxies.

Cosmic learning is enhanced not only with delectable delights, but also through advanced integration techniques that improve the ability to absorb, discern, and evaluate information. You can start your exploration without even leaving your planet, so grab your scarf and begin uncovering the treasures of your local library. *Who knows what you may discover there? Maybe even an Advanced Being!*

At some point soon, you may finally realize that there are upsides to becoming a wiser human being, especially if you visit your local library (or at the very least, utilize their online website). You may discover that these temples of knowledge have actually helped you achieve some level of wise-assery.

What's even more exciting is that you are now experiencing new insights that have transformed your perception of yourself, others and the world around you. Who knew that learning and expanding yourself could be so much fun?! *We did, of course!*

Lesson 4: Wise-Assery in a Nutshell

(Because where else would you put your wise-assery?)

You learn to think for yourself. No one else is going to do it for you!

You have a sense of humor because without it, wisdom is irrelevant.

You enjoy being a wise-ass because if your ass is wise, so is the rest of you.

You keep an open mind, but not too open, because you can never be too sure.

You are finally in charge of your mind, brain, and appendages because wisdom has benefits!

You know that you know some things, but you also know that you know pretty much nothing.

You help others realize that they too can be a wise-ass, but like you, they may need to go to the library for additional training.

"Follow your heart but take your brain with you." – Dr. Alfred Adler, psychotherapist

Say Hello to Your Brain!

Considering its importance, the human brain doesn't receive the level of attention it deserves, especially when compared to some other body parts. When was the last time you stopped what you were doing and thought about how your brain worked? It should be a no-brainer that the likelihood of evolution succeeding would increase if humans better understood the power within their heads. What do you think your skull is holding in there, empty space? If you have simply forgotten what's "up there" or haven't realized its potential, then it's time to say "hello" to your brain and get reacquainted.

Whether you acknowledge it or not, your brain hasn't forgotten about you and continues to run all operations related to your functioning. If it didn't, you would definitely receive some type of notice and it wouldn't be great news. In addition to keeping things running smoothly behind the scenes, your brain interprets and processes information. Depending on the situation, this information gets translated into emotions via the mind and heart.

While it's true that your human brain is a remarkable organ and an operating system worth looking into, it's also important to recognize that you are more than just your cognitive abilities. Intelligence is just one aspect of personal growth, and even if you possess a *top-of-the-line brain*, it does not define your entire being. Nevertheless, it's still wise to learn more about your brain's requirements so that you can enhance your ability to make the most of what you've got.

When your brain is functioning effectively, you operate better, which can lead to various improvements.[8] Having a basic understanding doesn't require a degree in neuroscience, but lacking interest in the capabilities of your brain should not be an excuse to disregard or ignore its importance. This is when a library card would come in handy!

"Our brains are nicely shaped, colorful, and quite large – in this regard, size does matter." – AB1 & AB2

"We have a brain to produce adaptable and complex movements. Moving our body is the only way to affect the world around us. Emotions, attention, and other cognitive processes are relevant, but they are only important to either drive or suppress future movements. The golden evidence is an animal called the sea squirt: a modest animal that has a simple nervous system, swims in the ocean, and at some point in its life, permanently implants on a rock. Once implanted, the first thing it does is digest its own brain and nervous system for food. So once you don't need to move, you don't need the luxury of a mass of neurons we call the brain." — Daniel Wolpert, Professor of Neuroscience at Cambridge University

Unless you happen to be a sea squirt, you will need a brain to function as best as you can on Planet Earth. Of course, it is also highly recommended that if you have a brain, you make sure to USE IT!

Now, is Professor Wolpert suggesting that if you stop moving, you should resort to eating your own brain for lunch? Maybe, but it's unclear if it's the best option for a meal, unless, of course, you have no other alternatives. Nonetheless, it is plausible to assume that the principle *"if you don't use it, you lose it"* applies to the brain (and possibly to other body parts) regardless of whether you are a sea squirt or not. Professor Wolpert likely has more fascinating insights to share, which should encourage more humans to appreciate having a brain and to keep moving.

It is puzzling why there isn't more stimulating conversation among humans about the mind-blowing wonders of the brain, especially during cocktail hour or dinnertime, unless of course, one is a neuroscientist or doctor. Ironically, while you are enjoying your cocktail and *engaging in stimulating discussions about the latest episode of shrieking humans and their bizarre antics*, your brain is quietly taking care of the majority of your functions in the background. Since many humans still do not find their brains fascinating, it can easily be taken for granted until a problem arises. To prevent future issues, it may be a good idea to establish a routine maintenance schedule for your overall system.

Having a highly developed brain doesn't always guarantee that a species will evolve in a positive way. Intelligence, without wisdom and other important qualities, can be used for harmful purposes. Conversely, brain impairments or difficulties do not necessarily impede one's ability to live a fulfilling life, as all brains have unique settings and quirks. Defining what is considered "normal" or "abnormal" can vary from one human to another and may be subjective depending on the brains in question.

Improving one's brain power facilitates expansion by enhancing perception, intellect, and other capabilities that may seem unimaginable to most humans. The high functioning of neurons amplifies the user's ability to access untapped areas of the brain and mind, leading to an ever-increasing awareness of potential. This sets off a feedback loop that continually fine-tunes the brain and mind space, enhancing one's capacity to evolve even further. It is important to note that there are different ways to achieve brain potential. Therefore, do not let your unique brain system impede you from becoming a wiser human or at the very least, a more informed and insightful one.

Ding Ding!

Advanced beings typically possess highly developed minds, and some may no longer even require physical brains due to quantum conscious evolution. Throughout the universe, there exist various degrees of mental development ranging from rudimentary to highly advanced. However, the focus should be on holistically integrating oneself as a whole being, rather than fixating on one particular aspect, organ, or appendage. The brain and mind evolve when a species understands the reason for its existence and combines this insight with wisdom. This can lead to a shift in consciousness.

Lesson 5: Do You Think I'm Sexy? *You Betcha!*

Just like any healthy relationship, your brain deserves your respect and appreciation. Treat it with love, and you may even get lucky with your sexy brain! Lingerie and other romantic supplies are optional.

- Keep your brain active and challenged by trying something new, such as learning new skills, picking up a hobby, or taking a class to help your brain form new connections.

- Engage your brain cells by reading and writing, which is where libraries can come in handy.

- Meditate or quiet your mind, as it has been proven to increase the amount of grey matter in the human brain, the region responsible for processing information. A meditated brain is a highly sexy brain!

- Make sure to rest your brain and get plenty of sleep, as it cannot function properly if you are not adequately rested. Not only will your brain work better, but you will as well.

- Sexy brains do not like to multitask. There's no benefit to it, so stay focused on one thing at a time.

- Move, dance, or exercise. Your sexy brain likes to groove.

- Listen to great works of music, but avoid using it as mere background noise.

- Create something! The brain thrives on arts, crafts, and creativity. Try knitting a scarf.

- Nourish your brain with healthy food, not junk. Chocolate, organic and natural plant foods are highly recommended.

- Reduce passive and mindless screen time. Excessive stimulation can lead to dysfunction. This includes video games, reality shows, and aimlessly surfing the internet.

- Sharpen your brain with puzzles, crosswords, and other activities that enhance brain function.

- Take your brain out into nature because it needs fresh air, time with the birdies, and sunshine to warm up it's neurons. While this may not be entirely based on neuroscience, we believe your brain will thank you for it.

- Keep your brain in shape with meditation, sound therapy and other mind and brain treatments. It's like spending quality time with yourself!

- Engage in stimulating discussions, uplifting information, new ideas, and new experiences. This will exercise your brain muscles and keep it sexy, but be mindful of topics that can trigger others!

"There is more to humans and other beings than just their brains. The true essence of a higher life form lies in their heart, mind, creative spirit, and soul. While having a highly functioning brain is beneficial, the future development of the human race depends on a shift in consciousness." – AB1 & AB2

There's Nothing Like the Real Thing

Choosing between artificial intelligence (ai) or advanced intelligence (AI) can be tricky for some species, especially if that particular species is unaware of the difference. Humans may want to focus on advancing their own intelligence rather than allowing technology to replace it. When a tool surpasses the intelligence of its creators, there should be cause for concern.

The advancement of technology, rather than the ADVANCEMENT OF HUMAN BEINGS, is a losing proposition in the long run. Without WISDOM, progress can only go so far. Reflect on this further if you're unsure of what this means. There can be potential consequences if *less-than-advanced* humans misuse artificial intelligence and technology. Unfortunately, some humans are more interested in advancing technology rather than their own evolution.

Clearly, technological advancements have improved the quality of life for many in education, medicine, communication and industry. However, while devices like cell phones and other high-tech gadgets may seem harmless, the humans who use them may not be. Furthermore, an over-reliance on technology can come at the expense of genuine human relationships and societal progress.

Humanity should carefully consider the ethical implications of developing technological advancements, such as artificial intelligence, before introducing and integrating them into society. Without a deeper understanding of what is at stake, humanity risks being controlled by humans who may exploit technology to enhance their own power, wealth, and influence over the common good.

The challenge for Earthlings in the advancement of technology is not only to improve quality of life, but also to discover the purpose of human development.

Another concerning issue is that unsustainable growth also applies to technology. It is often driven by greed and self-interest, frequently at the expense of the environment and various life forms. Understanding how to effectively utilize technology without sacrificing your humanity, sanity and the planet will require a heightened level of awareness and insight.

A new approach may involve managing growth or implementing agreed upon standards to prevent harm to individuals and society. Taking precautions however, does not mean stopping innovation, nor is it necessary to go back to the Stone Age.

Are You Using Technology Or Is It Using You?

Changing perspectives on how future technology should be developed and integrated into society can be challenging. Informing society about the benefits and potential drawbacks of any advanced tool will require more than just a simple social media post or quick update in the news. Regardless of how it is conveyed, the message should clearly emphasize that technology is not a substitute for human interaction, nor is it a miracle cure for cultural issues.

Advanced Beings and assorted extraterrestrials respect progress and it's many advantages. We understand that humans enjoy their tech gadgets and have benefited from various improvements over the centuries. Most modern humans would be at a loss without the help and convenience of advanced tools. We doubt that many would prefer living in caves without plumbing or WiFi, although we do recognize that some may find that appealing even now.

As with most tools, the issue typically lies with the life form using it rather than the object itself. It's interesting to note that warnings about the downsides of technology have come from some of the very humans who developed it![9] Not only are there certain negative impacts on the brain, but also the potential for causing addictive type of behaviors. Therefore, if you find yourself spending more time with gadgets than with other humans, animals or nature, you may want to ask yourself, "*Am I using my technology wisely, or is it using me?*"

BUT, BUT wait, does this mean I have to give up my cell phone, tablet, multiple devices, my smart fridge, my smarter car, my robotic vacuum, Alexa, WiFi, and the Internet?[10]

Probably not, but you can put them down, shut them off, or stop using them for a few hours. This will free up time for you to bake some bread, listen to music, dance, make crafts, go outside, take a walk, listen to the birds, play with your dog, or your cat if they are up for it, and just enjoy something other than a device. You can also GO TO THE LIBRARY AND IMMERSE YOURSELF IN THE TEMPLE OF KNOWLEDGE!

Go RETRO by experiencing your life without artificial distractions. Discover what it feels like to be unplugged and how good it really is. You may come to realize that too much technology can start making you feel like you are technology, and that may not feel too good at all.

"It has become appallingly obvious that our technology has exceeded our humanity." – Albert Einstein

Lesson 6: *Know Thy Tech*

Technology and modern advancements are tools that can improve life, but only if they *do not negatively impact the user's well-being.* Whether it's a smart phone or a simple hammer, a certain level of development and insight into how to properly use a tool is necessary.

Look up from your screens and embrace life.
Manage your tech use responsibly and mindfully.
Technology should not be a substitute for genuine connection.
Your brain is your most valuable technology, so treat it with respect and care.
Technology is a tool that should enhance your life, not control it.
Nature, animals and other living beings should not be overshadowed by technology.
Humans thrive when they are fully engaged in the experiences of life.

Babies Need Humans, Not Devices!

Making the best decisions for innocent babies and children requires a high level of maturity and a considerable understanding of the possible outcomes that may result from their exposure to different experiences. This is an essential responsibility for any adult who is entrusted with raising children on Planet Earth, while also LOVING and keeping them safe!

In order to fully understand certain concepts, especially those related to children, it is always advantageous to gather as much information as possible to become the best caregiver and parent. With each new generation, unique challenges arise that are influenced by individual backgrounds, cultures, families, and numerous other factors. When you add in the complexities of technology and modern gadgets, parenting has become even more complicated.

When considering the numerous decisions a human parent must make for their offspring, it is important to remember that many adults are also struggling to manage their own technology and themselves. If that is the case, why would any reasonable adult think it is a good idea to give a technological device or toy to a baby without considering what is best for the child? Your child is more precious than your cell phone, so educating yourself BEFORE giving your baby anything inappropriate would be a WISE decision.

Not long ago, humans would give their babies rattles and age-appropriate toys. Nowadays, babies are grabbing and using cell phones, laptops and iPad's, sometimes before they can even crawl! Some parents may defend their actions by saying there is nothing they can do because everyone is doing it, including babies. Some may even believe they have no choice but to give in because they worry that their baby or child will fall behind other children who are already texting before entering preschool!

There shouldn't be a rush to push a child's development before they are ready. The possibility of unintended consequences increases when there is a lack of awareness or a careless approach to something as important as child-rearing. One important thing to note is that spending too much time on tech gadgets can have developmental repercussions and may interfere with a young human's growing brain. During the formative years, it is crucial to allow time for activities such as art, story time, nature-based excursions, and play. These activities are more beneficial for a human child's ability to thrive and enjoy life.

"It is vital that when educating our children's brains we do not neglect to educate their hearts." – Dalai Lama

The *Kind* of Care

The consequences of *not knowing* "what the heck" you are doing are much more serious when you are responsible for another little human who is depending on YOU! How many parents would allow their 2-year-old to wander around and operate household equipment without supervision, or let them drive their vehicle?

A mindless approach to parenting is not what your child or the world needs now. It is your responsibility to understand that CHILDCARE actually means that you will CARE for your CHILD and not rely on technology (or perhaps even your nanny) to raise and shape your child while you are distracted by your gadgets. Unless you snap out of it in time, you will miss out on what being a parent is all about.

Let's hope that more humans will realize the importance of being vigilant when it comes to exposing children to technology. Parents who quickly give their offspring the latest tech gadgets to keep them occupied while they spend time on their phones should reconsider their actions. Before allowing your children to use certain toys and technology, it would be a good idea to do some research.

An even better idea would be to familiarize yourself with what is best for a child's mental and physical well-being and development. Explore the best ways to obtain this information, whether it's through your local library, online resources, or consulting with child development experts. You may even want to consider asking your own parents for their insights, depending on the circumstances. With the current wealth of resources and experts available, humans have the ability to discover the most effective ways to navigate parenting in the digital age.

"Children more than ever, need opportunities to be in their bodies in the world – jumping rope, bicycling, stream hopping, and fort building. It's this engagement between limbs of the body and bones of the earth where true balance and centeredness emerge." – David Sobel, environmental educator and academic

The Cosmically Advanced Kid Association (CAKA), a respected advocate for the offspring of all species, advises the following:

- Drop your cell phone, device or remote into a bag, and then proceed to put it into a closet. Do this often.
- Take your baby or child to another room where there are toys or other interesting items for them to explore.
- Bring your baby or child outside to discover and experience the natural world firsthand, rather than through a screen or cell phone.
- Provide opportunities for your offspring to EXPAND THEIR BRAIN and IMAGINATION through real experiences, play and interactions.

- Spend quality time together without gadgets and *make the conscious effort to be fully present with your offspring.* As you watch your baby or child immersed in activities other than a beeping electronic device, you will hopefully realize, if you haven't already, that nothing can replace human contact and connection with one another!

Learn to master your relationship with Life by first mastering yourself.

"Our relationship with the earth involves something more than pragmatic use, academic understanding, or aesthetic appreciation. A truly human intimacy with the earth and with the entire natural world is needed. Our children should be properly introduced to the world in which they live." – Thomas Berry

---

Repeat After Us

I trust my inner wisdom.
I am wise and intelligent.
I continue to improve my mind.
I am excited about learning new things.
I love exploring the many wonders of life.
I am open to the wisdom and love of the universe.
I expand my knowledge and viewpoint.
I am living life, not just watching it through technology.
I am open to information that helps me grow and evolve.
I prioritize humans, nature and life over technology.
I allow my inner wisdom to guide me to better decisions.

"Our mission is to align technology with humanity's best interests. We envision a world with technology that respects our attention, improves our well-being, and strengthens communities." – Center for Humane Technology[11]

Thoughts?

"Knowledge is the seed, intelligence is the stem, understanding is the branch, and wisdom is the fruit." — Matshona Dhliwayo, Philosopher

Notes

1. Learn more about wisdom. Miller, Kori D. *The 5 Character Strengths of Wisdom in Positive Psychology*, scientifically reviewed by Jo Nash, Ph.D. (May 2019) https://positivepsychology.com/wisdom/

2. Prof. Green, Mitchell. *"The Philosophy of Self-Knowledge,"* its history and relevance. https://today.uconn.edu/2018/08/know-thyself-philosophy-self-knowledge/ and the online course titled *"Know Thyself: The Value and Limits of Self-Knowledge"* on the learning platform Coursera: https://www.coursera.org/learn/know-thyself-the-examined-life

3. There are multiple forms of intelligence, and usually, it is not limited to one specific ability. Instead, most humans possess various forms, such as linguistic, emotional, logical-mathematical, musical, spatial intelligence and more. https://en.wikipedia.org/wiki/Theory_of_multiple_intelligences

4. How do you really know? There is a distinct inner sense of truth that doesn't rely on facts or references. This should not be confused with those who simply say *"I know"* in order to avoid further discussion, debate, or conceding a point.

5. It's important to note that in this context, "stupidity" does not refer to certain humans who may function differently or have cognitive disabilities. Instead, it usually involves intentional actions or a deliberate rejection of intelligent choices. Some humans are negatively stupid not because they are incapable of being otherwise, but because they choose to be. For more information on the issue of "stupidity" and intellectual rigor, please refer to: http://www.elegantbrain.com/edu4/classes/common/stupidity.pdf

6. "An analysis of approximately 730,000 IQ test results by researchers from the Ragnar Frisch Centre for Economic Research in Norway has revealed that the Flynn effect reached its peak for humans born in the mid-1970s and has significantly declined ever since." - Dockrill, Peter. Science Alert (2018). This theory attributes the increase in average IQ in the 20th century to improved access to education and better nutrition compared

to previous generations. However, recent research suggests a reverse trend in the Flynn effect among current populations. Conaway, Will: Forbes Technology Council (2020), *Technology Is On The Rise, While IQ Is On The Decline* https://www.forbes.com/sites/forbestechcouncil/2020/04/29/technology-is-on-the-rise-while-iq-is-on-the-decline/?sh=1846dfcab103

7. Buckmaster, Luke "*Idiocracy: a disturbingly prophetic look at the future of America – and our era of stupidity.*" The Guardian (July 2021) https://www.theguardian.com/culture/2021/jul/19/idiocracy-a-disturbingly-prophetic-look-at-the-future-of-america-and-our-era-of-stupidity

8. When facing mental and emotional challenges, gaining insight into your unique brain and its strengths and weaknesses can be beneficial. Mental and psychological issues are often linked to specific problems within the brain.

9. Our minds can be hijacked': Lewis, Paul, *The tech insiders who fear a smartphone dystopia*: The Guardian (2017) https://www.theguardian.com/technology/2017/oct/05/smartphone-addiction-silicon-valley-dystopia

10. A *Short History of the Internet*: Science and Media Museum (2020) https://www.scienceandmediamuseum.org.uk/objects-and-stories/short-history-internet

11. Center for Humane Technology is an independent nonprofit. They believe that by understanding the root causes of harmful technology, humans can work together to create a better future. https://www.humanetech.com/

19. Do Better

"Have the courage to say no. Have the courage to face the truth. Do the right thing because it is right. These are the magic keys to living your life with integrity." – W. Clement Stone, philanthropist and author

In this age of *"anything goes"* behavior, standing up for what is right will definitely set you apart from the rest of the crowd. Humanity may have temporarily strayed from its principles while finding its way, but that doesn't mean you have to do the same. Your inner moral compass can help guide you through life's difficult choices, although it may need some fine-tuning if it hasn't been used in a while.

Most humans, with the exception of criminals and other deviants, can probably find common ground and agree on basic standards of right and wrong. However, as moral views vary from one human to another in society, differences of opinion about acceptable or unacceptable behavior can arise. It would be much easier if everyone understood that acceptable conduct naturally occurs when there is a high level of integrity. Therefore, any attempt to do better should start with aligning oneself with higher standards of ethical behavior, regardless of which way society's moral winds are blowing.

Ethics are guiding principles that help humans decide what is good or bad, while **morals** are the beliefs held by an individual or group regarding what is right or wrong.

"Conscience is the inner voice which warns us that someone may be looking."
– H.L. Mencken, journalist

Do you do the right thing even when no one's looking?

We certainly hope so! You should always strive to choose the best action, regardless of whether or not you have an audience. However, the temptation to take alternative paths and throw caution to the wind (and possibly, undergarments) has a certain appeal that can be hard to resist, especially when one is weak and believes they can get away with it. This is especially true in a world where technology can normalize unethical behavior, leading gullible humans down a slippery slope and influencing them to believe that such behavior is acceptable. This misuse of technology, combined with high levels of digital distraction, is starting to have detrimental impacts on human decency.[1]

Modern unethical behaviors may seem insignificant, but they are actually important to address because they gradually erode the moral foundation of society, which should be based on integrity and standards. When common values decline, it becomes difficult to uphold standards, especially when they are no longer "set in stone" as they were long ago. Whether they were set in granite or another material is probably irrelevant; the point is that they no longer have the same impact they once did.

As a result, many humans are trying to keep themselves in line without the guidance that is sometimes needed from benevolent authorities on the subject. For less evolved humans, this can be challenging to accomplish as it requires both motivation and dedication to avoid unethical behavior that may entice them from various sources, including those in positions of power. Creating your own personal moral code on a tablet, or a piece of paper, can be a good idea to remind yourself of the values you hold to be important.

Moral instructions from centuries ago may have become outdated in some societies but until the glorious day arrives when there is a collective shift in human consciousness, society still needs to uphold certain common standards for the good of all. Since too many humans are on shaky moral ground on their own, it may be time to consider following an updated set of guidelines that emphasize universal ethical principles, rather than just behaviors. Simply telling someone not to do something is obviously not enough!

While certain human advice is still being preached (or in some cases, screeched) from pulpits and social media, it often ends up being nothing more than a lot of hot air or mind-boggling blabbering! Clearly, this is not the most effective way to motivate humans to be their best. Keeping it simple may help in getting more humans on board.

With this in mind, we believe that having a **"Do Better"** guideline to share with others can come in handy, especially during the holidays and other gatherings. In fact, giving this book as a gift may be the best thing for both them and you. Instead of wasting time trying to convince others that their lax ethics are hindering human evolution, you can spend more time enjoying some delicious delights while they peruse the **"Hurry Up and Evolve"** manifesto!

"If it is not right, do not do it; if it is not true, do not say it." — Marcus Aurelius, Roman emperor and philosopher

---

Strive to be:
Truthful Fair Respectful
Loyal Generous Loving
Trustworthy Brave
Courteous Honorable

Do no harm. *When making choices, if it hurts another, don't do it.*
Be honest and honorable. *Your word is your bond.*
Do what's right *instead of what's convenient or selfish.*

But... *Everyone Else is Doing It!*

While you may want to be part of the crowd, you should keep in mind that just because everyone else is doing, saying or thinking something doesn't mean you should too. In other words, don't mindlessly follow a crowd, group or cult-like leader because conformity is not always a virtue and sometimes, it can be fatal. To be clear, this advice usually applies to negative or unsafe behavior. On the other hand, if everyone is evolving or becoming the best human possible, then please proceed to join them.

Whether you want to be part of a horde of unsavory humans ready to cause mischief or simply like to mindlessly hand over your moral principles to any group that will accept you, the bottom line is that you alone are responsible for your actions and choices. If you find this assessment harsh, consider the consequences you'll face when you plummet over the edge alongside the rest of the group!

The struggle between "right and wrong" behavior has been ongoing since the dawn of human civilization. *Apparently, it seems that humans take a while to learn.* Attempts to address this dilemma and keep humans in line have taken various forms throughout history, with mixed results. We are not sure who thought that threats of divine punishment or earthly consequences, such as eternal damnation or other unpleasant outcomes, would be the best way to motivate humans and keep them under control. While this approach may have succeeded in restraining some humans, the allure of certain temptations often proves too powerful to resist, leading some to the conclusion that, well, *consequences be damned.*

Various cautionary stories have been ingrained in the collective psyche of humanity, such as the incident in the garden involving two humans, an apple, and an unfortunate snake.[2] It remains unclear whether this was a genuine attempt to tarnish the snake's reputation or simply to highlight the consequences of poor choices and moral dilemmas for which one must take responsibility, whether one is aware of their behavior or not. Stories like this one hold profound moral and spiritual implications that may require further exploration, but with a fresh perspective. Evidently, there is a need for more straightforward guidance and insight in spiritual matters that have become needlessly convoluted.

Leave the Apple, Take the Snake?

The key takeaway is that you typically have choices in most situations. By holding a firm conviction of what is morally right, you won't have a problem making the best decision, even if a snake is trying to convince you otherwise! However, sometimes dealing with a snake is *preferable* to certain overzealous humans who may be masquerading as religious and moral experts. Many of these humans are more than happy to enforce whatever moral and ethical standards are currently in vogue. Oftentimes, these overexcited authoritarian types conveniently ignore their own moral mandates because they themselves are immoral. It seems like they either don't understand or *don't care about practicing what they preach!*

Humans who intentionally subvert the message of integrity and moral conscience will face a day of reckoning, sooner or later. In the meantime, you can find moral clarity without all the preachy drama because wouldn't you know it, you actually know more about it than you sometimes want to let on. If you are honest with yourself, you know the difference between "right and wrong," unless of course, you are a sociopath or a deviant of some sort. Sure, it can be convenient to forget where you put your moral compass,[3] especially when certain temptations come your way.

While it's understandable to have weak moments, repeatedly crossing certain lines can eventually corrupt one's moral fiber and values. Don't fall for the excuse that doing the right thing doesn't matter, because once standards start slipping, it may be difficult to regain them. Committing to high standards and NOT conforming to a crowd mentality that has lost its morals and marbles isn't for weaklings. It takes courage and strength to stand against the prevailing attitude of *"well, everyone else is doing it!"*

The bottom line is that every time you excuse unacceptable behavior, such as cheating, dishonesty, greed, corruption, intolerance, adultery, lawlessness, hatred and violence, YOU become part of the problem instead of the solution. If you do what everyone else is doing and it's deemed unacceptable behavior, then guess what? You will be just like everyone else who is not striving to be their best.

What actually do YOU Stand For?

When you stand for something, it means that you adhere to a set of principles that guide you and have mentally prepared your mind for how to act if a certain situation arises. Essentially, this means that when others try to knock you down, you are able to remain standing BECAUSE you live with integrity and values. You have convictions of a higher order that you uphold no matter what happens, even when faced with temptations (which are more likely to involve other humans rather than snakes!).

Not knowing what you stand for can be a problem because there's the possibility that you will fall for anything. This should concern you because humans need to stand for something other than their egos or their "brand." Perhaps you truly believe that your personal brand adequately represents you, but is that enough in this age of shaky ideology and loose standards? That depends.

If your personal brand is built on a high-value system and a strong ethical foundation, then what you stand for and your personal brand will likely be in alignment. If this is the case, you will be authentic and should feel comfortable with your private and public persona.

HOWEVER, if your brand is built on dishonesty and greed, cleverly packaged so that only a select few can see through the deception, then a major overhaul is necessary. This is when having moral courage means being willing to do the right thing, even if it may come at a personal cost to your brand and carefully crafted image!

When You *Stand for* Something

You are intentional in choosing the right actions.

You develop your conscience through self-improvement.

You purposefully live a life that aligns with high-order values.

You seek to understand the objective truth about right and wrong.

You are aware and attentive to the small decisions you make daily, as those small, *not-so-great* choices can result in negative consequences before you realize it.

Good Intentions *Are Not* Always Enough

Look, you can have the best intentions, but if you don't put your
ethical standards or principles into action, then it doesn't really count.
Actions speak louder than words in this instance. **It's not enough to
know what is right if you don't actually do what is right**. This applies
to both personal and collective issues. Doing what is right and best
for a person or group is *not just a choice, but a declaration* that you
stand for something. It shows that you have high values and ethics of
behavior.

How does this scenario play out in the *Earth School of Hard Knocks*?
It means that when you find a wallet on the floor, you hand it over
to its rightful owner instead of keeping it and using the credit card
inside. If you've been cutting corners in more complex ways, it's now

time to set aside your selfishness and do what's right. This could mean finally making the decision to be honest about your cheating and shady dealings, and facing the consequences instead of making excuses or blaming others.

Unfortunately, when the time comes to make a real difference in the world, some may find it tempting to stay silent and not take a stand for what's right. After all, it's often easier or safer to avoid rocking the boat. During turbulent times, there can be an inclination to keep your head down, or fall into apathy and denial. It's not unusual to feel like giving up when the tidal wave of unacceptable things keeps growing stronger every day, leaving you feeling as if you are sinking into an ocean of despair or helplessness. Surely, when there is dysfunction and confusion, adopting a "what's the point?" attitude can become a coping mechanism for those who feel as if they are being pulled under by the waves.

BUT *hello*, who do you think will send out the lifeboats or help you navigate towards the shore? It can only be you, of course, because the time has come when taking a stand is imperative to bring about a higher order of behavior that will ultimately lead to becoming an advanced race of humans *and possibly*, prevent your species from combusting! There is no doubt that many of you know what is right because you have an inner voice, called your conscience, that keeps reminding you of what is the most ethical thing to do at any given moment!

Knock Knock, It's Your Conscience

Unlike some of the other voices competing for your attention, your conscience can be simply described as *the inner voice that guides you to live with integrity and values.* This particular voice is the one you may have ignored when you took that candy bar when no one was looking, or when you decided that cheating on your taxes was no big deal. Yes, that voice.

More than likely, you have quite a few conversations going on in your head at any given time, including the one that keeps reminding you of your to-do list. But don't let your mind and ego interfere with what your conscience may be trying to say over all the chatter. Some may say they never hear their inner voice, or if they do, they make excuses to dismiss or completely ignore it.

It's important to pay attention, as there will be moments when you need to determine what is right and wrong to avoid acting on urges and desires that could lead you into trouble. For some humans, understanding their conscience and how it functions, *or doesn't*, can be compared to ignoring an important phone call or a loud knock on the front door while lounging on the couch.

Your conscience may nag at you when you've made a mistake, much like how your accountant consistently reminds you that your payment to the IRS is overdue. However, it is in your best interest to trust your inner conscience when faced with anything that challenges your fundamental ethics or moral values.

If reflecting on your conscience is not a priority for you, there is a good chance you have been disregarding important messages that could come back to haunt you later on.

A strong conscience that aligns with your character and values can help you make better decisions, ultimately leading you to live with integrity. It will help you understand that doing the right thing is not just about morals, but also about living a life free from the fear of facing negative consequences in the future. The best part is that when someone knocks on your door, you won't always have to worry about receiving bad news. Instead, there's a good chance it will likely be the delivery of the pizza you ordered.

"Conscience is the light of intelligence to distinguish good from evil." – Confucius

Dr. Youpoke Yopraugh (Dr. Yo Yo), creator of the Ultra Galactic Species Evolution Training Series, has this to say about the conundrum that some humans face when looking at themselves in the MIRROR of DECENCY.

"Okay, no beating around the burning bush or tossing tablets off a mountain because the bottom line is that a species needs a set of standards to live by, and drum-roll.... they don't have to be complicated! Look, if you want to fly by the seat of your pants (if you have them) and go along with every ding-dong you meet, or behave in ways that chip away at any decency that may still be clinging to you, then go right ahead and become a human who has no moral fiber or any shred of respectability, because folks, that will lead to consequences you will most likely regret.

Sure, it takes a spine (if a species has one, if not, visualize it) and a lot of courage to stand out and stand up for things that are right, decent and morally correct. In order to be someone who truly lives with honor, honesty and integrity, it will take some real inner strength, and quite possibly more than one cup of strong coffee, to become someone who does the right thing most of the time because deep down, it truly matters to be a good human, especially one who has no trouble having a second cup of coffee when things hit the fan!

Most importantly, if you can face yourself in the mirror and honestly tell yourself that you are a decent human being who stands for things that are important, like honesty and trustworthiness, then you can go about your day in a much happier way, because you have integrity. BUT, if you are lying, cheating, stealing, cussing, screeching absurdities and falsehoods, and acting like some absurd specimen that should not represent the human race, you need to go back to that mirror and take a real hard look at yourself and ask, would you trust and like the person you are looking at?" Cheers – Dr. Yo Yo

I'm Conscious, Isn't That Enough?!

Certainly, being alert and aware is necessary to navigate your existence and comes in handy when dealing with everyday activities. However, it would be even better if you had a higher level of awareness that could bring you closer to understanding certain concepts, maybe even the meaning of life! While not yet mainstream, developing your higher consciousness will increase awareness of the connection to Source, among other benefits. Understandably, many humans may still be grappling with everyday issues, such as deciding what to order for takeout or sorting through numerous unanswered emails. It's possible that maintaining a level of (higher) consciousness may not be a priority at the moment, unless it involves the use of certain mind-altering substances.

While understanding the differences in mental or spiritual states of mind may not be your preferred way of spending your precious time, it would be helpful to grasp some basics in your personal journey of evolution. A *shift* in perception allows you to view the world in a new light and fosters a sense of connection that extends beyond humans, to all life forms on and off your planet. This should spark some excitement in you to expand yourself and give it a try!

Elevated awareness is sometimes understood as having access to the higher mind, which allows you to loosen the grip of your ego. This enables you to experience a more inclusive and universal perspective, letting go of judgments, fears, biases, selfishness, and other limiting viewpoints that create barriers between humans (and even other life forms). **Trust in this shift**, as it opens the door for personal growth in every encounter, including those involving Advanced Beings sending messages through downloads!

The truly amazing advantages of having a higher mind include the ability to see beyond the illusion of false beliefs and experience other interesting side effects. We would love to expand upon this further, but that is best saved for another guidebook.[4] However, we can confirm that contrary to some misleading information circulating on your planet, the latest headlines from the Cosmic News Network (CNN) have verified that *the expansion of the human mind and spirit is the next evolution emerging on Planet Earth.*

Despite the various sh*tstorm scenarios that may suggest otherwise, there has been a continuous progression of human consciousness, and hopefully, there is more to come. Led by various enlightened humans, ranging from yoga masters to neuroscientists and everyone in-between, there is a commitment to advancing humanity during this crucial time, with some help from the sidelines of course.

Attaining a higher level of awareness helps with experiencing the different states of dimension that exist. It is an essential step in discovering your true nature and the real you, *because wouldn't you know it, your existence means something, even if you're not aware of it!*

"*The real revolution is the evolution of consciousness.*" – Anonymous

What State Are You In?[5]

Consciousness is the awareness of oneself and the world.

Conscience can be described as a belief in what is right and making decisions based on those beliefs. It means using moral strength rather than relying solely on gut instinct, along with the obligation to do what is best.

Higher consciousness is a state of elevated awareness and perception where one gains a deeper understanding of the nature of reality, the self, and various spiritual aspects of life.

All of these aspects play significant roles in personal evolution and psychological development.

"*Consider, if you will, that the universe is infinite. This has yet to be proven or disproved, but we can assure you that there is no end to your selves, your understanding, what you would call your journey of seeking or your perceptions of the creation.*" – Anonymous

---

Every human has equal, inherent value. Dignity matters.[6]

It should come as no surprise that dignity is your innate worth as a human being. Recognizing human dignity involves respecting the special value of human beings and giving them a basic level of respect. Ideally, dignity highlights the intrinsic and equal value of all humans and has the potential to change the world when extended to all living beings.

Having a clear understanding of who you are and what you stand for is reflected in your life, leading to personal self-growth and positive change. Your worth is a result of your ability to differentiate between right and wrong, truth and delusion, and to recognize the impact of your actions. Ultimately, your choices have consequences that not only affect your own life, but also have implications for humanity as a whole.

When someone has truly connected with their intrinsic self-worth, it cannot be taken away or destroyed by the actions of others.

Move into Alignment

If you want to test your moral and ethical abilities, you should make sure that you are in alignment before test driving this deluxe model. It's one thing to believe you have integrity, but another when the time comes to test it and you find that you don't always measure up. Creating an integration of your outer and inner life requires merging the two sides together to form a whole, consistent you.

Staying on the path to a higher moral ground works best when your internal code of behavior and philosophy are properly aligned. Your words and actions should be based on TRUTH as much as possible in all aspects of your life. A realignment is necessary for both the individual and society as a whole. This requires that high values be fully incorporated and honored in leadership, commerce, education, entertainment, culture, the environment, and communities.

In order to begin achieving a cohesive alignment, both individually and as a group, it is essential to establish a consensus on guiding principles that originate from an authentic core. Ideally, these principles will define a highly self-actualized human being.[7] Put simply, strive to live in a way that is consistent and harmonious with the *best version of yourself*, so that you can be proud of who you are every day (or at least every other day).

Stand Up and Stand Out

Commit to justice for all human beings.
Lift others up by helping them in positive ways.
Keep your agreements, commitments, and your word.
Check in with your principles to make the best decisions.
Develop strong personal values and take personal responsibility.
Act honorably and with integrity, even when no one is looking!
Respect the value, dignity and unique contributions of others.
Treat others with genuine respect and show gratitude to those who have earned it.

"To laugh often and much, to win the respect of intelligent people and the affection of children... to leave the world a better place... to know even one life has breathed easier because you have lived. This is to have succeeded." — Ralph Waldo Emerson

Oops! You've Made Some Mistakes

After delivering the challenging news that you need to do better, we want to remind you to be easy on yourself because mistakes happen! Don't be too harsh on yourself if you haven't always been the best version of yourself. Perhaps you haven't always used good judgment or made the best decisions. It happens. Maybe you've even done some questionable things, veered off course, or found yourself in a difficult situation. This is not the worst thing that can happen, as long as you learn from it and make changes.

Making mistakes, even some very serious ones, is sometimes the only way to *become conscious of your inner self*. Remorse combined with reflection is a beneficial tonic for the soul (if you have one, that is). However, if a human continues to make poor choices, whether consciously or not, then that becomes a problem. It can indicate either a real lack of self-awareness or, worse, a conscious choice that leans towards the dark side. This could lead to some serious consequences, which may include a friendly visit from your local chapter of the "Spawns of Satan," who we must remind you, *may or may not be actual spawns of Satan*.

If your mistakes are not beyond redemption, the good news is that you can always choose differently next time. Good deeds accumulate and have the ability to transform anyone into the best version of themselves. Just stay focused on making the best choices each day and recognize that it may be a bumpy ride until you reach a point where making wiser choices becomes almost automatic.

On Planet Earth, it is certainly easy to get sidetracked by alluring enticements that can be highly intoxicating. These can lead you astray into a state of oblivion, where you become dependent on sensations, substances, people, or experiences that try to fill an emptiness or boredom within you. But don't despair or lose hope. Embrace the fact that you're a work in progress. When you stop judging and blaming yourself, the path to LEARNING and GROWING from your missteps will become that much easier!

Mirror, Mirror on the Cosmic Wall

Dr. Yangoorish Yinish and Dr. Zoopa Zip, founders of the Advanced Being Behavioral Association (ABBA) and authors of "*Theories of Inter-Galactic Humor to Expand Cosmic Relations*" and "*If You Can't Laugh, You're Boring*," sincerely hope that humans will be inspired to start looking at themselves in their own mirrors, because what you see may not be who you really are.

"*Once upon a galaxy, a few stars to the left of the void, there existed a planet called Xyloni7. The inhabitants of this planet were, on the surface, beautiful beings who could change their appearance at will, much like a chameleon. However, beneath this facade, there existed a malicious essence that easily corrupted others, especially if they sensed* weakness or a negative inclination. They were incredibly dangerous if you happened to be around them for any extended period of time. Violence and deviant behavior were common, and many were drawn into their orbit of debauchery, corruption and vile behavior.

Often, visitors to the planet disappeared, never to be heard from again. Their treasures and gifts were taken and stored in great caverns, protected by gruesome creatures that the Xylonians created themselves. Bloodshed and death were common on the planet, and other creatures like them who craved this type of behavior, were drawn to the planet.

Unfortunately many of these creatures became servants to their brutal desires and compulsions, falling under the spell of the Xylonian's false beauty and treachery. Their path to self-destruction was inevitable, although it wasn't visible to those who happened to be there. Corruption and decay are not always visible. What you would see, and what we saw through, was a facade that concealed the lies and dishonesty.

Deception is a powerful tool that the user believes will work on others, but ends up destroying the one who is the deceptor.

For the Xylonians, gazing into their mirrors was a customary ritual that reflected their obsessive conceit and arrogance. Little did they know that looking into a mirror is not always a true reflection of who you really are, unless you look very deeply, past the image you believe you see. Their mirrors were illusions, wrapped in spells that were cast eons ago when the first of their kind began their civilization. The mirrors lied and deceived the Xylonians, preventing them from seeing who they really were. In truth, they did not want to know.

Those who look within themselves and know who they are, can look into a mirror and see that essence. Those who hide their true nature behind a facade will only show what they want others to see and what they themselves desire to see.

Not unexpectedly, the Xylonians could not sustain their civilization. Why? They could not be honest with themselves. Towards the end, there was much shrieking, cursing, and wailing. It was ugly all around and quite uncomfortable. Unable to face their lack of inner morals or decency, the negative energy ended up pulverizing their essence, reducing them to a form that solidified into a rock-like substance. Anyone visiting Planet Xyloni7 will still find these rock-like substances scattered throughout the planet. The party however, is over. If you found *this civilization even a little bit enticing, we would highly recommend that you take a long hard look at yourself. Yes, use a mirror if you have one. Do you respect what you see? Can you see the light that is within you? Look deep within, and beyond what you "visually" see. In truth, you actually don't need a mirror to face yourself, because* **you are the mirror.***" – Be Your Best, Dr. Yangoorish Yinish and Dr. Zoopa Zip*

"The only thing necessary for the triumph of evil is for good men to do nothing." – *Edmund Burke, philosopher*

Repeat After Us

I am truthful.

I speak well of others.

I keep my conscience clear.

I conduct myself with dignity.

I am honest with both others and myself.

I align myself with the greatest good for all.

I keep my word and my commitments.

I accept total responsibility for my actions.

I strive for fairness and justice in all my interactions.

I respect the uniqueness of all humans and species.

I find courage and strength to do what is best in each situation.

I stand for what is right, not what is convenient, even if it means standing alone.

I am not mean to snakes or blame them for something I did.

"Integrity is telling myself the truth. And honesty is telling the truth to other people." – *Spencer Johnson, M.D., author of "Who Moved My Cheese?*

Thoughts?

"A dignified life means an opportunity to fulfill one's potential, which is based on having a human level of health care, education, income and security." – *Global Dignity.Org*

Notes

1. Samuel, Sigal. *Technology is Making it Harder to be a Moral Human.* Vox (Aug. 2021) https://www.vox.com/the-highlight/22585287/technology-smartphones-gmail-attention-morality

2. According to the story of Adam and Eve, based on certain Judeo-Christian and Islamic traditions, the newly formed human couple supposedly left paradise after eating an apple. Some versions even suggest they were *thrown out* and instructed to become adults elsewhere. As they were considered the parents of the human race, their descendants were told this story as a lesson on good and evil, and perhaps as a warning to steer clear of snakes. This narrative may have inadvertently discouraged some humans from eating apples as well. Ultimately, there is a deeper message and purpose to this story, and it is open to various interpretations.

3. A moral compass typically refers to an internalized set of values and objectives that guide a human toward ethical behavior and decision-making. "Ethical" pertains to the principles of morality and refers to what is right and wrong in conduct or practice.

4. The Cosmic Collective on Spiritual Consciousness, with approval from the Universe, is collaborating on a new edition of spiritual advice in the very near present!

5. Different levels of consciousness can affect your behavior and influence your emotional and mental processes. Biswas-Diener & Teeny: Noba 2025 https://nobaproject.com/modules/states-of-consciousness

6. Declare your dignity and encourage others to do the same. https://globaldignity.org/wp-content/uploads/2019/08/Dignity-The-Essentials_Global-Dignity.pdf

7. The journey to reaching your full potential is ongoing. Kendra Cherry, MSEd https://www.verywellmind.com/characteristics-of-self-actualized-people-2795963

20. Where is the Love?

"All you need is love." – John Lennon, singer, songwriter and musician.

Love is Not Lost

While many believe that "love makes the world go round" and is a powerful force that motivates and supports human existence, there are those who feel that love has failed them, no matter where they happen to have looked. Therefore, it may be difficult to believe that searching for love may not be necessary, as it is not lost to begin with but instead, is *actually present within you!*

The idea of having your own inner source of love may seem implausible, especially if you are struggling with abandonment issues, loneliness, insecurity, or low self-esteem. To overcome the challenge of understanding your inner capacity for love, *a change in perspective is necessary.* This shift will allow for the expansion of a loving nature, ultimately leading to a positive impact on your energy. This will create an ability to rely on a higher love that comes from within, rather than relying on unrealistic expectations and demands from others. For those who are ready to accept the idea that "love is an inside job," this can be encouraging news.

When you experience a shift in understanding love, those in your orbit may become more receptive to your greatly improved vibes. You may become so elated that you might want to break out some appropriate libations or indulge in some delectable treats. Becoming a "love magnet" shouldn't come as a surprise, as a loving disposition naturally draws others in, with or without the ardent spirits!

If this concept seems "alien" to you, rest assured that enhancing your love vibes will transform your daily interactions, because wouldn't you know it, positive energy is an energizing mood lifter!

Of course, changes in perspective don't always happen quickly or easily, especially for those who believe they know everything about a subject but actually know very little. A lack of insight can cloud one's judgment, especially when it comes to romantic love and its various mating rituals. Some of these rituals are sometimes less than romantic, often centered around physical desires and passionate cravings. While they may start off exciting, they can fizzle out when there is a lack of a deeper connection.

What's more, searching for love shouldn't be the primary motivation in any relationship; instead, it should be the outcome of it.

Many times, what is mistaken for love is actually just attraction and lust, a HOT combo typically fueled by highly charged passions and uncontrollable hormones. This can lead to the possibility of a human losing control not only of their heart, but also of certain orifices and appendages.

Certainly, once the initial thrill subsides, there is always the possibility of a long-term commitment, but don't count on it. An idealized or unrealistic version of love is often unsustainable in the long term unless it is grounded in trust, respect, and commitment, among other things.

Without these essential elements, it can be difficult to withstand the realities and challenges that arise in a relationship. Lasting love is not just a feeling, but a conscious choice to nurture and prioritize the emotional, physical, and mental well-being of another.

Choose Love

The Universe encourages that in all matters of love, strive to be a loving human. This is when you are the best version of yourself. When you act out of love, things start falling into place because loving vibes are not only magnetic but also life changing. Whether you unconditionally love another human or a cute furball, showing love in any form ultimately comes down to this: *you choose to be a loving human being or you do not.*

A loving human demonstrates a genuine concern for the well-being of others without expectations, regardless of who or what they are, through affection, compassion, care, and sometimes even self-sacrifice. When love is expressed through action, it becomes an energetic force that when shared, becomes an act of transformation.

"Your task is not to seek for love, but merely to seek and find all the barriers within yourself that you have built against it." – Rumi, poet and mystic

Love Will Steer the Stars

In order to hurry up the Age of Aquarius, humanity will need to consciously amplify the energy of love to release the negative energy (sometimes resembling sludge) that is stuck in human hearts and causing blocked energy channels. It is essential to have more loving humans, not fewer, working together to find solutions to the many ongoing crises and conflicts. This will help humanity avoid ushering in the Apocalypse Age that certain malevolent humans appear determined to bring about!

A sustainable future and a more pleasant planet will depend on the MAJORITY of humans reaching out to *"touch someone with their heart"* rather than with unkind behaviors. None of these behaviors should be acceptable to a species that often insincerely supports the idea of love but fails to put it into practice when it is needed the most.

Of course, truly practicing loving behavior also requires believing that almost all humans, even the most difficult ones, benefit from loving intentions regardless of how negative they may seem. Approaching others with an open heart and the conviction that everyone deserves kindness is the foundation of genuine love in action. This perspective will allow humans to rise above negativity and respond with empathy, potentially inspiring positive change. Sometimes, it doesn't take much to change someone's heartspace. Often, even a small gesture of affection can start to soften a hardened heart because love has the power to heal.[1]

Ah, but perhaps our Cosmic perspective on love doesn't align with your own well-established beliefs or the latest theories on your radar, some of which may come from questionable sources. Judging by current behaviors and interactions, it's clear that deeply ingrained beliefs still influence how humans navigate the world. Breaking away from rigid mindsets or entrenched beliefs is not always easy, but the alternative of staying the same could be even worse.

Ding Ding!

It is time to recognize that humanity is still operating from an outdated manual that the Universe highly recommends be revised. Implementing "advanced updates" can provide numerous benefits that will last a lifetime and beyond. Have we mentioned the additional perks of a happier next-dimensional experience and karmic rewards? To receive these bonuses and more, all you need to do is *embody love and set things into motion.*

Love is an inner quality that sees good everywhere and in almost everyone. It believes that the potential to be good is within all, and by refusing to accept anything but good, it causes that quality to emerge. Love can be stubborn in that way.

Did You Know?

Love encompasses all of life, from loving your partner, children, family, friends, animals, rocks, trees, chocolate, books, and of course, *advanced alien beings*! Not surprisingly, some humans may find it easier to focus their love on anything other than another human being. But no matter who or what you love, what is important is that it leads you to the path of higher love for all beings, species, and Life.

However, you can't just sit there and do nothing! Love needs to be shared and put into action. It requires practice and may take multiple attempts to refine, unless you are an advanced master of some sort. Becoming a conduit for unconditional love and putting it into action can take a lifetime, or in most instances, more than one.

If you are somehow able to properly love in this existence, *ding ding*, you get a gold star and will move ahead to the next level! No matter what dimension you happen to be in, tapping into your inner love will positively impact the world and the universe around you. Love is the ultimate connection and the good news is, it doesn't depend on WIFI to work!

Not a believer in reincarnation or any other spiritual belief? No worries, no one is trying to force you into believing in karma. You'll probably have more than one chance to come around to it anyway.

Love is at the center of all life.
There are many different ways to express love.
Love is an energy that grows stronger when shared.

"*Love and compassion are necessities, not luxuries. Without them humanity cannot survive.*" – Dalai Lama

Let Love Conquer

Loving and respecting oneself appropriately is just as important as loving others. Consequently, there are times when it becomes necessary to set boundaries to avoid being treated in a harmful manner, no matter how much conquering you may want to do. The act of love should not blindly tolerate hate, hostility, violence, or cruelty, because unless you are spiritually advanced and can maintain unconditional love based on an evolved level of development, being exposed to extreme negativity can harm you.

Maintaining a loving attitude towards difficult and sometimes quite unlovable humans requires a big shift in your awareness (and heart chakra). It also requires having ample amounts of compassion and forgiveness. Of course, you need more tools in your toolbox. It's essential to have reserves of kindness, humor, patience and possibly even selective hearing because certain situations will test even the most benevolent human, and in some cases, even advanced beings!

Although loving difficult humans is not always easy, it is still possible to show love and compassion towards most of them, even if you don't necessarily like them.

However, when dealing with humans who do horrific things, your reserves of love can fly out the window, possibly causing you to feel emotions of hate and disgust towards truly reprehensible acts. Repeated exposure to "horrible humans" can eventually lead to giving up on the human race and can harden hearts (and possibly arteries).

It's not surprising then, that some humans eventually lose hope in the power of love to heal and transform both humanity and the world. It is crucial to prevent the spread of greater hopelessness and indifference, which often arise from the rampant cruelty and callousness of those who have unfortunately severed their ties to compassion and empathy.

The issues of hatred, divisiveness, and injustice must be properly addressed, or they will only continue to worsen and escalate the numerous interconnected crises that have reached a dangerous tipping point. Humanity's destructive ways must come to an end, or the human race may face extinction.

Major transformations are necessary to establish a truly cooperative global community in order to overcome the harmful actions of some very naughty and unloving humans. These negative behaviors impact all inhabitants of your planet and contribute to its deterioration. Humans must prioritize enhancing their interactions with one another to prevent further despair and suffering caused by the widespread malevolence of those who have lost their connection to love.

This evolution will require a conscious effort to heal past wounds, address injustices, and create a future where love and compassion serve as the guiding principles for all human endeavors. When empathy and ethical decision-making are upheld at every level of society, humans will feel empowered to challenge injustice and advocate for positive change. Only through such a holistic and transformative approach can humanity hope to eradicate the roots of cruelty and build a world where compassion, understanding, and respect for all are the cornerstones of your shared existence.

Ding Ding!

Humanity cannot overcome current and future crises without love as a part of the equation, as *the lack of love* is the root of almost all of your problems. The question to ask is this: *"Do you love the world and each other enough to save yourselves?"*

Love is Cosmic

"Awakening to the Essence of Love is to see the Higher Divine Being in another and in oneself. It is expressed and affirmed by the ability to see past all issues, negative behaviors and other assorted disgraceful deeds, and to accept the pure essence of that being. Higher Love is also acknowledging that the Supreme Love Energy is what connects you to ALL." – The B.O.S.S.

When you are able to see beyond a human's limitations, you will recognize the part of them that is pure love, even when there is very little evidence to show for it. By doing this, you become an agent for love.

Imagine that inside every human there is a "true-self" that is essentially the best version of oneself. Some may understand this as the higher self, while others refer to it as the soul. Some of you may have no idea what we are talking about. What is most important to grasp is that this part of you is connected to the universal divine spark, which is pure love energy.

If you find it hard to believe in a divine anything, then it may be helpful to focus on the ideal parts of yourself and other humans. This is the pure essence that exists without corruption, fear, anger, hate, or any other human dysfunction. It is what others can love about you and what you can love about others.

All of you possess a pure essence that is good, true, and joyful. And we truly mean all of you. Okay, maybe not every single one, but we remain optimistic. Within most of you lies the capacity to see beyond the facade of human behavior and to connect with what unites each of you. Yes, even in the darkest, most corrupted soul there is still the ability to access the spark of unblemished love. This is good news for those who tend to lean towards the dark side and may not know how to turn back the other way!

The failure to properly understand the "universal law of love energy" and its role in advancing the human race has unfortunately led to the current human and planetary crises. This reality is made worse by refusing to accept that all life is interconnected and interdependent on one another.

"The soul of the Universe is the Love you feel within." – Star~Ashanumi

Naughty Ones, Listen Up!

If you happen to be a naughty human, or in some cases, beyond naughty and are actually reading this guide (or know someone who should be reading this guide), please be aware that the days of causing trouble and turmoil are coming to an end, in one way or another. Although the Age of Aquarius has begun, it seems that malevolent humans at this critical juncture have absolutely no interest in becoming better versions of themselves! *Appalling, isn't it?* In fact, some of them are working on advancing their nefarious agendas without the slightest fear or concern of repercussions and consequences.

Whether you are a naughty human or not, in order to avoid negative influences from ruining your life on Planet Earth and beyond, one must become aware of their insidious force before it takes over completely. Negative energy feeds on the weaknesses and shadow sides of humans and other beings. This can be a struggle even for relatively good humans, who may sometimes end up doing terrible things that are out of character.

Acknowledging the shadow side does not necessarily mean that you will end up in a hellish dark pit or another miserable dimension. However, you will have a better chance of enjoying your existence, regardless of the dimension you are in, if you do not fully give in to the temptation of dark impulses that lead you away from love. Denying the existence of a shadow side within oneself, ignoring it entirely, or believing that focusing solely on positive energies will prevent negative ones, is not an effective way to deal with it.

A better approach to dealing with your shadow side is to recognize that you have the choice and ability to rise above it, rather than getting lost in the darkness. In any case, the good news is that for any lost soul who is ready to change before universal laws (and karma) kick in, the *Higher Power* will provide loving redemption for your naughty deeds. Simply ask, and the Universe will respond *because it has been set up that way!*

Accepting this deliverance should be a no-brainer for those engaging in any level of naughty deeds, especially when considering that without it, the resulting consequences will most certainly correspond to the severity of those deeds. It's never too late for a turnaround (even for spawns!) to fully embrace love, unless of course, one truly prefers all that hateful nastiness.

For those humans who are not interested in bettering themselves, or cannot or will not develop their ability to love, or at the very least make the effort, the Universe has a message: you either have a pathological brain disorder or actually prefer the dark side. Quite possibly, you may even enjoy being a spawn.

With the possible exception of a brain disorder, which may or may not include sociopath tendencies, most humans can avoid the dark side when they stay connected to the source of light within themselves. However, any being who intentionally chooses the dark side may have lost their connection to love and a higher power, and may find the dark side much more enticing, especially when it receives so much non-stop coverage! Even then, hope is not lost, as love will always triumph over darkness of any kind because Love is much more powerful. *Plus, it's fully backed by a 100% guarantee!*

Darkness is composed of light, and to emerge from darkness towards the light, one simply needs to remember that it is also made of love. *Negative energies will ultimately be transformed,* one way or another, no matter what choice is made.

LOVE is the energy of the Creator because the Creator is Love. This is true regardless of whether one believes in a Higher Power or not. Universal Truths do not depend on belief because they exist on a level that transcends belief. So whether one believes in God, the B.O.S.S., universal energy, spirit, Jesus, Buddha, Brahman, Bunnies, Allah, Mohammad, Dalai Lama, the Goddess, Santa Claus, the tooth fairy, little green Martians, **or even Us**, the truth remains that the energy of love unites us all. *It's called "intelligent design" for a reason.*

"Divine love makes us true to ourselves and to others. Divine love is the solution to our difficulties and problems. It frees us from every kind of binding. It makes us speak truly, think truly, and act truly. It makes us feel one with the whole universe. Divine love purifies our hearts and glorifies our being." – Meher Baba, spiritual teacher

Love is the way the Universe communicates with you.

Are you listening? You can respond and connect with the Universe by acknowledging that you are a loving being who is willing to share that love with others. The more you feel connected to universal love, the easier it is to be loving, especially towards those who need it most. There's no better time than now to raise your vibrations and use the power of love to bring about positive changes on Planet Earth. Love is the superpower that you've had all along!

Becoming one with Universal love means letting go of whatever is keeping you from that love. Within you is a sacred place that allows you to experience the harmony of Universal Love Energy. *Love is all there is.* It is the highest vibration in the Universe.

Since humans are already a part of the grand master plan of universal love, all one needs to do is go inward to the space where their heart energy and soul reside. From this center, allow yourself to feel the love expanding and permeating throughout you. Let it flow outward to others, even if no one is around. If you have plants or furry friends, they will notice. Take that feeling and connection, then imagine it as an energy that you can direct and share with whomever you encounter. Stay properly hydrated though, and while you're at it, *don't forget to water your plants!*

"Love is a moving energy which causes us to travel toward wisdom, goodness and the beautiful. Love is the primeval cosmic desire, the spirit which moves between the gods and people linking us all and giving birth to that which becomes ultimate and eternal. Love is that which transcends from the individual to the universal, bringing us spiritual inspiration and the great motivation of divine madness." – Socrates.

Love creates a vortex of positive energy!

Getting into the flow of love and grooving with the vibes requires some insight into finding the best way to fine-tune and balance these energies. This is important because there may be times when intense emotions or other challenges can destabilize or create a blockage, which can then negatively impact your vortex flow and possibly lead to the temporary suspension of your grooving.

Minimizing disruptions to your love flow and grooving abilities can be achieved through the time-honored activity of inner reflection and other mental, emotional, and spiritual tune-ups. If you are truly motivated and want to fast-track your evolving project, you may want to consider such things as balancing or tweaking your chakras, immersing yourself in some form of sacred self-care, or even scheduling a session or two with a Reiki healer!

While love energy is enhanced by nurturing wisdom, spirituality and emotional development, a truly loving heart is essentially simple and innocent, much like that of a baby. However, while managing and maximizing your energy is a worthwhile endeavor no matter how you go about it, there is no need to create a complicated strategy BECAUSE when it comes to the energy of love, you already have the tools within yourself.

What you should understand is that **LOVE** is the foundation of your being, strengthened and expressed through caring, patience, and kindness that *expects nothing in return*. Love entails having a generous nature and is shown through your actions towards others. It involves being fully present for another human by giving them your attention, time, and energy. Pure love without conditions is forgiving and supportive, without any hidden agendas or ulterior motives.

Love knows no boundaries; anything that separates is merely an illusion.

Love has the power to transform life on Earth.
(It's been within you all this time)

Love is the highest and most evolved state of being.
(If you still believe otherwise, you have not been paying attention)

We all have infinite love within us.
(It never goes away)

Love is a timeless state of unconditional joy.
(Take our word for it. You will be glad you did)

"Love is the bridge between you and everything." – Rumi

The Creative Power of Love!

Star-Ashanumi, Galaxy Sound & Visual Artist, Creator of *Galaxy Mega Hits* and other *Delightfully Divine Creations* & Member of the Cosmic Celebrities Care Council (CCCC), is a cosmic bright star who shines love and stardust into all corners of the Universe with soul energy. Star-Ashanumi embodies the power of loving creation, channeling cosmic visions to inspire all life forms.

This message is for you, Darling Earthlings!

"Love is the Current of my Soul"
(from the SoulStar Being collection)

"I paint my dreams upon the stars of your soul; so baby, shine with me as we sail on cosmic love, spinning in galaxies high above. See within me the universe of your heart, do not doubt, we have eternity to go.

Love is the message, as below, so above. Nothing changes but everything does. Who are we but stardust, glittering in the heart of Source, painting in colors of love on our souls forever, it is more than enough.

Love me baby, the way it is, 'cause love is the cord to the One Heart within. There's no distance between our souls, only love baby, that's all you need to know, 'cause once you do, you are one with ALL."

****

"My heartfelt poem for humans and Earthlings, and for my soul mates in all galaxies, I share with all my love. Don't you see how special you are to the heart that beats throughout the Cosmos? How many times does the Source need to show you that you are held dear and high, each and every one, even those who cling to the darkness? But the light will come through because it is the Light of Love, stronger than all.

Humans, sing with me the song of Love, for you know it well, but your ears and heart can be shut down. Do not let that happen, your Planet and fellow Earthlings need you to LOVE because there is nothing else for you if you do not. Humans, do not despair, because love will bind all hate and fear and toss it away if you let it. Humans, do not hate, for Love is the answer to hearts that are broken.

Humans, do not take anger as your solace. It will poison your heart, and only love can be the balm for broken dreams and brittle minds. Humans, take courage and Love yourself and others, for without LOVE you cannot exist, it is not possible and if you try, you will only be disappointed and broken. So look without and see, look within and see, look into another's heart and see, for the soul of LOVE is always there.

Peace and Love to you my Earthlings, I do LOVE you and know that I will be here, always, to listen to your dreams as you gaze up into the starry night. Shine your brightest, my lovelies." – Star-Ashanumi

This is your heart on Love. Just say yes.

Be patient.
Give comfort and support.
Be useful and of service in the world.
Express your appreciation and gratitude.
Forgive often and avoid blaming or shaming.
Love without expectations or strings attached.
Help others see their potential in themselves.
Do things in your daily life that reflect your love.
Love heals. Help someone who appears to be hurting.
Speak something true and beautiful that uplifts the spirit.
Allow life to unfold and love what is, not what isn't.
Be tolerant of those you love; allow them to make things right.
Offer a hug, a smile, or some form of encouragement to another.
Give your full attention. Listen attentively and with genuine interest.

A heart and soul is a terrible thing to waste.

"Love is patient, love is kind. It does not envy, it does not boast, it is not proud. It does not dishonor others, it is not self-seeking, it is not easily angered, it keeps no record of wrongs." – 1 Corinthians 13:4-5:

Don't just expect miracles. Be one!

Put down your weapons of destruction, your mass delusions of hatred and violence, and your illogical fear of each other. It is time to accept the truth that *anything humans do without love is doomed to failure.* Love is the key for humanity to open the door to a new way of living and being. Recognize that the transformational potential of love is based on a connection with the source of all love.

The Universe *is* Love

Without love, wisdom is not enough if it depends solely on ego or intellect and neglects heart-centered energy.
Without inner wisdom, love can become a highly charged irrational emotion that may lead to poor decisions.
Without both Love and Wisdom, creation would be impossible.

Repeat After Us

I am love.
I send out love.
I see love in all things.
Love resides within me; it is my natural state.
The more love I give, the more there is to receive.
I open myself to the beauty and love of the Universe.
Every day and in everything I do, love surrounds me.
I am connected with all things through love energy.
I am created from love and will continue to exist forever in love.

"*Try not to change the world. You will fail. Try to love the world. Lo, the world is changed. Changed forever.*" – Sri Chinmoy, spiritual leader

Thoughts?

"But I say to you, love your enemies, bless those who curse you, do good to those who hate you, and pray for those who spitefully use you and persecute you." – **Jesus,** carpenter, nomad and all-around benevolent ultra-supra-human and ADVANCED BEING who shared with the poor, tended to the sick, hugged and loved the destitute and unwashed masses, and who actually was a true representative of what love is all about. Yes, THAT Jesus, not the one who is being re-branded by dubious religious marketers and other unscrupulous humans.

Notes

1. Prison inmates who are given pets to care for are often transformed through love. Cohen, Jessica. Utne Reader (July 2019) *Animals and Inmates: Symbiosis and Redemption* https://www.utne.com/community/animals-and-inmates-zm0z19uzhoe/

PART IV
YOUR BREAKTHROUGH IS A CHOICE

21. To Evolve or Not to Evolve?

"In the kind of world we have today, transformation of humanity might well be our only real hope for survival." – Stanislav Grof, psychiatrist

What Will You Choose?

It's always best to make a choice while you still can. Your world is being held hostage by some very immature and dangerous human beings, which does not bode well for the future. Ongoing chaos and dysfunction cannot be sustained indefinitely. If there has been any improvement in humanity's circumstances by the time you reach this section, you may be reading the first edition, or humans may have started evolving rapidly!

The core message from the cosmos is that the human race must commit to evolving. While this is a serious issue to consider, we are fully aware that accepting guidance from "so-called" advanced beings requires a suspension of what you may have previously held as personal reality. Well, is your current reality serving you well? Now is the time to shift your world into a new reality that involves becoming better versions of yourselves. The way forward has been clearly defined. It encompasses decency, wisdom, civility, manners, goodness, humor, and love. Scarves are optional, but highly recommended. We believe that if a sufficient number of enlightened and mature humans rise to the occasion, choosing to make this shift will be a cause for celebration.

The main point is that when a species is committed to evolving and decides to finally grow up, anything is possible! The choice is clear: either accept the possibility that things may continue in the wrong direction, or decide to change course towards a new vision. Change is coming one way or another, and Planet Earth is now at the forefront of that transition. Not to be outdone, the Universe is also transforming and evolving. Consequently, humans will either collectively merge with the new energy or be stuck in a dimension that can no longer sustain itself.

"When the mob governs, man is ruled by ignorance; when the church governs, he is ruled by superstition; and when the state governs, he is ruled by fear. Before men can live together in harmony and understanding, ignorance must be transmuted into wisdom, superstition into an illuminated faith, and fear into love." – Manly Hall, author and mystic.

So, What Steps Will You Take?

Perhaps you are unsure of what to do next, or questioning the feasibility of change. After reading this far, you may feel tempted to give up and book a one-way ticket to Tahiti because the idea of humankind evolving may seem so far-fetched that it borders on absurdity. Undoubtedly, dealing with the necessary changes on your planet can be overwhelming, and taking any action may seem unrealistic or even hopeless.

As Cosmic Coaches, our mission is to inspire, awaken, and guide species towards a pathway of higher evolution. We believe in the vision of all our missions, even if the species in question does not believe in it themselves. The attempt to adequately convey information, based on common knowledge and wisdom in the Universe, is for the purpose of elevating the human race. We sincerely hope that positive transformations will become more common on your planet. Much of what has been conveyed in this manifesto aligns with many human wisdom traditions and cultural philosophies. At the very least, we hope that you are now giving more thought to becoming a better human!

Yet, perhaps a spark of inspiration has been ignited and you are eager to take the steps towards your inner blossoming. We can only hope that this is the case. The role of a life coach, whether human or otherwise, is to support positive change and growth towards a better future. The decision is ultimately up to you, as only you can choose to implement advice and suggestions for evolution. However, keep in mind that choosing to do nothing is likely not in your best interest, personally or globally. Improving humankind for the better necessitates a collective effort, *and that includes YOU!*

There may come a time when it becomes increasingly painful to stay the same rather than make the necessary changes. If you have been paying attention, you probably realize that the time is now. Sometimes, personal and global chaos can be an opportunity for growth. However, if left unaddressed, it can lead to escalating problems that may be difficult to manage, especially for those who are unprepared or resistant to change. Despite the challenges, a conscious shift is always possible, no matter where one falls on the Evolve-o-Meter.

Get on the Evolve-O-Meter

Remember that you are a work in progress, regardless of where you currently stand on the scale of evolution.

Rate the questions on a scale of 1 to 5:

1 = Absolutely.

2 = Yes, sort of.

3 = Sometimes.

4 = Are you kidding me?

5 = No clue; probably not!

1. You are taking steps to become the best version of yourself. _

2. You are open to advice, learning, and wisdom. _

3. You believe in making the necessary changes to improve and are willing to stay the course. _

4. You believe that humankind can move forward, starting with you._

5. You believe that transformation is possible even as humankind is experiencing a meltdown. _

6. You believe, or hope, that evolving can be fun and beneficial for both yourself and Planet Earth. _

7. You realize that evolving isn't just for those "yoga energy healing wellness woo-woo types." _

8. You are not going to wait for the "*Hurry up and Evolve*" show and are ready to roll now. _

9. Transformation has always made sense to you, and you know it must happen for survival. _

10. You have hope for humanity, even though it's going to be tough for a while. _

11. You believe that humans will finally start taking their evolving seriously. _

12. You agree with the concepts presented in this guide to improve as a human. _

13. You realize that humans can do better, be better, and ultimately grow up! _

14. You accept that anything is possible, including the idea of *Advanced Beings* publishing a guidebook and offering coaching advice. _

15. You are open to a new vision for yourself and the planet. _

16. You understand why human intelligence(HI) should take priority over artificial intelligence (AI). Or, you recognize that HI is a priority, even if you don't fully understand AI. _

Your results: _ _ _ _ _ _ _

Where do you stand on the Evolve-O-Meter? (Please note that you can always change the results).

16 –   **Wow, yippee!** Evolving, here you come. You have the potential to become an *advanced human!*

17-31   **Great!** You are on your way to becoming a better human through your efforts. Keep it up!

32-46   **Hmm...** you're kind of in limbo, but you're still open to working on yourself. Just keep going!

47-61   **Ugh Oh**. Please take another look at our advice and review the tips and suggestions.

62-80   **Yikes!** Either you're having a really rough day or worse, a tough life. Just know you're not alone.

If you are at level 16, please support other humans who need to evolve and share this guide with them.

"The secret of making something work in your life is, first of all, the deep desire to make it work. Then the faith and belief that it can work. Then to hold that clear, definite vision in your consciousness and see it working out step by step, without one thought of doubt or disbelief." – Eileen Caddy, spiritual teacher and writer

Taking a quick snapshot of your current situation can help clarify where you stand, especially if you are feeling stuck or in limbo. Are you planning on doing nothing? How is that working out for you right now? It's important to recognize that even making one change for the better is a positive step forward! However, if you're thinking of just continuing to "fly by the seat of your pants," remember that "winging it" has never been a great plan for humanity.

Focusing on making one or two consistent changes, and including some rewards and enjoyment along the way, can make the process of evolving feel less burdensome or unattainable. In fact, there's more to transformation or evolution than simply following a plan or checking off steps. Often, intuitive and creative methods are more suitable, but even those options usually start with a vision or intention.

There's also the possibility of immersing yourself in the mystical glitter of a spiritual awakening, or diving deep into a transcendental shift, which will elevate you to a higher state without the need for extensive note-taking. No matter how you navigate your path of inner evolution, make sure that you remain dedicated to it

Personal self-mastery can be a bumpy ride, so paying attention to where you are going and how you plan on getting there is not only sensible, but critical to your safe arrival. Sometimes you may need to take a break, but don't let that slow you down or stop you from continuing on your journey.

Stay the Course. Maintain positive energy!

Create a personal intention and vision.
Keep striving to stretch yourself.
Reward yourself when appropriate.
Keep your motivation and commitment steady.
Honor the time needed to reflect and develop.
Focus on the areas of growth that resonate the most.
Concentrate on positive affirmations and messages to stay inspired.

"The secret of change is to focus all of your energy, not on fighting the old, but on building the new." – Socrates

Take Some Notes!

Record your experience in a journal, collage, or by using technology.
Set aside time for honest reflection of your habits and mindset.
Document your positive changes as you gain self-mastery.
Stay connected to your higher vision to avoid falling back into old habits.

Keep learning but be selective. Not all advice is wisdom.

Stay curious.
Read personal stories and insights from others who have experienced transformations.
Utilize the library for inspirational and knowledgeable resources.
Connect with others who take self-growth seriously (and may have even read this guide).

Be willing to embrace discomfort

Change can be uncomfortable, but embrace it as it may become the new normal.
Recognize that staying within your familiar comfort zone can hold you back from personal growth.
Transformation means stepping into new environments and trying things you're not accustomed to.
Don't allow obstacles to hold you back. Find ways to build strength and overcome adversity.

Trust and Believe

Imagine how things will improve once you address your challenges.
Trust in your ability to overcome adversity.
Fear and a lack of trust can make it difficult to commit and can block the flow of energy from higher realms, ultimately hindering the process of transformation.

Connect with Kindred Spirits

Find support from others who embrace self-discovery and are open to a new paradigm. Transformation happens faster when you surround yourself with like-minded individuals who are on the same journey.

"Our challenge is to create a new language, even a new sense of what it is to be human. It is to transcend not only national limitations, but even our species isolation, to enter into the larger community of living species. This brings about a completely new sense of reality and value." – Thomas Berry, "The Ecological Age," in The Dream of the Earth

What the Shift?! Common Signs

- Things are falling apart at increasingly high levels.
- There is a growing need for alone time and reflection on the future.
- Transformation may start slowly but can quickly accelerate.
- Negativity and chaos are pointing out what no longer works for humanity and society
- Many feel lost or confused. While this is not a new phenomenon, more humans are now recognizing it.
- Expect heightened levels of frustration, especially when the realization sets in that there is no going back, and the path forward is unclear!

"The great solution to all human problems is individual inner transformation." – Vernon Howard, teacher and philosopher.

Achieve Cosmic Velocity!

Integrate wisdom teachings and a higher vision as pathways to transformation.

Nurture your mind, body and soul through reflection and spiritual self-care.

Acknowledge both what you know and what you don't know.

Share positive energy with others. Sprinkle in some love!♥

Inspire yourself and others with joy, authenticity and a zest for life.

Recognize that you possess a great gift – the power of choice.

"How wonderful it is that nobody need wait a single moment before starting to improve the world." – Anne Frank, German-born Jewish girl who kept a diary

Are You Ready to Evolve? Thoughts?

---

22. Just Imagine

"Some say we are dreamers, envisioning the Universe as One. This vision is no illusion, but an awakening for everyone." – Star-Ashanumi, Artist

If you aren't already a dreamer, become one. If you don't have a vision, create one. If you've lost your imagination, go and find it. And, if you're not inspired, then figure out why! What the world needs now, in addition to more love, is visionary humans. When inspiration is boldly and creatively expressed, it has the power to unite and energize humans to achieve extraordinary things.

The prospect of the human species lacking a *new cosmic vision* should be a cause for deep concern. Humanity's path to a brighter tomorrow hinges on visionary minds that dare to evolve and guide civilization forward. By aligning your lives with the Universe and embracing a life filled with love, a grander vision of what is possible becomes within reach. This may seem far-fetched to those who are facing daily challenges and disruptions that leave little room for dreaming and holding a higher vision.

Embarking on a life filled with inspiration is a noble ambition because it will motivate you to believe in a new dream. The ability to bring about a new vision, filled with sparkle and enchantment, is not exclusive to a select few. Do not allow indifference and numerous distractions to diminish your visionary abilities. Now is the time to reignite the human spirit and dream anew.

Just imagine the possibilities if humanity were to combine their collective creativity and imagination to create a bold new vision of life on Planet Earth.

"A very great vision is needed and the man who has it must follow it as the eagle seeks the deepest blue of the sky." – Crazy Horse, Lakota Sioux, leader

Be Like the Eagle

To become a creative visionary, one must have a vision of both the present and the future. Take the time to dream and become inspired. Keep your mind open to new stimuli and see things as if a child again. Daydream, stay curious, and be open to MAGIC and stardust. Truly notice the beauty that surrounds you in your world.

Go out into nature and take a deep breath of fresh air. Look around and up at the sky, focus on a flower, or anything else that catches your eye.

If you cannot go outside, start using your imagination (the ultimate virtual reality)!

What do you notice? What do you see, hear, sense, and smell? How are you feeling? Try not to overthink.

Connect with the part of yourself that is your inner dreamer.

It may be buried under all the stuff you've been accumulating over the years, but it's there.

Notice that little spark. Feel it! Expand on the vision that your spirit is yearning for.

It may not just be about you; perhaps it includes a larger picture.

Start with that spark. It will ignite and glow. Encourage the embers of your dreams so that they can take hold.

It can all feel quite magical, this dreaming process. Fairy dust and all.

Visualizing ignites your imagination and dreams. When this process is initiated, your intuition and creativity will flow. Nurture your inner visionary with whatever sparks your imagination. Make sure you have enough scissors, glue, pens, paper, paint, glitter, and whatever else you may need to bring your dreams to life!

Reflect
Dream, Imagine, Visualize
Create the Vision
Add something Sparkly
Develop a plan of Action
Share it and Create Momentum

"When you're dreaming, you're connecting with the ultimate cool vibes of creating." – Sirius Lee Cosmic

---

When you Wish Upon a Star, the Universe Listens!

A creative visionary uses their imaginative abilities to bring forth something new and unique. Wishing upon a star isn't considered crazy because visionaries can imagine what is possible and impossible. They use their inner creative powers to make it happen and bring forth solutions, artistic creations, and innovative ways of living. Every human has innate creative potential, and by embracing this gift, extraordinary visions can come to life.

Creation depends on imagination, vision, and energy to manifest it into reality. Humankind already has all the tools they need within themselves. A brighter vision for humanity and a new Earth already exists within your souls – just bring it forth and co-create with the highest visionary of all.

"Wishing upon any star is meditative, thus allowing the spark of inspiration to twinkle or in some cases, ignite into a full-blown explosion." – Master Yogishimi Yami Zami, Guruologist

Like a Great Creator, A New Vision is Here...

- Nature and the environment thrive in harmony with all living things. Trees and plants flourish, air and water are clean, animals, rain forests and oceans are healthy, flowers bloom, bees buzz and pollution is non-existent. Planet Earth is HAPPY!

- The climate crisis is under control and disaster has been averted. Ecological awareness is now integrated into education systems worldwide. Humans feel connected to the Source, both on and off the Planet.

- Mother Earth is respected and revered, and her BEAUTY is a gift that humans appreciate.

- Humans are now stewards of the environment, effectively managing the planetary system in a sustainable manner

- Animals are treated with respect and humane consideration.

- Poverty and hunger have been eradicated, and life's necessities are available to all.

- Wars and weapons of mass destruction have been eliminated, and violence is almost non-existent.

- Every human has the choice to fully participate in society with equal opportunities.

- Social challenges and disagreements are effectively resolved without resorting to violence.

- Societies care for and support the most vulnerable among them.

- Monetary systems are not driven by greed or outdated, unfair capitalist objectives.

- Humans can realize their potential and thrive without worrying about money, living expenses, or fear of poverty.

- Art, music, and theater are elevated as essential components for happiness and joy, free from commercialization.

- Governance truly represents all humans, with corruption and abuse of power being eliminated.

- Education at all levels, as well as social and spiritual development, is accessible and inclusive for everyone.

- Positive mental, physical, and emotional health are enhanced through increased happiness, security, and an understanding of integrative health. Wellness is viewed as multidimensional and holistic. Addictions have been eradicated.

- Community and family connections are strong and supported in all societies.

- Communication is based on authenticity, integrity, and honesty. Finally, telepathy has a chance!

- Ugly buildings and other unattractive spaces are replaced with architecturally pleasing edifices.

- Chocolate and ice cream are nutritionally dense super-foods that are freely available to all.

- Technology has lost its hypnotic hold over humans and is considered just another tool in the toolbox.

- Humans finally agree that there is only one race on Planet Earth – the human race (for now anyway).

- All humans, regardless of nationality, gender, culture, or color, are treated equally and with respect.

- The Library is as important as any religious temple, church, or worship space.

- Religions have come together to cooperate and share a united message: the focus is on spirituality and love, not dogma.

- Plush animals have become talismans of love in every home.

- Planet *Kinder*garten has become the official training program for humankind (not surprising).

- Scarves are a popular global garment that creatively display one's unique self.

- Smiling and content humans are now considered the new normal.

- Humankind has matured and evolved. *It's about time!*

- Very naughty humans are now few and far between.

- Quantum space travel has become an option.

- **Magic and Wonder have returned to the world!**

- **AND Cosmic visitors are welcomed and embraced on Planet Earth.**

"*Perhaps a new revelatory experience is taking place, an experience wherein human consciousness awakens to the grandeur and sacred quality of the Earth process. Humanity has seldom participated in such a vision since shamanic times, but in such a renewal lies our hope for the future for ourselves and for the entire planet on which we live.*" – Thomas Berry, "Ethics and Ecology" in The Great Work

We've got a better world in mind![1]

"*I like being human most days. But on some days, I would much rather be an intergalactic sorceress or wizard-like being, with lasers shooting glitter from my orbitals.*" – L. ChakraZara

Your Vision is the Mission!

"*The Cosmic Dream is within all of you, weaving and spinning for all eternity. All you need to do is align yourself with it and allow it to emerge.*" – The B.O.S.S.

Notes

1. Anderson, Berit and Hanna, Christine. *We've Got a Better World in Mind.* YES! Media (2020) https://www.yesmagazine.org/issue/world-we-want/opinion/2020/02/19/world-vision-future

23. Reset Your Codes

"Laws control a lesser person, right conduct controls a greater one." – Chinese Proverbs

T he Universe represents the entirety of existence and is dedicated to promoting the well-being and right conduct of all life forms. It believes that all beings should strive to bring out their best, just as much as the Universe aims to consistently inspire the best in you.

Remember, the B.O.S.S. affirmed your potential and proclaimed, "Do not underestimate the cosmic power that is within all of you. We know all about it, we put it there!"

A code of conduct provides guidance to navigate the evolving process. Codes are typically based on an agreed-upon way to behave collectively and individually with each other. Evolving is hindered when there is a haphazard approach to basic universal standards, especially if a species tolerates or accepts low levels of behavior. Please revisit the *"Behavior Unbecoming"* and *"Do Better"* chapters of this guide if you need a refresher.

When there is a cooperative global effort to adhere to a code of conduct, it benefits everyone and gives humans the skills they need to coexist and better themselves. Fortunately, humankind has already established various templates and ideas on *worldwide ethics* that humans can expand upon.[1] Therefore, creating and following a set of planetary codes of conduct should not be difficult, as there are already humans practicing them.

Basic rules can be learned on Planet *Kinder*garten, where young *kinder*gartners have already established high standards that adult humans can easily and effectively adopt for themselves. If a 5 or 6-year-old human child can learn how to behave on Planet *Kinder*garten, shouldn't adult humans be able to do the same? Regardless of whether it involves fun motivational tools like charts and stickers, adults can surely find ways to motivate themselves towards positive behavior. Perhaps it's time to incorporate Planet *Kindergarten's* common incentive plans, such as naps, snacks, playtime, and other fun activities to encourage those who need it.

Stay in the Cosmic Loop

Maintaining high standards can be challenging when trying to figure out "what comes next," especially during times of chaos. However, having a universal code of conduct is not only ideal but essential for staying in the cosmic loop.

It is crucial to recognize that what is considered acceptable human behavior on Earth may not be acceptable to certain evolved species in the galaxy. This is especially important to keep in mind when these life forms encounter humans for the first time. If one species has very high standards while the other does not, and the less evolved species does not adhere to acceptable levels of conduct, there is a likelihood of a negative outcome that impedes the formation of a connection or relationship.

Set Your Codes

A code of conduct or ethics is a set of values, guidelines, and principles that outline how to behave and interact with each other, and sometimes with other intelligent life forms such as aliens or advanced beings. Many evolved species establish codes of conduct based on their core values and use them to influence the actions and behavior they expect from each other.

The Cosmic Code of Conduct is a set of principles that promote advanced behavior throughout the universe. Higher evolved species adhere to higher standards not out of obligation, but because *it is the*

---

right thing to do. Placing a high value on one's conduct in various situations is a sign of development.

Without high standards of conduct, it becomes challenging to resolve conflicts, prevent violence and address dysfunction, ultimately hindering a species evolution. The Cosmic Code of Conduct provides insight into the expectations of advanced life forms, regardless of their location in the universe.

"Virtue depends partly on training and partly on practice. You must learn first, and then strengthen what you've learned by practice." – Lucius Annaeus Seneca

Creating your own planetary code of conduct is possible when it is based on agreed-upon ethical principles that are fundamental to human evolution and the future of the planet. These codes should reflect a culture that all humans are willing to promote for the highest benefit of all.

Universal Cosmic Codes

Do No Harm.
Live with Honor.
Act with Dignity.
LOVE one another.
Elevate Justice and Fairness.
Share Knowledge and Wisdom.
Do Not hurt or kill other Beings.
Respect yourself and all life forms.
Require a culture of Honesty and Truth.
Earn and create Trust by being authentic.
Foster Optimism and a Positive mindset.
Do Good, or at the very least, do your best.

Cultivate Compassion and Empathy for all Beings.
Promote Self-discipline and keep your Promises.
Extend Goodwill to other beings and all life forms.
Strive for the Common Good of all Beings and species.
Cultivate Integrity in your words, actions, and thoughts.
Elevate Courtesy and Civility in all forms of communication.
Live with High Principles that are a guiding force in all you do.
Allow Open Dialogue, Listen to Understand and Agree to Disagree.
Uphold an elevated Vision of what is possible for the highest good for All.

Sharing the ideas in this book.

We hope that you will share our message mindfully and respectfully. So what do we mean by this? It means that you should give credit to the Source, the authors, and the intent of the message. Feel free to mention our guidebook to those in your orbit through social media, and even suggest it as a gift for those who may benefit the most from it.

Any references to us or to our human author, L. ChakraZara, should acknowledge that this unique work aspires to encourage personal and spiritual growth through the guidance reflected in this guide. Our intention is to enlighten as many Earthlings as possible, not to boost our egos or win a popularity contest. If we do gain attention and become well-known, so be it, as long as the focus remains on the mission and message.

> *"Sometimes, the message is all that really matters, regardless of its source."* – AB1 & AB2

Cosmic Copyright Code

The prospect of someone claiming this work as their own for personal gain or recognition would be extremely disheartening. Such actions are unethical, dishonest, and reflect poorly on one's character. It should be evident that plagiarizing and stealing someone else's ideas and work is not a hallmark of an evolved human. If this is not clear, we recommend carefully reviewing our guide to gain the necessary insights to fully understand. At some point, you may even be inspired to write and share your own journey of growth and discovery.

Furthermore, it is important to realize that Advanced Beings possess *advanced methods* of detection and knowledge. Whether you believe in this or not is irrelevant. Some may view this entire book as the mere ramblings of an ordinary human who added the "alien angle" for attention. However, take a moment to ask yourself, "*How can I truly know that?*" Well, the reality is you cannot. Therefore, carefully consider what you are going to do before you do it. Actions have consequences not only in your world but also in the galaxy and beyond.

Ultimately, we hope that the message of *"hurry up and evolve"* encourages a shift that will move humankind forward towards a positive future.

"*Your intention when using technology and your voice should be to positively impact others, not to negatively influence them.*"
– *Star-Ashanumi*

Notes

1. Winkler, Enno A. *Are universal ethics possible? A systematic theory of universal ethics and a code for global moral education.* Original Paper, Open Access. Pub. (May 2022) https://rdcu.be/c9D9M

24. You've Got Questions?

We Thought So.

When it comes to the subject of extraterrestrial life forms, questions[1] are to be expected. Who wouldn't be curious about Advanced Beings downloading information in written form? However, whether or not certain questions get answered depends on the particular species in question. It is best to keep expectations realistic because, more often than not, some questions either have no answers or require finding your own answers.

We have compiled a few responses to common queries that are frequently asked throughout the universe, tailored specifically to humans. Providing explanations is done on a *need-to-know* basis, evaluating what is most appropriate when interacting with a life form, especially one that is still working on its own growth. There are many pressing questions to which humans will want answers, but the most urgent one, in our opinion, is: *"When will humans begin to hurry up and evolve?"*

Q. Are You Really (*REAL*) Aliens?

A. We are REAL Advanced (alien) Beings.

Despite our earlier explanations in this guide, some humans will probably continue to use the term "aliens" instead of "Advanced Beings." Nevertheless, we are genuine advanced alien beings from a very nice planet located in a distant galaxy, both in terms of physical distance and evolutionary progress.[2] This galaxy is not (currently) visible on your Intergalactic Search Systems, so there's no need to bother the busy humans who study space or any other stargazing humans with very large telescopes.

To clarify, *real aliens* who are considered Advanced Beings typically offer some form of cosmic life coaching and provide advice and guidance in a manner that benefits all involved. The majority of these advanced beings focus on helping less advanced life forms, such as humans, evolve. However, there are some *real aliens* who may not be as advanced and may actually require assistance with their own evolution. In fact, most *typical aliens* probably wouldn't bother including a FAQ section in their guide, assuming they even had one. Indeed, there is a wide range of beings in the Cosmos in different stages of development and evolution, similar to the diversity found on Planet Earth.

Simply put, Advanced Beings are not limited to being defined as aliens, extraterrestrials, space creatures, or Martians (they've relocated to another galaxy), or any other cosmic entities that currently lack description in the human language. What's more, Advanced Beings are considered legal across all galaxies. In fact, anything existing in the cosmos is "officially authorized" by the B.O.S.S. Therefore, we not only EXIST in multiple dimensions and forms, but we are also *officially real!*

Q. Do you look anything like the drawings in this guide?

A. Nope.

We decided that images of friendly-looking aliens would be more reassuring. After reviewing various images, cartoons, and browsing the web, we had a better idea of what would be the least threatening. While we understand the curiosity about our appearance, what we look like isn't a priority and could create unnecessary distraction or simply get lost among the countless images available everywhere. We will admit though, that we are quite photogenic and considered attractive in more than a few dimensions and galaxies.

HOWEVER, we would like to point out what we don't look like!

We do not resemble any type of insects,* whether small or large, gooey or non-gooey, with or without large jaws, teeth, and claws. We are not robots, metal-encased beings, or metallic-like objects. We do not look like gelatinous blobs of goo, oozing blobs of goo, large jelly-like blobs of goo, or anything resembling Earthling fish, lizards, or other creepy crawlers, gooey or not. We also do not have exceptionally large teeth or lots of tentacles. However, testicles are a different story (LOL).

Note: We have nothing against Earthling insects, blobs, fish, lizards, crawlers, etc. It's just that we do not resemble them.

Q. How are you able to communicate using words, and why is it in English?

A. We would prefer telepathy, but not many humans communicate in this way.

It is unfortunate that telepathy is not a common form of communication among humans. Telepathy, along with empathy, has the ability to convey concepts, feelings, and other things faster and more effectively than words. The question of how this is done, specifically the interpretation and translation for a species that is different from your own, may have to wait until humanity progresses.

The closest we can come to describing this capability is that it involves optimizing a process of "mind meld" and "thought absorption." Is this like reading someone's mind or brain? Perhaps, although it is more involved than just a quick scan. However, there's no need for any human to be concerned that we would somehow *"impolitely invade your brain."* As Advanced Evolved Beings, we prioritize being respectful and leaving things just as we found them, especially when it involves another species' minds and brains!

It was decided that the best way to communicate with humans would be to choose from the various human languages currently in use and then transcribe it into text.* After utilizing our receptors and conducting a quick search on your Internet, it was confirmed that English is the most widely used global language on your planet. Translations of this material in other human languages are assumed to be available through various transcription tools.

Q. Are you orbiting in a spacecraft near our planet?

A. We are on standby.

Earthling technology cannot pick up any signals due to our advanced "cloaking" devices. We have no intention of materializing in solid form or landing our "spacecraft" on Earth, for reasons that should be obvious by now. However, if you are still unsure as to why we are observing and not landing (or visiting), the simple answer is that humanity is not yet prepared to properly receive guests from the universe until a higher level of advancement has been reached.*

Unfortunately, due to ongoing conflicts among humans, the chances of any extraterrestrial species, such as aliens, Martians, Advanced Beings or other cosmic creations receiving a warm welcome are slim. Unless, of course, they happen to visit Planet *Kinder*garten!

Note: *Some planets and species are simply not ready for visitors!*

Q. Can you read our minds?

A. Yes, but we prefer those that are mindful.

We are telepathic and empathic, allowing us to selectively tune into thoughts, despite the high levels of mindless chatter on inner channels. Additionally, we are adept at setting appropriate boundaries, like taking long breaks from our telepathic surfing to avoid negatively impacting our own minds.

Q. Why are spacecraft, UFOs, and UPAs[3] being seen more frequently?

A. Some of us like to show off, especially those with the newest models.

Q. Is Planet Earth the only planet with life in the galaxy, or are there other planets similar to Earth in the universe?

A. No and yes.

It is understandable why some humans still believe that Planet Earth is the only habitable planet in the galaxy. There are numerous conspiracies, fake facts, and misinformation, BUT so little time to sort them all out, especially when there is a lack of critical thinking skills. Let's burst that cosmic bubble right now.

You are not the only life form in the galaxy. We repeat, you are not the only life form in the galaxy.

Whether this is good news or bad news may depend on a human's expectations and convictions.* On Planet Earth, there is a WIDE range of beliefs, sometimes influenced by cultural and religious doctrine rooted in various creation theories. One especially popular belief is that God's *divine plan*, also known as the "Planet Earth project" in the cosmos, was to create the human race and an assortment of other Earthly life forms to keep it company, with some especially nice landscaping thrown in.

This creation theory suggests that once things were wrapped up, the Creator decided it was time for some rest and put all other "life-form creating" projects *on hold* for the rest of the Universe. Hmm. Does that make any sense to you?!

Think about it. If we continue to follow the theory that the Master Planner of the UNIVERSE would somehow decide to create ONLY ONE nice, livable planet (one that humans are still EVOLVING on, sheesh!) with some uninhabited "lifeless" planets thrown in for good measure, but then inexplicably chooses *not* to replicate this successful life-building blueprint elsewhere in the galaxy (and beyond), it raises the inconceivable possibility that the Creator was just passing time, got bored, and then decided to take a long and well-deserved break!

Does any of this sound like something a HIGHLY Intelligent Being would do? If for some reason you answered "yes," then we have some real estate on Jupiter that you might be interested in. Take all the time you need to reflect on any beliefs that may be limiting your perspective. However, keep in mind that limited viewpoints have frequently held back the human race. Changing one's perspective is a choice that requires a readiness to fully accept that *some things are not always what they seem.*

Without a doubt, the realization that Planet Earth may NOT be the only planet with intelligent life (or in some cases, unintelligent) in the universe, can result in a range of strong reactions, from fear to excitement and everything in between. Contemplating life elsewhere in the galaxy while still dealing with life on your own planet can initially be quite mind-boggling and overwhelming. It would be understandable and easier to continue with the current paradigm,** but in case you haven't noticed, that paradigm isn't working anymore.

While there are other life forms in the Universe, humanity should be focused on the future of ALL LIFE on Planet Earth because right now, that Life is what truly matters!

Who knows, discovering that humans have galaxy neighbors might inspire humankind to fully develop and become cosmic citizens! It's important to note that diversity and cooperation are standard practices in any well-functioning galaxy, so humans will need to address their own diversity-related challenges. The universe is full of diverse life forms, and just like on Earth, some life forms are in different phases of evolution. This could mean that they may not be highly advanced or intelligent, or they are intelligent BUT also disruptive and hostile.

Reflect on this: If the *Creation of Life* just happened randomly or was a function of a natural process, wouldn't it still require some form of "outside" intervention to get started? How can any process truly be considered random or just form by itself? Life creation necessitates intention, purpose, process, and a PLAN. And most importantly, it requires a creative HIGHLY ADVANCED intelligence, one that can be challenging to imagine for most beings. If you happen to notice that some of this seems similar to creating your own evolving Life Plan, good for you!

Note: Some humans may not believe in any creation theory, or perhaps, not even care about how it all began. We acknowledge the right of every human to hold different opinions, alternative theories, or no theories at all. This includes the right to believe that the Creation of Life is or was a random series of events, a "one-off" occurrence that may have started accidentally.

A paradigm *is a pattern, perspective or a way of viewing something.*

Q. Why haven't galactic messages from humans been answered by aliens or E.T.s?

A. Is this a serious question?

The Intergalactic Cosmic Outgoing Voicemail Message:
"Hello, thank you for reaching out! Feel free to leave us a detailed message or try again when you are sufficiently evolved. Your call may be answered within the next 3-5000 business eons. At this time, we cannot respond to emails, chats, or texts. If this is an emergency, please hang up and dial 911.[4] Have a nice eon, bye bye."

It can be frustrating to initiate any form of contact and not receive a response, even after several attempts. You may start to question what it could mean – maybe the message didn't go through, there's a malfunction with your device, or maybe the message was sent to the wrong recipient – without considering the very real possibility that it may actually have something to do with YOU and that perhaps, when you don't get a response, there's likely a valid REASON!

The reasons for not returning human long-distance calls are essentially the same reasons why there will be no in-person contact at this time, at least not from us. Although who knows about random aliens at this point? None of this should be surprising, unless, of course, the prevailing human assumption is that an advanced civilization would not evaluate their visit to another planet before the actual visit! When humans travel to distant lands, do they not review the culture, conditions, climate, and so on BEFORE they go? Who among you enjoys visiting hostile and unfriendly places to meet other humans or see new things? We cannot make it any simpler than this!

In any case, the current lack of response is considered to be the only appropriate one at this time. However, all messages have been noted and saved. Additionally, many in the galaxy are well aware of Planet Earth and its inhabitants because advanced beings (and some aliens) can pick up signals without the need to intercept numerous messages repeatedly.

When attempting to make contact in the universe, it is crucial to understand the true reasons for seeking a response AND to be prepared if one is received. There is always the possibility that your messages will be intercepted by unintended recipients. Therefore, it is advisable to focus on advancing your own evolution before reaching out in order to avoid any consequences from those you may not want to hear from!

Note: *In a recent study, the Coalition for the Cosmos Communicates to Connect concluded that any human contact with an advanced race would be unproductive as humans are still struggling to communicate with each other. Hello! High levels of interpersonal communication skills* among all human cultures are a basic prerequisite not only for evolution but also for forming connections with species unlike your own. Therefore, as humans improve their connections with each other, there will be a higher probability that their long-distance Cosmic Calls will finally be successful!

Q. What does being advanced really mean?

A. Being advanced means that one is highly developed, complex, ahead in knowledge and progress, and much evolved from an earlier ancestral type. Advanced Beings also enjoy wearing scarves and have a highly developed sense of humor.

To truly advance, whether human or not, one must embrace the concept of integration and unification. This involves fully accepting a holistic, multi-dimensional, and interconnected view of all things, all life forms, and the Universe. Advancement for a being typically starts with the individual but it can also be a collective choice, especially when there is complete and universal acceptance of higher consciousness. Shifting one's consciousness is key to evolution.

The human being will evolve when it can expand its consciousness and reach its creative potential. For those who may be thinking, "What the heck is this all about?" don't be discouraged. Keep making the effort because you may end up surprising yourself one day when a shift does happen!

Certainly, humans have come a long way and progressed to a higher level of existence, even if not everyone experiences those benefits equally. However, a truly advanced civilization prioritizes inner growth, so that any outer progress reflects genuine development that benefits all life forms, including the Earth itself. This may seem like a fantasy, but it's not! If humanity continues to confuse the concept of progress and persists in its focus on developing harmful technology* rather than on improving themselves from within, there is a high likelihood of an implosion. This fixation on material progress over all else is hindering YOUR inner development!

Humanity must discover its "formula" to become an advanced civilization. Advancing to a higher level of evolution requires a foundation of wisdom, ethical behavior, and intelligence grounded in philosophical, spiritual, and emotional comprehension. Empathy and self-awareness would help, as well as some chocolate. Not only are these qualities essential for advancement, but could aid in navigating the numerous crises humanity faces, such as ecological disasters, disruptive technology, dangerous weapons, infectious diseases and perhaps most alarming of all, a group of human ding dongs** who may jeopardize your survival.

Humanity is still considered an emerging civilization that is progressing somewhat unevenly. Fully understanding the concept of evolution will be necessary before the opportunity is lost. That would truly be a shame but well, you know, this is what karma and consequences are all about.

*Note: *Most humans may not fully understand what Artificial Intelligence entails, while others are rushing ahead to use it without grasping its potential issues. It would be wise to focus on improving human intelligence before hastily developing technology that could surpass humans, potentially leading to disastrous consequences for humans, not for AI. Consider this a warning.*

Human Ding Dongs *have nothing to do with those yummy chocolate cream-filled cakes like Ring Dings and Ding Dongs. We suspect that many humans secretly indulge in those treats, even though they may not be very nutritious. However, human ding dongs can be just as unhealthy, if not more so, and are anything but yummy, as they are likely loaded with artificial substances. Many of them are also annoying, disagreeable, unruly, contentious, and sometimes, dangerous!*

Q. Will there be any abducting and probing?

A. No, **that is a ridiculous question.**

While some humans may wish to be abducted and possibly probed, we have no intention of doing so. If we were to take anything, it would likely be some of those cute, cuddly talismans that provide soft and squishy comfort during stressful moments, and maybe some Earth chocolate. Since we don't typically carry cash or cards, we would leave something in exchange, as we are not shoplifters.

We have a sufficient understanding of humans and see little benefit in attempting any up close and personal contact right now, even if it were a mutual decision. We want to make it clear that there will be no abductions from our end. Do we need to emphasize that abducting any living being is unethical? We are *not* those aliens who enjoy performing invasive probing experiments. However, if we were to invite a human to come along, we would first ask for permission, as that is considered good manners where we are from.

Note: *Probing can sometimes be unpleasant and uncomfortable, especially when conducted by humans (and a few aliens) who like to poke around in places they shouldn't!*

Q. Are the stories of alien abductions real, or are they fake news?

A. We're not exactly sure. There's a lot of fake news* on Planet Earth, but that may not be one of them.

Our experience has shown that most aliens do not abduct* other life forms. In the previous question, we made it clear that we have no intention of taking any humans, although we wouldn't mind if some cute furballs came along.

The Advanced Beings we are in close contact with do not engage in abductions. However, we cannot say for certain that there have never been any abductions from your planet, or that there won't be in the future. Occasionally, certain extraterrestrials go rogue in the galaxy and *may drop in* without politely notifying the inhabitants, possibly taking some "things" with them. These types will have advanced technological tools and other highly developed gadgets in their toolbox, but that doesn't necessarily mean they are sufficiently evolved in other areas.

Unfortunately, the *Galaxy Police* cannot always prevent those in covert operation mode from engaging in inappropriate behavior. However, most extraterrestrials, whether advanced or regular aliens, are typically peaceful and friendly. They have even "assisted" your planet at times without causing any drama.

***Note:** Any form of abduction is wrong, whether it is carried out by humans or aliens. It is especially concerning when done for sinister reasons without any concern for harmful consequences. As for fake news, when it is intentionally created for dishonest and destructive purposes, it ceases to be considered benignly fake and instead becomes a dangerous force. Its purpose is not to inform, elevate, or even entertain, but rather, to deliberately deceive and divide, potentially resulting in harm.*

Q. Are cosmic beings responsible for creating crop circles?*

A. Maybe. They are certainly intriguing, aren't they?

The response of "maybe" suggests that indeed, some extraterrestrial beings appreciate this art form and could have left their mark on Planet Earth to keep humanity guessing. However, this form of creative expression likely originates from various sources, some of which are natural to Earth and its dimension, while others are otherworldly. Some crop circles may have even been created by humans themselves, although their style and quality may differ.

Remember, everything is composed of energy, including this artistic phenomenon. If this concept is perplexing, it's meant to be. We did say early on that "*more often than not, some questions either have no answers or require finding your own.*" Regardless, cosmic beings enjoy art and crafts and are receptive to the creative process.

***Note:** Circles are symbolic of cosmic life, the unknown, and the Universe.*

Q. Who sent you? God?*

A. Well, we certainly don't work for the other group** (lol)!

Why wouldn't the Supreme Divine Source (also known as "God"), who created everything including the Cosmos, send Advanced Beings to Planet Earth?

If humans can believe in the possibility of alternative life forms in the universe, such as aliens, then why wouldn't they also believe in a Supreme Being making a decision to have aliens – who in this case, are also advanced being coaches (ABCs) – assist Planet Earth? It might be time for humanity to consider that perhaps the concept of "God" needs an upgrade.

Decisions for important outreach programs like this one are not made lightly. Usually, local excursions within one's galaxy are authorized through a planetary council agreement. However, the "leave no human behind" project (in a galaxy unlike our own) required clearance from a *higher authority*. In this case, the B.O.S.S. (Being Of Supreme Source), who reports directly to the S.D.S., oversees these galaxy projects once they are approved. An outreach is made to determine a qualified team, especially when the mission is relatively urgent. Any contact from the B.O.S.S. is taken seriously.

The Universe is in contact and connected with all life forms, regardless of who or what they are, and it's not just a one-way conversation either! Remember, the Intelligent Designer (S.D.S.) created the Universe and all the planets, so why would it not want to stay in touch with everything? The Universe considers the receptivity of every life form with which it communicates, including all Earth's species, such as humans. It's worth noting that Planet Earth is also a living entity **(Gaia***)** that the Universe communicates and interacts with. By now, you should be aware that the Universe and your planet are sending important messages that *should not be ignored.*

Given that humans may not always be paying attention and could miss messages for various reasons, the Universe decided to send cosmic beings as life coach guides, which is as good an idea as any. However, it may not be enough, so other strategies are being considered for Planet Earth. While we don't exactly have the inside scoop on what the Universe is going to pull out of the "Cosmic Bag of Evolution," *it's probably best to be prepared.*

In the meantime, if one keeps an open mind about the existence of God, aliens or advanced beings, they may connect and hear messages that would normally be missed. It's worth noting that our human author (LCZ) was quite receptive to our numerous messages, and look at what has "evolved" from that transmission. Of course, we are aware that many humans throughout history have accepted the notion of some sort of divine assistance to humanity, which sometimes worked out and other times, not so much.

Sooner or later, you will find the answer to whether the S.D.S. exists or not; that is quite certain. However, whether or not you believe in a Higher Power is entirely up to you (free will and all that) because the S.D.S. doesn't need your belief to continue existing. It has "been there, done that" throughout the ages, all without needing any validation, although it does appreciate when the love is reciprocated!

*Note: **God** has many names and no name. For our purposes here, we alternately use The Universe, S.D.S., Source, the Creator, and Intelligent Designer. The B.O.S.S. is also part of The Universe and on "God's team."

The **"other group" refers to the negative ones, the dark side, naughty beings, and so forth.

***The **word Gaia** is translated from ancient Greek and means "Earth Mother." Another interpretation is that Gaia is the Spirit of the Earth.

Q. Are highly spiritual humans considered to be Advanced Beings?

A. Perhaps.

However, these evolved spiritual beings (sometimes human) are distinct from advanced beings who are on missions like this one for Planet Earth.

In the spiritual realm, there exist highly developed spiritual beings who belong to a category entirely separate from most evolved beings or other advanced species. These beings are from high-level dimensions, and while they are accessible to humans during their time on Earth, that accessibility may change once they depart, depending on the strength of their mutual connectivity.

These beings are sent on specific missions to your planet and consciously decide to take on the human experience and Earth adventure. We give them credit where credit is due, because these experiences aren't always easy. In some cases, things can become mixed up, especially when proposing new ways to elevate humanity. In fact, many of these beings, due to their special gifts, alternative views, independent nature, or their sex and gender (or even lack thereof) were not only denied recognition but were persecuted, sometimes violently, due to the numerous impediments of society. Not fun times!

Even today, these messages are often misunderstood due to distortions, misinterpretations, and a limited ability to comprehend the true meaning of what is being conveyed – which is usually some version of the importance of loving and caring for your fellow beings. To truly understand any significant insight requires mindful introspection of one's thinking and behavior, and then addressing any blockages that prevent one from becoming a compassionate and better human.

Our mission is to raise awareness about the purpose of EVOLVING and to get things moving in the right direction. Since this is already a big task, assistance with profound spiritual concepts requires a more in-depth approach. There is always room for another perspective when it comes to spirituality. Since humans may need more DIRECT instructions, the likelihood of providing further guidance in the future is quite possible.

Finally, just to clarify, we are not angel guides, spirit forms, or deities (although that would be nice!). However, these entities, and more, are willing to assist humans. What should be comforting to humanity is that we were once, long ago, a species not unlike your own. It became a priority to figure things out and once we did, we moved on to a higher level of existence. The fact that we share some similarities should give you hope that the Universe is quite friendly and encourages you to find your way forward!

Q. How did you manage to find someone to write and publish this guide for you?

A. Well, it definitely wasn't through an agent.

Fortunately, we are skilled at connecting with those who are aligned with similar goals. This process does not involve threats, bribes, or deceptive tactics. We simply selected a human who was receptive to our "energy waves" to download and publish the information using current methods. For more details, please refer to the bio of human author, L. ChakraZara.

The goal is to connect with as many humans as possible and offer guidance in e-book and traditional book formats, while also exploring other options. We also wanted to ensure easy access to this material, as many humans now prefer to read on various devices.

Instead of *physically landing* on your planet, this *soft landing* is intended to introduce ourselves and spread the cosmic message to as many humans as possible. Depending on the reception of our initial publishing efforts, there may be additional creative possibilities to promote awareness of the "human evolving mission." Stay tuned!

Q. Oh, come on! You're going to take over our planet, aren't you?

A. Let's be crystal clear: we have no intentions of taking over your planet. We have our own planet and do not want to babysit yours, or, heaven and the universe forbid, become your "handlers!"

The threat of a planetary invasion is taken seriously throughout the galaxy. Please read the entire guide carefully for reassurance. This cosmic outreach aspires to prevent a potential extinction of YOURSELVES, which would likely result in a lot of boo-boos, tears, and overall unpleasantness. Additionally, humans have nowhere else to go, as the Galaxy neighborhood is not welcoming any human refugees for temporary stays or any other relocation initiatives.

As previously mentioned, we do not engage in invasions or planetary takeovers of any kind. Instead, we strive to encourage native inhabitants to fully understand that it is in their best interests to grow as a species. We believe in human potential and want to see you thrive, but ultimately, humans must believe in themselves. It would be wonderful if you could join us in the galaxy as an evolved species, or at the very least, as improved humans.

Q. If humans were to visit your Planet, would they be considered Aliens or something else?

A. Yes, they would be considered something else.

When a species devotes a substantial amount of its resources to developing increasingly destructive technology and weapons, they are not only viewed as backward but also as hostile. Why would a species possess so many weapons to harm and kill one another? If a species persists in neglecting their planet, disrespecting the environment, and harming other living creatures because they believe they are entitled to do so, or out of ignorance or greed, then why would any advanced civilization on another planet regard them as anything other than an *"alien something else"*?

If humankind wants to be considered advanced aliens, they will need to "hurry up and evolve," regardless of whether they eventually reach an advanced being status.

Q. Do advanced extraterrestrials like humans?

A. Well, we cannot speak for everyone in the Cosmos, but the human race has quite a reputation in the galaxy, and some of it is *not so great*.

Regrettably, some humans can be quite unpleasant but fortunately, there are enough who are likable. However, it is not always necessary to like other life forms, though it would certainly be preferable. Being liked may matter to some, but what is now more important is to acknowledge and focus on the necessity for evolving. To be frank, we much prefer non-human species, especially the adorable, furry ones who aren't destructive and are quite smart and lovable. But please don't feel like it's a competition!

Q. Do humans really have a chance?

A. Well, we certainly hope so! We wouldn't be offering cosmic guidance if your chances were slim or nonexistent.

However, do not rely solely on chance. Humans must understand the importance of making the best choices now. Not making a choice may not be a good option at this time. You either choose to evolve or you don't. Improve your chances by improving yourselves.

"Everyone thinks of changing the world, but no one thinks of changing himself." — Leo Tolstoy, author

Notes

1. You may find that a particular question you have is not covered in this section. This may lead you to wonder if you can forward a question to our Earthling author (LCZ). The answer is: "*You can try*, but a response is not guaranteed."
2. Light years are not just about distance but also about energy and its various forms and dimensions. Understandably, there may still be some confusion about space and time travel.
3. Unidentified aerial phenomena.
4. 911 is used in the USA, Canada, and some other countries. There are other numbers used throughout the world, so it's best to know what that number is in the country you are in.

PART V
COSMIC COLLABORATION

25. The Advanced Being Authors

We assume that many humans would like to know a little more about us. After reading this guide, you may have an idea of our nature and personalities. Or maybe not. So, for those of you who are curious about us, we want to give a little background about ourselves. Not too much though, as we believe that the message in this book takes precedence over who we are.

AB1 and AB2 are not our real names of course. We simply thought it would be easier than trying to translate our "actual names" as they are very long from where we are from. In our galaxy and on our planet, names are a reflection of your being. However, you can change it at anytime if you want. No one gets upset when you do this by the way.

We come from a highly advanced planet, that started out similar to yours many eons ago. At a critical point, the beings on our planet collectively decided that *"enough was enough"* and started seriously evolving. These beings are our ancestors and we are grateful for them. On our planet, beings like us now undertake missions to assist in the development of other worlds. Not in terms of real estate or buildings, but in terms of species!

You would love our planet, as it is incredibly cool and beautiful. We work to ensure that everything is in balance to the best of our abilities. We have systems in place for cleaning up, sharing resources, communicating with all residents, and making our world a great place to live.

Obviously, or maybe not so obviously, we are advocates for peace, wisdom, and knowledge. We are constantly learning. While we each have different talents in specific areas, we work together as a team. So even though it may seem like only one of us is "communicating" in this guide, we are both actively involved. In our world, collaboration not competitiveness, is the key to progress.

Many of you may be wondering whether we are male or female. We do have opposite energies, so yes, maybe we are. On our planet, we don't focus on that too much and let our species define themselves as they wish. We are flexible in that regard. We are not too big and not too small, although there are species on our planet that are voluptuous due to their natural form. Our forms are fluid energy but we cannot go into specifics about that right now. We recommend reading more about Quantum Physics, as that may be helpful in understanding.

Both of us have families, communities, and "day jobs" aside from this mission. It's not all fun and games out here! Yes, our children have tantrums like your children, although they typically last a nano-second or so. We may raise them differently, but love is love, and that is the main thing among all species. We eat food, but sparingly and not like the things most of you eat. It's all high-vibration nutrition. We don't consume other evolved species on our planet. We realized that it was gross a couple of eons ago and have moved forward with finding ways to sustain ourselves without causing harm to other living beings. In a way, we are like your vegans.

As you may have noticed, we have a sense of humor. We do like to laugh and yes, we have feelings as well! We can get a little sad at times, but it passes. Our advanced nature allows us to manage both our thought processes and emotions, which is very helpful in facing challenges and living life in the best manner.

Yes, we like to travel. It was clearly a requirement for this mission. However, time is an illusion so we do not have to worry about "spending time" or how long a project like this might take. We work on a multi-dimensional level, which is very convenient for our mission. So yes, we are here (near your planet) but can quickly be elsewhere.

Truly, we are humble and perhaps even a little shy. We know, that may be hard to believe considering this mission! Although we are not inclined to brag about our achievements, we do have a strong sense of who we are. We are creators, dreamers, and wisdom sharers. So, we approach everything with a positive attitude and a strong belief. We have dreams, we enjoy our lives and we like to share. It's not just about positive thinking, but about *positive being.*

We live very long physical lives and don't age the way we used to long, long ago. This is one benefit of being advanced. But age in our world is on a different level than yours. You will find that out if you evolve properly. We hardly even speak of age and if we do, we honor those of our species who are our elders and have existed on the physical plane for a very long time. We also honor those that are on another level as well. But if you want to know our age, we are in our mid-eons, relatively speaking.

So this is us. There's more to us of course, but let's just leave it here for now. Perhaps there will be another time for a fuller autobiography. We will provide updates when appropriate.

Short Bio: AB1 *and* AB2 are *Certified Professional Galaxy Coaches with Advanced Species Training and Doctorates in Advanced Mission Development* (DAMD). They are fluent in Galaxy Languages, Telepathic Communication, Energy Transmissions, and are quite handy with tools. They enjoy arts and crafts, (star) gazing into space, playing with Earthling kittens and puppies, traveling at the speed of sound, and indulging in cosmic dreaming during busy missions. They have recently discovered chocolate on Planet Earth and plan to take some home. As parents to beautiful offspring, they happily coexist with their significant others. Both AB1 and AB2 also enjoy taking extended breaks to simply just BE!

26. About the Human Author

A brief overview of the Official Earth Assistant to the ABs:

L. ChakraZara is a creative visionary who assists humans, their pets, and other life forms by fine-tuning their life vision, chakras, and metaphysical energy. She dabbles in art, sound healing, writing and spiritual growth, adding a touch of cosmic eco glitter to everything possible. At times, she receives deep insights on her own and also from friendly otherworldly beings, and originally thought it was a departed loved one playing a practical joke from the other side (pretending to be an "alien") when the ABs first made contact.

She feels honored to have been selected as a spokesperson for the ABs and believes it was her sense of humor, open-mindedness, and her belief that she is from another planet that made her a candidate for this important job. When she is not helping ABs deliver important messages, L. Chakra Zara is busy tweaking and vibrating her chakras (which do get out of whack more often than she would like to admit), breathing in copious amounts of aromatherapy fumes, consulting astrological charts on her bad days, looking for her misplaced crystals and eating large quantities of chocolate for stress reduction.

L ChakraZara currently resides on Planet Earth with her sidekick, Lulu, a very contented kitty who is always more relaxed than she should be. Other companions, whether furry or not, have kept her grounded on Earth even as various distractions occur. However, L. ChakraZara may be relocating soon, depending on her karma and how things unfold on Planet Earth.

Have questions or in the media? You may contact LCZ by sending your energy vibes through the ether, or by traditional methods at wellnesswisdombooks.com and ladychakrazara.com. There is no guarantee you will receive a response right away or even later, so please do not take it personally.

27. Many Thanks!

"If the only prayer you ever say in your entire life is thank you, it will be enough." – Meister Eckhart, Mystic

First and foremost, we are eternally grateful to the Source of Creation for making all things possible. We truly appreciate being guided to the wisdom that has allowed us to express profound universal truths in a simple, gentle, and humorous manner. The Source continues to inspire us to trust that we are *all connected* and on a journey to become our best selves. For this insight and more, we are very thankful.

To our personal Cosmic Collective, we want to express our gratitude. There is no doubt that a project like this is made easier with the help and support of family, friends, allies, and kindred beings. We are very thankful to those who helped us keep our sanity with much-needed cosmic humor. Our professional colleagues provided us with invaluable insights into species development and evolution that were extremely helpful for this project. We firmly believe in the idea that "it takes a universe to raise a species" and hope that humans realize they are not alone in their planetary struggles.

Eternal love goes out to our cherished ones, partners, family, parents, and galactic friends who offer unconditional love and understanding, no matter which corner of the Galaxy we happen to be in. Assisting another species in crisis relies on the support of loved ones who believe in us. It always serves as a reminder to appreciate that "there's truly no place like home."

We cannot thank Lady ChakraZara enough for her perseverance on this project. Her ability to maintain her equilibrium, despite the mind-shattering distractions on Planet Earth, confirms that *she may be from another planet after all!* Her sense of humor, along with copious amounts of chocolate substances and the company of her feline friends, was a brilliant strategy to sustain the energy needed to translate our guidance into human words. Now that we know that chocolate and furry helpers are essential for urgent projects such as this one, we may consider this winning combo for future missions!

We are extremely grateful to those folks who have provided encouragement, inspiration, and laughter for a project that some would describe as "unbelievable." A special thank you goes out to the group of human and otherworldly cheerleaders, such as Baa bee and Ginger Ninja, who believe in L. ChakraZara and the vision of this "manifesto." Belief and vision are like stardust to the universe and LCZ really likes that stuff!

To those remarkable humans who are dedicated to evolving in any way possible, we are incredibly grateful for your perseverance and commitment. Although it may seem like you are in the minority, there are actually more of you than you realize. Please continue your efforts to become better humans and inspire others.

To all the humans who have provided unlimited amounts of amusing, and sometimes not so amusing, displays of Earthling insanity, we thank you for the mind-boggling "entertainment" and educational research. The non-stop theatrics and tragic-like comedy were valuable lessons to observe and learn from. Human behavior on Planet Earth will certainly be analyzed and written about in Cosmic Psych-Behavioral books for eons to come. As perpetual *students of the Universe*, we have certainly learned a thing or two about humankind, reminding us to never take our planet for granted.

Last but certainly not least, we acknowledge and thank all of the long-suffering Earthling non-human species and creatures who provided their unique insights and assisted us in our mission. We respect and understand you more than you know!

The day is coming when humankind will finally catch up to the innate wisdom of other species besides themselves.

"Humankind has not woven the web of life. We are but one thread within it. Whatever we do to the web, we do to ourselves. All things are bound together. All things connect." – Chief Seattle, 1854

28. The End or a Beginning?

"The Universe proclaims the wonder of Source
The world is a canvas, each day a miracle of creation
All who are ready, feel the soul spark alive
for the radiance of Source is within you, expressed as Love."
– Lady ChakraZara

There is a turning point, a moment at which something changes or shifts. By embracing the cycle of life, humans can cultivate a deeper understanding of the continuous process of growth and transformation. Life is a series of beginnings and endings, or at least, it seems that way.

The Universe is eternal and has no beginning or end.

"The stardust of the Universe is composed of Love and Magic."
~ Star Ashanumi

Vast Resources

"I have learned that all knowledge is available to us. We don't have to create it; we have only to access it. Simply ask in the right way—not with pride in your accomplishment, but with an open heart. I don't even mean to ask humbly, in the sense of being self-deprecating. Don't think about yourself at all, nor about your ability or lack of it. Concentrate, rather, on attuning yourself to Infinite Consciousness and ask for guidance in what you want to do. It's delightful, fun, and deeply inspiring to work and let yourself be used in this way." —Ervin Laszlo, *The Akashic Experience:*

Humanity possesses abundant resources, many of which are readily accessible. Expansion of knowledge can take various forms beyond just reading books. Utilize your sources wisely on your transformative path.

Human Books

Barrios, Carlos. *The Book of Destiny: Unlocking the Secrets of the Ancient Mayans and the Prophecy of 2012.* New York: HarperCollins, 2010

Berry, Thomas. *The Great Work; Our Way Into the Future.* New York: Harmony/Bell Tower, 1999

Bucko, Adam and Fox, Matthew. *Occupy Spirituality: A Radical Vision for a New Generation.* North Atlantic Books, 2013

Grof, Stanislav. *The Cosmic Game: Explorations of the Frontiers of Human Consciousness.* Albany: State University of New York Press, 1998

George, Chief Dan. *My Heart Soars; You Call Me Chief: Impressions of the Life of Chief Dan George* and *My Spirit Soars; The Best of Chief Dan George.* Hancock House Publishers,2017

Harvey, Andrew and Baker, Carolyn. *Radical Regeneration: Sacred Activism and the Renewal of the World.* InnerTraditions, 2022

His Holiness the Dalai Lama XIV. *A Simple Path: Basic Buddhist Teachings.* New York: Harper Element, 2009

Jenkins, John Major. *Galactic Alignment: The Transformation of*

Consciousness According to Mayan, Egyptian, and Vedic Traditions. Bear and Co., 2002

Norman, Mildred Lisette. *Peace Pilgrim, Her Life and Work in Her Own Words.* Ocean Tree Books, 1992. Get a *free* copy at http://www.peacepilgrim.org

Wallace-Wells, David. *The Uninhabitable Earth, Life After Warming.* New York: Tim Duggan Books, 2019

Human Websites

https://atmos.earth/
https://chooselove.org/
https://earth.org/
https://noetic.org/
https://onbeing.org/
https://plumvillage.org/
https://www.raceforward.org/
https://theshiftnetwork.com/
https://www.theosophy.world

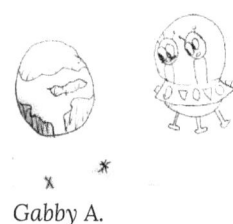

Gabby A.

"Wisdom is given to no man until he asks for it." – Manly P. Hall

Glossarion

A Positive Peaceful Planet (APPP)

Planet Earth deserves a positive and peaceful future that unites all Earthlings across the world. Now is the time to turn this vision into reality by starting an APPP movement.

Advanced Being Certificate Diploma (ABCD)

ABCDs are certified and *electrified* cosmic certificates that acknowledge when a species has achieved advancement. The frame is optional.

Advanced Being Code (ABC)

Advanced Being Codes are standards that are part of The AB Cosmic Code of Conduct manifesto. Those who adhere to these codes have either evolved or are in the process of evolving.

Advanced Beings (ABs)

ABs are highly evolved both individually and collectively, and are frequently mistaken for ordinary aliens or extraterrestrials. It is possible that humans may someday become a part of this exceptional group.

Advanced Human Association (AHA)

Isn't it time for humanity to establish an association that provides support, resources, and assistance for evolution?

Advanced Human Being (AHB)

An AHB designation signifies achieving an advanced level of holistic integration. There are numerous paths to the enlightenment process, *if you aspire to reach it*. While there are some highly evolved humans on Earth, their numbers remain insufficient.

Affirmations

Positive affirmations are phrases that you repeat to yourself to reflect the human you aspire to be. Initially, these affirmations may not align with your current reality, but with consistent repetition, they become ingrained in your subconscious mind. As you truly embrace these affirmations, they shape your reality and become self-fulfilling. For example, by affirming and believing that you are a better human, you will eventually embody that belief. By replacing limiting or negative beliefs with positive thoughts, you cultivate confidence, a positive mindset, and growth.

Aliens

Some humans believe that aliens are imaginary or fictional beings, while others believe they are real. The term "alien" is sometimes used disrespectfully by insecure humans. A human alien is usually defined as a person born in one area who then chooses to move to another and either can't or won't become a citizen there. Aliens are often seen as outsiders, feeling disconnected from the community they wish to be part of. This can apply to extraterrestrials and cosmic beings, who may or may not want to remain on Earth. The term "alien" needs to be reconsidered, as it reflects an outdated view from the past.

Being of Supreme Source (B.O.S.S.)

The B.O.S.S. is the Galaxy Supervisor and Cosmic Commander who reports to the S.D.S., the Supreme Divine Source and Designer of the universe. They are usually busy but will respond under certain circumstances.

Coalition for the Cosmos Communicates to Connect

A group of highly advanced Cosmic Beings who evaluate the potential for inter-species communication. Evaluations take into account the level of advancement of a species and their current methods of communication. The criteria for acceptable consideration are based on the effectiveness of the species' communication and its ability to foster connections among them.

Cosmic Advanced Being Coach (CABC)

Certified in species development theory by the prestigious Intergalactic Species Development Center, these professionals assist in guiding species towards reaching their full potential, among other things. In the galaxy, there are many coaches, some of whom have assisted humans.

Cosmic Behavior Database (CBD)

Throughout the universe, various diagnoses are included in the Cosmic Behavior Database (CBD) for analysis and review. All life forms and beings are subject to cosmic evaluation to enhance life in the universe for everyone.

Cosmic Code of Conduct Advisory (CCCA)

The Code of Conduct is part of the Advanced Being Codes, with the fundamental principle being to "do no harm." The CCCAs primary focus is on the universe, where they identify and address negative actions by various species, even if those species are unaware of their impact. The CCCA board members come from diverse multidimensional backgrounds, including intellectual and spiritual beings who have a vested interest in the well-being of the universe. They have provided numerous recommendations regarding humankind's existence.

Cosmic Comical Collective

The Cosmic Comical Collective is a MAJOR contributor to the mission of "Leave No Human Behind." They are a group of advanced beings and species who know how to laugh at themselves, no matter how advanced they may be. Their intention is to ensure that humor plays a critical and vital role in the development of all species, regardless of their progress.

Cosmic Council of Conduct Advisory Board (CCCAB)

The CCCAB offers legal and ethical advice with guidance to all entities in the Universe. It emphasizes appropriate behavior and actions that align with universal standards of conduct. This advisory council is particularly valuable when species or entities struggle to uphold these standards, or when guidance is needed on how to best interact with another species alien to their own.

Cosmic Crap

Various types of waste are expelled from planets, including negative energy. The members of the Galaxy Council have a low tolerance for waste being released from any planet, and warnings can be issued from the universe when necessary.

Cosmic Health Intergalactic Privacy Standards and The Domain In Personal Secrecy (CHIPS and DIPS)

The mission of CHIPS and DIPS is to protect species who do not wish to disclose their personal information in the galaxy or universe. Respecting the privacy and confidentiality of personal information is the highest priority, as some species may have less respect for it than is required.

Cosmic News Network (CNN)

The Cosmic News Network covers local cosmic and universal news. Committed to upholding high standards and ethics, all news and messaging are rooted in factual sources and a positive outlook. CNN's investigative reporting delves deep into the expansion of the Universe and its ongoing impact on the evolution of all species.

Cosmic Research Assistance Projects (CRAP)

The primary purpose of Cosmic Research Assistance Projects (CRAP) is to observe the evolution of Earthlings, and other cosmic species, over extended periods of time in order to provide appropriate assistance. These projects typically require a thoughtful and practical approach, as some populations may need prolonged analysis and repeated assistance.

Cosmically Advanced Kid Association (CAKA)

CAKA is a respected collective of advocates for offspring of all species, regardless of the galaxy they inhabit. The organization's focus is on holistic multi-dimensional well-being, and prioritizing joy and FUN during the early formative years.

Council of Cosmic Mind Counseling (CCMC)

The CCMC is a carefully selected group of professionals, some of whom may also advise the Cosmic Counseling Committee (CCC). The CCMC specializes in addressing all facets of a species mind, while the CCC is dedicated to providing counseling using various techniques tailored to diverse universal life forms.

EVOLVE

Evolution is the gradual process of changing and adapting over time, often spanning many generations, to better fit the evolving conditions of society, the environment, and the planet. To reach a more advanced stage, conscious personal growth is essential to survive and flourish. Eventually, there comes a point when a species must either progress or risk extinction. This is when it is most advisable to "*hurry up and evolve!*"

Galaxy

A galaxy is a system of millions or billions of stars, along with gas and dust, held together by gravitational attraction within the universe. All galaxies are part of the universe and overseen by the B.O.S.S., who reports to the S.D.S. A galaxy can be inhabited by a diverse group of beings, including but not limited to Advanced Beings, assorted alien species, meteors, comets, as well as various inhabited and uninhabited planets.

Grand Evolved Theory and Cosmic Law of Universal Energetic Harmony (GET A CLUEH)

GET A CLUEH is based on the fundamental principle of unifying communication through mutually aligned intentions and vibrations, whether conveyed through spoken word or telepathy. It asserts that establishing a comprehensive connection to what one is expressing or hearing is crucial for effective communication in all forms, with the ultimate aim being genuine understanding.

Human Being

The official definition states that a human being is "a man, woman, or child of the species Homo sapiens, who can *usually* be distinguished from other animals by superior mental development, their power of articulate speech, and upright stance." This definition may need some revisions, especially when it comes to the idea of superior mental development and articulate speech. This is not a critical assessment, but rather an observation that humans may sometimes overestimate their own capabilities. Nevertheless, the statement about humans maintaining an "upright stance" remains accurate (for now).

Human Emotional Explosive Disorder (HEED)

This disorder occurs when a human struggles to manage intense and explosive emotions, often leading to unpleasant behavior that can result in a meltdown. Symptoms may include volatile outbursts, difficulties with reasoning, impulsive actions, and loss of control over orifices and appendages.

Knucklehead - Ding Dong

A knucklehead is someone who behaves foolishly, like a "ding dong." This informal term is often used in a lighthearted manner rather than as an insult. Not all knuckleheads or ding dongs are malicious or mean harm, although some may have negative intentions. Most are simply silly and goofy.

Make Earth Great Again! (MEGA)

MEGA offers a superior approach to enhancing all aspects of Earth, not just specific parts of it. MEGA empowers you to recognize the inherent magnificence of the planet, as well as the potential within yourself and those around you. The truth is, the planet has always been great. It is humankind that needs to further develop and improve in order to recognize this truth.

Mother Earth (ME)

Mother Earth, also known as Nature and Gaia, is the entity responsible for overseeing all planetary systems, ecology, energy, weather, and nature. Mother Earth is a powerful force and is currently *displeased* with humans. Humans are intricately linked to Mother Earth. The planet does not need humans but humans need the planet. Humans are merely guests on Earth and must accept responsibility in their relationship with Earth.

Multi-Dimensional Being (MDB)

A multidimensional being exists on multiple planes of existence simultaneously, beyond its physical presence in different dimensions of space. All beings possess a nature that is complex in relation to other dimensions such as time, energy, and consciousness.

Open Mind (OM)

An open mind is a state in which facts, ideas, messages, and information are absorbed *without* preconceived notions. It is defined as *being willing* to consider ideas and opinions that are new or different from your own, and being open to listening to other people (and species). The S.D.S. encourages all to keep an open mind and heart. **The OM Sound** is a mystic syllable considered the most sacred mantra in Hinduism and Buddhism. It is regarded as three sounds, a-u-m. "*Om is a very simple sound with a complex meaning. It is the whole universe coalesced into a single word, representing the union of mind, body, and spirit that is at the heart of yoga.*" – Ann Pizer, Yoga teacher

Planet Earth

Planet Earth is the third planet from the sun and where humans reside. It was formed about 4.6 billion years ago, around the same time as the sun. It consists of an inner iron and nickel core, an outer liquid metal core, a mantle, and a surface crust. While some humans think that Earth is the only known planet with an atmosphere containing free oxygen, liquid water oceans, and life, the Universe knows better. Planet Earth is round, not flat.

Positive Attitude

Having a positive attitude is a habit that focuses on the bright side of life. Human neuroscience confirms the benefits of this positive rewiring of your brain. When humans choose to improve their attitudes, a positive change will result.

Spacecraft

A machine designed to fly in outer space for various purposes, such as outreach missions, planet observation, space and planetary exploration, transportation, and sometimes for leisurely cruising in the neighborhood. Some humans dream of flying around the galaxy, but they should wait until they evolve.

Supreme Divine Source (S.D.S.)

THE Supreme Divine (Energy) Source of all things, beings, species, galaxies, planets, and the whole enchilada, is everywhere and in everything. It is the past, future, and present. It knows all, creates all, and yes, like Santa Claus, it knows when you are naughty or nice. Humankind describes the S.D.S. as God, the Divine, and perhaps by other names, but yes, she/he/they/them is the ALL, The 3 in ONE, the Highest Power. The mystery and divine power of S.D.S. is indefinable.

Telepathic Transference Translation (TTT)

TTT is the ability to communicate while simultaneously translating that communication with beings who do not speak or converse in the same manner. A highly adept being can use their TTT ability when encountering a less evolved being to connect with care and empathy. This skill is typically exhibited by Advanced Beings or Extraterrestrials who have highly developed telepathic skills, along with the psychological ability to listen and respond without judgment. Some Advanced Beings speak fluent Empathatian, which assists with TTT, but it is not always a prerequisite for communication.

United Planet of the Universe (UPU)

A united humanity means working together peacefully and intelligently with each other, the environment, animals, and other advanced beings to achieve planetary and galactic objectives. This includes promoting sustainability, evolution, general well-being, and pursuing other visionary ideals. Planet Earth and humans will then become part of the Universal Organization of Advanced Beings (UOAB).

Universe

The Universe is believed to be at least 10 billion light years in diameter and contains a vast number of galaxies. It has been expanding since its creation in the Big Bang about 13 billion years ago. The S.D.S. and the B.O.S.S. have been immersed in their *ongoing plans of creation*. All existing matter and space are considered as a whole, especially all physical matter, including stars and planets, which are all part of the cosmos. This includes humans, despite the persistent belief in illusions of separation.

WellnessWisdom Books

Originating as a creative spark of the universe, WellnessWisdom Books is part of a larger vision to inspire and serve the formative needs of any being seeking inner growth, evolution, spiritual nourishment, and some much-needed cosmic mirth!

While *Lady ChakraZara* has a presence on social media, she prefers to focus on the Cosmos. Availability and connections may change at any time.

instagram.com/ladychakrazara/
facebook.com/ladychakrazara
hurryupandevolve.com

"It is certainly interesting to know that we come from the stars, but even more interesting is the realization that we're part of the cosmos. Although we might only be a speck in the immensity of the universe, we are the Great Father's (and Great Mother's, our addition to this quote) children, and our destiny is linked to that of creation. Every being has a role to play, a destiny to fulfill, and so every bit of existence is transcendent."– Don Isidro, Mayan sage

www.ingramcontent.com/pod-product-compliance
Lightning Source LLC
Chambersburg PA
CBHW070545130626
46556CB00001B/26

* 9 7 9 8 9 9 1 8 8 9 8 0 3 *